# ICONIC JEWISH WOMEN:

*Fifty-Nine Inspiring, Courageous,*
*Revolutionary Role Models for Young Girls*
*(A Perfect Bat-Mitzvah Gift)*

D1712858

## ALIZA LAVIE

Producer & International Distributor
eBookPro Publishing
www.ebook-pro.com

**ICONIC JEWISH WOMEN:**

*Fifty-Nine Inspiring, Courageous, Revolutionary Role Models*
*for Young Girls (A Perfect Bat-Mitzvah Gift)*

ALIZA LAVIE

Cover deisgn: Maria Sokhatski

Contact: aliza.lavie@gmail.com
ISBN 9798863033334

*"Our sister, be thou the mother*
*of thousands of ten thousands"*

Genesis 24:60

# Contents

Acknowledgements ........................................................................9

Introduction: Iconic Jewish Women ............................................. 13

1. Sarah Aaronsohn: Hero of the Nili Spy Network......................25

2. Bella Abzug: "Battling Bella" ......................................................32

3. Grace Aguilar: Groundbreaking Poet and Thinker...................37

4. Shulamit Aloni: Social Justice Warrior......................................42

5. Esther Arditi: The First Woman to Receive Israel's Military Medal of Distinguished Service....................................................... 48

6. Ruth Bader Ginsburg: Supreme Court Justice and Defender of Equal Rights ...................................................................................54

7. Osnat Barzani: The First Female Rosh Yeshiva .........................59

8. Miriam Ben-Porat: The First Female Judge on Israel's Supreme Court .................................................................................................. 64

9. Rachel Bluwstein: Famed Mother of Modern Hebrew Poetry.. 69

10. Bruriah: A Sage Woman in the Talmud.....................................74

11. Geulah Cohen: The Story of a Fierce Fighter............................79

12. Deborah: Prophetess, Judge, Military Strategist, Leader, and Poet ................................................................................. 84

13. Esther: From Beauty Queen to Leader ............................... 89

14. Ada Fishman Maimon: Revolutionary Founder of a Women's Labor Movement .................................................95

15. Anne Frank: A Young Jewish Diarist in the Holocaust .........101

16. Rachel "Ruchie" Freier: Hasidic Judge and Community Organizer ........................................................................107

17. Glikl of Hameln: Astute Merchant Who Left behind a Treasure .........................................................................112

18. Lea Goldberg: The Immigrant Who Became a Great Poet....118

19. Hannah Greenebaum Solomon: Founder of the National Council of Jewish Women ................................................ 123

20. Bracha Habas: The Land of Israel's First Female Field Reporter .........................................................................128

21. Regina Jonas: The First Female Rabbi................................ 133

22. Judith: Hero and Savior .....................................................138

23. Helena Kagan: Jerusalem's First Female Pediatrician ......... 143

24. Emma Lazarus: The Statue of Liberty's Poet.....................148

25. Leah: A Mother of the Israelite Tribes .............................. 153

26. Nechama Leibowitz: Teacher............................................. 157

27. Rita Levi-Montalcini: A Tenacious Scientist despite the Nazis .........................................................................162

28. Zahara Levitov: The Pilot with a Tragic Love Story ...........166

29. Deborah Lipstadt: Warrior against Holocaust Denial and Anti-Semitism..........................................................171

30. Zivia Lubetkin: Resistance Fighter in the Warsaw Ghetto ... 175

31. Hannah Maisel-Shohat: Agricultural Sustainability Teacher ..180

32. Selma Mayer (Schwester Selma): Founder of Israel's First Nursing School ............................................................ 185

33. Golda Meir: Israel's First Female Prime Minister ............... 190

34. Lise Meitner: Nuclear Physics Pioneer .................................. 196

35. Doña Gracia Mendes Nasi: The "Queen" of the Jews .......... 201

36. Miriam: One of Three Leaders in the Wilderness ............. 206

37. Rachel Morpurgo: The First Modern Hebrew Poetess.......... 211

38. Fanny Neuda: Pioneering Composer of Prayers for Women ..216

39. Yehudit Nisayho: A Mossad Agent in the Capture of Adolf Eichmann ............................................................... 220

40. Ida Nudel: Guardian Angel of the Refuseniks ...................225

41. Bertha Pappenheim: A Life Dedicated to Advancing Women..230

42. Rachel: A Mother Awaiting the Return of the Children of Israel..................................................................235

43. Rebecca: A Life of Blessings and Love.................................. 240

44. Elynor "Johnnie" Rudnick: Trainer of Israel's First Air Force Pilots.................................................................. 244

45. Ruth: The First Known Convert to Judaism......................... 248

46. Salome Alexandra: Hasmonean Queen.................................253

47. Sarah: Matriarch of the Nation .............................................257

48. Flora Sassoon: Philanthropist, Businesswoman, and Scholar ....................................................................... 260

49. Sarah Schenirer: Founder of the Bais Yaakov School System ......................................................................... 264

50. Hannah Semer: The First Female Editor of an Israeli Daily Paper .................................................................................. 269

51. Hannah Senesh: Paratrooper and Poet ...................................273

52. Ada Sereni: The Woman in the Black Dress........................ 278

53. Naomi Shemer: Composer of Israel's Most Treasured Songs..283

54. Mania Shochat: Founder of HaShomer and Mother of the Kibbutzim ..................................................................... 288

55. Henrietta Szold: Zionist Leader and Founder of Hadassah .. 293

56. Hannah Rachel Verbermacher: Leader of a Hasidic Community ............................................................................ 298

57. Lillian Wald: A Nurse Dedicated to Impoverished Immigrants.......................................................................... 304

58. Stefa (Stefania) Wilczyńska: Mother to Jewish Orphans during the Holocaust.......................................................... 309

59. Zelda: The Poet from a Hasidic Dynasty ............................. 314

More Inspiring Jewish Women ...................................... 319

The Wide World of Bat Mitzvah Ceremonies: A Journey through Time and around the Globe.................................323

Timeline of Iconic Jewish Women ...............................339

Glossary ................................................................345

Sources ................................................................ 366

# Acknowledgements

How do you write to your sister far away and share a private, personal, intimate journey in contemporary language? You get help from good people — and you listen to the younger generation.

On my book tour for A Jewish Woman's Prayer Book, I encountered many communities and was exposed to different bonds within the Jewish oneness. I remember, in particular, a lecture I gave in Boston, at a moving ceremony in which women who had turned eighty celebrated a bat mitzvah together. "We never had a bat mitzvah, and it was something we felt was missing," they told me. As they spoke of their lives' journeys, I experienced the excitement they felt at their delayed celebration, with its formal entry to a shared community, a circle of women, and a chain of generations. At that moment, I knew that one day I would devote a book to bat mitzvah girls.

I was fortunate to have many wonderful people help me along the way. Mostly, I enjoyed listening to girls who were turning twelve — from around the world and from Israel; from the city and the country; observant, traditional, and secular. All enthusiastically answered the call, reading the life stories and celebration ideas in the book and experiencing the ceremonies. Their mature and constructive comments were unapologetic and unhesitating, and guided me in presenting the women, ceremonies, and sites; they made the book stronger, and, I hope, accessible to more girls and the people reading with them. Mothers, aunts, and grandmothers also shared how their bat mitzvah had influenced them or, alternatively, what effects not having such a celebration had had for them.

I listened to women's stories. Their experiences had held such meaning for them that women born in Italian communities — Venice, Rome, and Turin—could describe their bat mitzvah dresses to me seventy-five years later. In fact, the bat mitzvah dress was a theme that arose time and again when I spoke to women and girls.

It is my great hope that this book will encourage girls and their families to infuse the formal year of joining the Jewish people with profound meaning, both personal and communal, creating a celebration that carries the gift of identity and belonging more generally and, in particular, a connection to the women who came before.

Writing this book required a wonderful and sensitive team, and I am forever grateful to my mother, Miriam Mashiach, of blessed memory, my mother-in-law, Dina Lavie, and the women in my family, along with friends, scholars, colleagues, and experts who were there to lend a hand.

This book is published with the generous assistance of the Keshet Foundation, who enhanced the book by facilitating its translation to English and its presentation to a new audience. The most significant decision I made was to select Deena Glickman, a skilled and brilliant translator who also became a good friend. I was also delighted to work once again with Tirtsah Arzi, who had edited the original Hebrew book and stepped up to help with research and reviewing the new English manuscript.

The original edition of this book, published in Hebrew, was written for girls in Israel; it was crucial that the English edition speak to women and girls around the world. To this end, the lives of many women were studied, and decisions were made about which revolutionary women should be included and what activities should be suggested. The goal was to ensure that a wide breadth of readers would be able to craft a celebration that spoke to them.

In selecting the women who would be added to the English edition, I was helped by many people who have studied the subject in theory and in practice, in the world of education and within the community. Special thanks go out to Prof. Gur Alroey, Howard Blas, Blu Greenberg, Rabba Sara Hurwitz, Meredith Jacobs, Scott Lasensky, Prof. Pamela Nadell, Daphne Price, and Prof. Kenneth Stein.

My gratitude to my talented, beloved friend, editor Alma Cohen Vardi, who read the book and was passionate about it, and to Eran Zmora and Yoram Rose, the publishers at Kinneret, Zmora, Dvir, who loved the book and chose to publish it. Many thanks to Benny Carmi and the staff at eBookPro for publishing the book in English.

To my extended family, no small number of whom signed on once again to help with research and collected information enthusiastically, I extend my gratitude and love for encouraging and advising me, for reading and commenting.

I am grateful to the loves of my life, my daughters Yarden, Arbel, and Amit-Chana and my son Dror-David, my daughter-in-law Stav and my sons-in-law Yehonatan and Matan, who became my research assistants. And to my dear husband, Tzuriel, my everlasting gratitude for the support, for partnership in my journeys, and for the security that at any time I can consult with you about my worlds of research. I accept all of the family jokes about me with love.

To my granddaughters Ofir, Shachar, Neta, Nitzan, and Tavor-Simcha and to my grandsons Ori-David and Eitan-Tzuri: this is for you, and for the children of your generation.

Finally, I accept responsibility for the choice of the women included in the book and grieve those I did not have space to include. Their absence is but a catalyst for the next project — I promise.

September 2023/ Tishrei 5784
Tel Aviv

# *Introduction:*
# ICONIC JEWISH WOMEN

**M** azal tov! I hear you have a bat mitzvah coming up. You may be expecting to study a **Torah** portion or subject and give a speech, to read from the Torah at synagogue or temple, to take on a project that gives back to the world, or to have a large event for your family and friends. You may be excited or nervous — or you may feel like you're having a bat mitzvah only because your parents want you to. You may be asking questions: What is a bat mitzvah? What do the words "bat mitzvah" even mean? Why do societies choose to mark a specific birthday? Why did Judaism choose age twelve, or age thirteen? What does this celebration look like for girls like me around the world? What did it look like for my grandmother or great-grandmother? And what should this moment mean to me?

## *What Is a Bat Mitzvah?*

Let's start by defining what a bat mitzvah is. The easiest way to understand it is to think about how we change as we get older. As we grow, we find ourselves earning more privileges and taking on more responsibilities. As a child, you went to bed earlier and as you grow older you go to bed later; as a child, you had many things done for you, but as you grow you're expected to take on chores around the house or even in your community.

Within Jewish tradition, this change is clearly defined: the **Mishnah** states that girls at the age of twelve (and boys at the age of thirteen) find themselves reaching a new status. The age of bat mitzvah — the age of *mitzvot*, or commandments — means you are now considered an adult Jew, with all of the privileges and responsibilities that new title entails.

While boys have traditionally marked their change in status by making their first blessing over the Torah or reading from the Torah, girls have had no specific ritual. But in the past 150 years girls have begun to mark the occasion, too. Around that time, the Italian Jewish community created a bat mitzvah ceremony: dressed in white and surrounded by their community, the girls would recite the **Ten Commandments** and read the Song of Deborah (see chapter 12) together before the open **ark** in the synagogue.

Today, bat mitzvah celebrations are common. In some communities, girls say a blessing over the Torah or read their Torah portion; in others, girls take on a commitment to a volunteer or *hesed* project. Some girls study religious texts before their bat mitzvah and hold a *siyum*, a ceremony marking the completion of study, while others — especially in Israel — choose to connect to significant sites in Jewish history. Some hold a big celebration with friends, family, and community; for others, a small event with personal meaning is more fitting. Some communities hold celebrations at age twelve, as per the Mishnah, and others have moved girls' celebrations to age thirteen. Because no specific ceremony developed for girls over time, girls today can shape a celebration that expresses their feelings on becoming full-fledged Jewish women and ties them to their heritage.

# My Journey with Bat Mitzvah

A few months before I turned twelve, my parents and I made a plan to mark the occasion on the upcoming **Sukkot** holiday. My extended family — grandmothers Hannah and Rosa and relatives from around Israel, where I live — was invited; everyone took part in a scavenger hunt with tasks and riddles that we had prepared in advance, running from station to station in the open areas around our home. My father had built a bigger **Sukkah** than usual that year and after the hunt we all gathered, happy and hungry, under the Sukkah's fragrant roof, to enjoy the delicious treats that had been prepared by my mother and aunts.

My parents, Miriam and Menashe Mashiach, were both educators — but neither had seen bat mitzvah celebrations in their own families. It was simply not something that was done in their communities at the time. I was the eldest daughter, and their wish to celebrate my coming of age ultimately created a framework that has stayed with my family until today.

My own daughters, born in Israel, each chose their own path when it came to celebrating their bat mitzvah: My eldest, born around **Hanukah**, guided a tour on the Burma Road, a bypass road to Jerusalem paved during the **War of Independence**, and spoke about Mattathias and his sons and Judith (see chapter 22) in her speech. My second daughter, Arbel, born on the festival of **Shavuot**, chose to lead her guests climbing the cliff she was named for, where she gave a speech about Ruth (see chapter 45) and her route to the nation of Israel. With the women in the family, she read a prayer written for the traditional Italian bat mitzvah. My youngest daughter chose a challenging trek in the caves of Beit Guvrin and rappelling in secret caves from the time of the **Bar Kokhba Revolt** (132–136 CE), marking the occasion with a dance she had choreographed herself and a speech that related to the daughters of Tzelofhad and the historic precedent they made in demanding their own inheritance (Numbers 27:1–4).

## Choosing Your Own Path

Your bat mitzvah is an invitation to pause as your status changes and think about who you are. How do you connect to the different circles in your life — your family, your friends, your community, Jews around the world, the global community? How does your new status affect you on a religious and spiritual level? How does it connect you to your history and to girls who are like you and unlike you around the world? What does this change mean to you? What are the privileges and responsibilities that you will now take on as a full-fledged member of the Jewish people?

Your bat mitzvah year is an opportunity to foster relationships with family and to deepen bonds with community. This is a year that gives you a chance to open a window into a deeper discussion with yourself, to listen carefully, shape your identity, and think about where you belong.

Any change or event demands preparation; your bat mitzvah is no different. Take this time to prepare, to learn, to think, and to shape the bat mitzvah celebration that is meaningful to you.

## How to Use This Book

Your bat mitzvah is the perfect time to meet Jewish women who lived, wrote, and were active in the distant and recent past. But this is not a history book. It is a book that introduces you to women whose lives are characterized by words like "responsibility," "giving," and "initiative." These are women who added something significant to the Jewish people and the world, epitomizing the words *tikkun olam*, repairing the world. Many of them are women who refused to take "No" for an answer or simply would not give up on their dreams. Many ignored what was expected of them as women in order to create something that they knew was vital. Many made tremendous sacrifices to transform the world around them for the better. Each chapter in this book tells the story of one inspirational Jewish woman and then suggests four different ways in which you can mark your bat mitzvah in her honor and make your own contribution to the world around you.

In writing about the women in this book, I tried to tell the story of each woman's childhood and family. I used details from their worlds to express each one's individual voice. Their stories can help you, as you near your bat mitzvah, to find your own voice and express it. Each of these women is fascinating and inspiring, though you may never have heard of some of them; many are not remembered or celebrated as they ought to be. The book both tells you more about these unique women, pioneers in their fields, and offers you the opportunity to be a partner in bringing them back to public awareness. You may also notice that some of them are linked to one another — some knew each other or were inspired by one another, some connected to similar ideas or ideals, some were even related.

Some of the women in the book are entirely forgotten; some are well-known. Some made contributions to society that were even greater than male colleagues — but were forgotten because they were women. Some have only recently been discovered, and others are just waiting for you to discover them. At times, during my research, I found myself angry when learning about a woman who should have been well-known. I also found myself stunned to find how much was possible for women even long ago — how high and how far they could fly if only they could dream.

The women in this book are only a few from a very long list; they were selected with great care. I chose them based on their actions, but also at times because their character spoke to me. I hope that they speak to you, too, and move you. At the end of the book, I have included a list of only some of the other inspirational Jewish women I was unable to include; you may want to learn more about them as well.

My hope is that you use the stories of the women in this book to discover your own identity and your own path, and to learn more about your gifts and what important provisions they give you on your journey. Sometimes — I say this from experience — you may find answers through them to questions that have been occupying you.

I invite you to read this book and choose a woman whose life story speaks to you, or who arouses curiosity and creativity within you. Get to know the woman you've selected. Hold imagined discussions with her (I found it very helpful myself), pick a way to mark your celebration based on the suggestions given in the chapter, or create your own, a ceremony of transition from childhood to Jewish adulthood that is appropriate for you and only you.

The suggestions in each chapter tie the woman described to activities you can take upon yourself to mark your bat mitzvah. They are divided into four categories, which you can pick and choose from as you see fit. First, each chapter contains a suggestion for a topic you can study in depth. Second, it recommends a hesed activity you can take on to give back to your family, community, or society. Third, it describes a location you can visit that is connected to the woman you have read about. Many of these locations are in Israel and are ideal if you are planning a trip with your family to mark your bat mitzvah (specific addresses and information like hours of operation are not given in the book; these are easily found on the internet). Even if you are not able to reach the places, many can be visited virtually through their websites or on map sites. Finally, you are offered a wild card, an activity that is a little different or challenging. These four options are all ways for you to join the chain of Jewish women, adding your voice to those of the women who came before you.

So, for example, you can learn more about climate change in the spirit of Hannah Maisel-Shohat (chapter 31) or visit Neot Kedumim, the biblical landscape reserve, in honor of the matriarch Leah (chapter 25). You might want to create a share table at school to commemorate Doña Gracia Mendes Nasi and the soup kitchens she built in her community (chapter 35) or make a patchwork quilt to celebrate Hannah Greenebaum Solomon (chapter 19).

But you can also choose to incorporate a number of women in your bat mitzvah celebrations. Perhaps you'd like to pick women who functioned within one field — politics, science, spiritual guidance, art — and relate to them all. You can mix and match women from the book and activities that speak to you. You may want to create a bat mitzvah celebration that begins a year before your bat mitzvah and challenge yourself — visiting twelve places you'd like to see, writing twelve poems, meeting people from twelve different religious communities. You may want to incorporate your interests or hobbies — art, sport, cooking, or dance.

If you wish, you can also pick another woman who influenced you, whom you value and love, who is not in the book — a teacher you admire, a grandmother, a family member you never met, the person you were named for. You may want to adopt an idea from the book and apply it to the person you've selected.

The possibilities are endless. Only you know what combination of study and action will most speak to you and express your commitment to your community, beliefs, and values.

The book also contains a number of other resources for you to use:

* A list of women who were not included but are certainly worthy of further study, who may speak to you as well
* "The Wide World of Bat Mitzvah Ceremonies," a chapter that tracks the history of the bat mitzvah and contains prayers written specially for women and descriptions of women's ceremonies, which may inspire your own celebration
* A timeline, to help you navigate when each woman in the book lived
* A glossary, which gives explanations of terms marked in bold in the book
* A list of books that were consulted in writing this book and that might be useful for further reading

## Planning Your Bat Mitzvah

Begin by meeting with your parents or whatever team is helping create your celebration. In order to keep organized, you may want to open a file on your computer or buy a new notebook. Consult with your parents or family about the woman or women you wish to follow and the activities you would like to take on. You can write down all of the ideas that come into your head when you plan the bat mitzvah you dream of. Ask yourself: How would you like to celebrate? Who would you like to include? Where would you like to hold the celebration? What would you like to focus on?

Make sure that your initial ideas for a celebration fit in with the planned budget. When thinking about costs, take into consideration the number of people you are inviting and fees for activities, food, locations, transportation, and more. You may find that some of your ideas can be accomplished with the help of the people around you.

Once you have chosen a woman or idea to connect to, dive in. Begin by searching online; sites like Wikipedia can give you a start and you can learn more by clicking on Wikipedia's sources or doing a simple Google search. Check if books have been written on the woman or topic you chose. And if someone in your family or someone around you knows more details, you can interview them. Search for pictures and videos. These can help you if you want to tell your guests more about the woman you've selected in a **dvar Torah**, lecture, speech, or even a creative means — a movie, dance, or song.

As a link in a chain of Jewish women, you may want to connect to girls and women who marked their bat mitzvah one generation ago, ten generations ago, a hundred generations ago. You may want to ask older women from your family and your community whether they celebrated a bat mitzvah and, if so, how. It might be meaningful to you to incorporate elements of your mother or grandmother's life in your own celebration, or one of the ceremonies in the "Wide World of Bat Mitzvah Ceremonies" might tie you in to the sisterhood of women from long ago.

You can return to old customs or create new ones, adopt a practice from one of the many Jewish communities, choose ancient prayers or integrate a literary creation or poem that speaks to you, focus on a specific woman or on prominent features of hers that touch your life. Or you can create your own ceremony, that other girls may want to adopt after you.

It's your turn. This is your opportunity to connect to the women who came before you and add your own voice to a never-ending succession of active and engaged Jewish women.

## A Note about Translation and Dates

In order for this book to be accessible to all, I have used English names for places and people. When a term is given in another language, it is in italics, and is either explained in the chapter or appears in the glossary.

Chapters list the years that each woman lived or give estimated dates. Two types of dates appear in each chapter — first, the usual form, using the years as they are generally given today, and second, the Hebrew dates, based on the Jewish calendar that began roughly 5,800 years ago. This calendar relates to both the sun and the moon (as opposed to the general calendar, which is based only on the sun), and has its own names for months. If you'd like to learn more about your Hebrew birthday, you can find tools online; in fact, these tools can also help you discover what your Torah portion is.

# For the Adult Reading This Book
## with the Bat Mitzvah Girl

Since my books on women's tradition — *A Jewish Women's Prayer Book* and *Women's Customs* — were published, women often turn to me when debating how to mark important life cycle events for themselves or family members. Often young women, teachers, mothers, and grandmothers ask me what the "right" way is to celebrate a bat mitzvah. In meetings with groups of mothers, I hear distress: "We don't know what the place of a bat mitzvah is today." "Our daughter wants a party but we feel that a party isn't enough." "Something is missing. Perhaps we didn't receive it, and don't know what it is — but we would like to give it to our daughters."

This book was born out of questions that have occupied me for nearly twenty years, since I learned of the celebrations held in Italy some 150 years ago. Who decided that a ceremony should be formed to mark a young girl's transition to adulthood? Who was sensitive to the importance of celebrating the occasion before an open ark? Who wrote the prayer that the girls read at the ceremony? And who chose Deborah the Prophetess as a role model? Why was it that during the period of the **Yishuv** and after the establishment of the State of Israel no institutionalized coming-of-age ceremony was developed for girls? Many of the questions I have asked myself over the years are answered in this book, which illuminates other initiatives and rituals.

"Logic and pedagogic principles almost mandate that the girl's arrival at the age of mitzvot be celebrated," wrote Rabbi Yechiel Yaakov Weinberg, known as the *Seridei Eish*, considered one of the greatest rabbis of the Lithuanian world after the Second World War. "This discrimination between the boys and the girls regarding celebrating maturity deeply offends the human emotion of the growing girl." Many years have passed since then — but we have not yet learned the importance of the celebration of adulthood through a bat mitzvah.

Each generation must adjust the bat mitzvah celebration anew, in language that repeatedly evolves, using constantly improving forms. The language and terms have even changed since I began working on this book ten years ago.

The need is an important one, and it is yours to remedy. This book offers numerous paths for building a bat mitzvah celebration. Your job is to listen to the dreams and wishes of the bat mitzvah girl, to search with her for the ceremony, activity, or celebration that will give the occasion meaning and remain with her years later.

Is she a successful dancer but uncomfortable speaking in front of an audience? Build a celebration based on dance — or offer her a workshop to help prepare her to speak before her guests. Does she like to cook? Or research natural phenomena? Perhaps she dreams of becoming a pilot? Working as a scientist or doctor? Find the figures in the book who will speak to her.

You, along with the bat mitzvah girl, can find ways to express her aspirations, both known and hidden. The process of realizing the task together is an experience in itself, an experience of togetherness and building engagement and empowerment.

The book invites the bat mitzvah girl to join generations of Jewish women, a Jewish sisterhood. All of the women in this book are distinguished not by fame or status but rather by the responsibility each took upon herself. Each woman, in her own time and in her own way, used her skills and abilities for the Jewish people, with some sort of inner voice leading her to her version of *tikkun olam*. It was important to me to emphasize to the young readers that the heroines in this book are "famous" because of their efforts in action or learning, because of giving up their own personal comfort and sticking to a goal they set for themselves, even in times of hardship and loss, even in the face of failure. The ceremonies described in this book are coming-of-age ceremonies that express values of giving and responsibility, that connect to Jewish history and Judaism today.

As noted, this is not a history book; quite the contrary, it is an invitation to the girls and women around you to join the circle, to continue to ensure that each woman in her time and in her way can take flight. It is an invitation for Jewish girls and their families to meet heroines, even those who have been forgotten with time, and to tell their stories — and, in doing so, to expose young girls to literature, research, and national memory.

As chair of the Committee on the Status of Women and Gender Equality in Israel's **Knesset,** I had a custom: each committee meeting opened with the description of a woman and her life story. I asked all participants who initiated a discussion to tell us about a woman who impressed them, a role model in their life, an untold story.

I invite you to work with your bat mitzvah girl not only to tell one story and hold one event — but to add to the rich Jewish tapestry of culture, values, study, and community.

# 1

# SARAH AARONSOHN

## *Hero of the Nili Spy Network*

S arah Aaronsohn was the first daughter born after four boys. Her parents, Efraim Fishel and Malka Aaronsohn, had come to Zikhron Yaakov from Romania in 1882 with their firstborn son, Aaron. Sarah's oldest brother was already a teen when she was born, and she held a special place within her family.

Zikhron Yaakov, and, in fact, all of the **moshavot**, did not have a high school. Most children finished elementary school and joined the workforce. But in the Aaronsohn house, education was crucial. Aaron was already a well-known scientist — an expert in botany — and he encouraged Sarah to keep learning on her own. Alongside her regular chores, Sarah studied languages. She was fluent in Hebrew, French, and Turkish, and had a basic knowledge of Arabic and English.

Sarah could cook, embroider, and sew, but she also rode horses, took long hikes, and dreamed of the Jews conquering the land from the Turkish, who ruled at the time. Her first gun was a gift she received for her fifteenth birthday from her brother Aaron, whom she adored.

Sarah loved dancing and enjoyed life, and many men fell for her. The first was Avshalom, who was her age and lived in the nearby *moshava* of Hadera, whom she met when they were teenagers. Together they dreamed dreams, rode horses, and trained with weapons. Avshalom, a poet and a sensitive soul, loved both Sarah and her younger sister Rikva, and had a hard time choosing between the two.

The three spent their youth together. But it appears that Avshalom chose the younger sister, and Sarah decided to distance herself. She accepted the proposal of a wealthy Turkish merchant, married him, and left the land.

It was there, far away, in the large Turkish city of Constantinople (today Istanbul), that she first heard of the great war that had erupted — what was later called the First World War. Sarah learned of the terrible decrees that the Turkish had imposed on the *moshava* from letters she received from her sister Rivka and her friend Avshalom. While the letters appeared to be innocent, crucial information was concealed beneath the many stamps they affixed to the envelopes.

Sarah, who was closely tied to her family and friends, chose to leave her husband and return to her land. The road back was not a simple one in those days, and the train trip took her three weeks and left a strong impression; the Turks were massacring the Armenian people, and Sarah witnessed the murder of children and women from her window. It was clear to her that the Turks would not hesitate to do the same to her Jewish brothers and sisters. She was convinced that they must be actively fought, and she discovered that her family and friends agreed: in her absence, Aaron had established a spy network to give information to the British, who were fighting the **Ottoman** — or Turkish — Empire; Avshalom, it turned out, was the most skilled and important spy in the group.

The network, which included other Aaronsohn family members and a few dozen friends, chose the name "Nili," an acronym from a biblical verse: *netzah Yisrael lo yishaker* ("the Glory of Israel does not deceive," a quote from I Samuel 15:29). It was not easy for the Aaronsohns to convince the British to use their services, and, even once they had agreed, the British were skeptical about basic information — numbers of soldiers, types of cars — they received. Nili was capable of giving important and complex information that the British did not always appreciate; the network's members found themselves frustrated.

On her first night at home, Sarah was briefed by Aaron on the underground's secrets: how information was sent covertly, the code in which they wrote, the signals for the British ships that arrived once a month in order to collect information. The next day, Aaron departed for Egypt, and Sarah stayed on at the agricultural research station her brother had founded in Atlit. She was put in charge of organizing all of the material that the field people had attained in order to transfer it to the British.

During the day, Sarah would manage the research station and her father's home in Zikhron Yaakov; at night she would convert her friends' notes into code and watch for a ship that might arrive, at risk to her life. When a ship appeared on the horizon during dark, moonless nights, Sarah would race to hang clothing on a line — yellow, red, and green signaled whether she had information and whether it was important or even crucial.

In early 1917, the underground's state was not good. All of Nili's members were out of the country, and Sarah was alone, overseeing the activity. These were critical days, immediately before the British conquest of the Land of Israel, and very dangerous ones — the Turks were beginning to sense that an underground spy network was active in the land's north. The ring was tightening.

"Save yourself," Aaron begged Sarah when she visited Egypt. "Stay here; others can continue your work in the Land of Israel." But she would not hear of it.

"Save yourself," the British commanded her. "Board the ship that's on its way and come to us." But Sarah sent other people she was concerned for on the ship, and, with uncommon bravery and a sense of duty for her role and the people she was overseeing, maintained business as usual.

Or almost as usual.

Because meanwhile, an accident occurred, threatening the entire spy enterprise.

While in Egypt, Sarah had received a flock of carrier pigeons from her British operators. She would tie a coded message to a pigeon's leg and the pigeon would quickly fly, with the message, to the British in Egypt.

But one pigeon was lost along the way; it landed directly in Turkish headquarters, not far from the research station. The Turkish officers may not have known how to decipher the code — but they now knew without a doubt that spying was taking place in the area.

Did someone inform on Sarah and her friends? We do not know. But on the first night of **Sukkot** in 1917, the Turks arrived in Zikhron Yaakov. Sarah and her father were on their way to synagogue for prayers. They were both caught and tortured. Yosef Lishansky, one of the underground members who was also in Zikhron Yaakov, was able to escape. The Turks threatened the community's leaders: If Lishansky was not turned in, they would destroy the entire *moshava*.

Sarah was tortured for many days, but did not speak; she refused to reveal any information or inform on any of her friends. When the Turkish investigators decided to transfer her for trial in Damascus, Sarah feared she would not be able to withstand the torture. She asked to change her blood-soaked clothes before traveling, and the Turks agreed. She was taken to her brother's home in chains. And there, in the bathroom, she shot herself.

Sarah did not die immediately. For three days, she was treated by the *moshava*'s doctor, Hillel Yaffe. For three days, she begged him to kill her, or at least let her die, and the Turks ordered him to make every effort to keep her alive. At the end of three days, Sarah died.

Exactly two months after her death, Turkish Jerusalem surrendered to the British.

# ADD YOUR VOICE

## Explore

Nili was only one of many Jewish underground movements that existed during Sarah Aaronsohn's time. What do you know about Jewish underground movements? Before the State of Israel was founded, Nili was only one of the groups working in secret to fight for a land for the Jewish people. Research the **Lehi**, **Etzel**, and **Palmach**, and look into the differences between their ideologies and activities.

But there were also Jewish underground movements in other times and places. What do you know about Jewish underground movements in the more distant past? Find out more about secret movements during periods like the Spanish **Inquisition** and the Holocaust. Research the Jewish resistance that fought against the Nazis; you may want to look into Mordechai Anielewicz and his activities in Warsaw or Zivia Lubetkin (see chapter 30).

## Give Back

Aside from his work in Nili, Aaron Aaronsohn was also a botanist who discovered what is believed to be the "mother of wheat," a breakthrough that was vital for agronomists the world over. In 1909, he was invited by the American Ministry of Agriculture to share his knowledge; while there, he raised funds from wealthy Jews for a project that he felt would benefit not only the Land of Israel: a research station in Atlit that studied the land's crops.

In his spirit, learn more about HaShomer HaChadash, an organization that aims to protect Israel's agricultural land and forests. It recruits volunteers to work the land and protect it from fire, theft, and violence. Its projects include education — a youth movement, a high school, and a pre-army program — as well as activities for the general public on holidays. If you are visiting Israel, you can volunteer some time with the organization (see their website for more information). If you are not planning a trip, you can raise money for one of their projects or look for a similar organization in your community with which you can volunteer.

## See Something New

The *moshava* in Zikhron Yaakov, where Sarah Aaronsohn was born and died, is a beautiful place to visit. Founded more than 140 years ago, the *moshava* has been restored. You can visit the synagogue that the Baron de Rothschild built in memory of his father (Sarah's destination when she was caught by the Turks), or see the Aaronsohn house, which is now a museum. A tour of the house includes the tunnel that was dug from the house to the outside, which served the underground members for meetings, and the museum, which immortalizes the heroism of Nili's members.

Hadera Park, planted on the banks of the Hadera Stream, contains a monument to Avshalom Feinberg, Sarah's close friend and partner in the Nili underground, who was killed on his way to find Aaron Aaronsohn when contact with him had been lost. The Hadera Stream was one of the country's most polluted water sources; it has been cleaned up and restored, and the park planted around it operates along ecological lines.

## Get Out of Your Comfort Zone

Invite your guests to a navigation or spy game. You may want to use a geocaching app or a program that lets you develop your own game or challenge. Divide your guests into groups, with each group needing to navigate to a specific meeting point or hidden treasure using clues or riddles. You can even name your groups the Turks, British, and Jewish underground.

# 2

# BELLA ABZUG

## *"Battling Bella"*

B ella Abzug — then Bella Savitzky — embarked on her first feminist revolution at the age of thirteen. Her beloved father had passed away and Bella, who grew up in a religious home in New York and had always been angry that she had to sit in the women's section in the synagogue, stood up and recited the Mourner's **Kaddish**, a prayer that was reserved only for men. For a full year, she would come to the synagogue in the morning before school and say Kaddish, and no one dared object.

Bella was born in 1920 — the year in which women were given the right to vote in the United States, she was known to note proudly — to Emanuel and Esther Savitzky, both refugees from the **pogroms** in Russia. Her father was a butcher and her mother a housewife.

As a child, Bella was full of life, mischievous, and loved to sing; she was known to have a beautiful voice. Her older sister, Helene, was a gifted pianist, her father was a singer, and the family sang together on a weekly basis.

Bella's political activity began at age eleven. She and her friends from the **HaShomer HaTzair** youth movement would position themselves at the railroad station and raise funds for the Jewish community in the Land of Israel. Bella, who was always a gifted speaker, would give speeches about the **Zionist** enterprise and her friends would collect money from the passengers, who were moved by her words.

When Bella decided to study law, only her mother supported her; the rest of her extended family suggested she marry a lawyer instead. Bella applied to Harvard University, but was rejected because she was a woman. So Bella remained in New York and studied at Columbia University, which had offered her a substantial scholarship.

From the moment Bella received her license to practice law, she focused on civil rights, minority rights, and women's rights. She never dreamed of making a lot of money; she only wanted to make the world a little better.

In 1948, Republican Senator Joseph McCarthy began his hunt for people who were engaged in communist activities. Bella chose to defend the common people who were in danger of being fired due to suspicions about being communists.

Bella first became known in the public sphere due to a case she did not win. Willie McGee from Mississippi, an African American truck driver, had been accused of raping a white woman and was sentenced to death; the jury deliberated for two and a half minutes. Bella acted as his lawyer during his appeals in Mississippi and the Supreme Court. Mississippi was a hotbed of racism, and public opinion had already decided that McGee was guilty. When Bella arrived in Jackson, Mississippi, before the appeal, no one would rent her a hotel room; Bella, who was pregnant at the time, was forced to sleep on a bench in the bus station. And while Bella was not able to reverse Willie McGee's sentence, she did manage to successfully argue for a stay of execution twice.

It was not only in the courtroom that Bella defended her principles, but also on the street. She believed that protests and demonstrations were an important way to effect change. She was active in organizing a great march against nuclear testing in 1961, a march in which thousands of women from fifty-eight cities all over the U.S. participated. As a result of the march, a women's movement was founded, "Women Strike for Peace," which led the United States, the

33

United Kingdom, and the Soviet Union to sign the Limited Test Ban Treaty. The movement, led by Bella, then began to speak out against the war in Vietnam.

But Bella aspired to do even more. Instead of fighting laws, she wanted to make them herself, and, in 1971, she was elected a Democratic congresswoman. She was one of 13 women in a congress of 435 representatives. Many people did not like her very presence there. They did not like the fact that she fought for her beliefs, for minority rights, and against the war in Vietnam. Her opponents called her "Battling Bella," claimed that she swore, said that she was a communist, and even criticized her form of dress — primarily her colorful hats. But she ignored them, and focused on getting her job done.

Bella was one of the first members of Congress to support gay rights, introducing the Equality Act of 1974 along with Ed Koch. She sponsored the Equality Credit Opportunity Act, which made it illegal for money-lenders to discriminate along racial, gender, or religious lines. And she continued to be a supporter of the State of Israel and Zionism, leading the charge against the United Nations' 1975 resolution that stated that "Zionism Is Racism."

If she could have, Bella wrote in her diary, she would have created a coalition of women, minorities, youth, poor, elderly, workers, and the unemployed, a coalition that would turn the country upside down.

During her three terms in the House of Representatives, the war in Vietnam ended and many laws she had worked on were passed, advancing women's rights and the rights of other minorities.

Bella, along with other prominent American feminists such as Shirley Chisholm, Betty Friedan, and Gloria Steinem, founded the National Women's Political Caucus to support and foster women's participation in politics.

After an unsuccessful primary race for the Senate, Bella did not step away from her mission. She was one of the founders of the Women's Environmental and Development Organization (WEDO) in 1991, a global organization promoting human rights, gender equality, and the environment, and lobbied the United Nations to ensure that these topics were on their agenda. She worked on national commissions for women's issues. She did not stop creating change until her very last day.

Bella was also a wife and mother; her husband was her greatest supporter and one of her daughters followed her into the world of politics and leadership, founding the Bella Abzug Leadership Institute (BALI) for young women.

# ADD YOUR VOICE

*"Let's be honest about it: she did not knock politely on the door; she took the hinges off of it."*

*(Geraldine Ferraro)*

## Explore

United Nations General Assembly Resolution 3379, adopted in 1975, stated that "Zionism is a form of racism and racial discrimination." The resolution caused a great stir around the world — some people felt that it itself was an **anti-Semitic** statement — and was eventually revoked in 1991. Bella Abzug was a vocal opponent of the resolution, stating: "Zionism is a liberation movement."

This topic is a complex one. What led the United Nations to pass the resolution? Why was it revoked? Look into the history and the different voices on the subject. Who supported the resolution and who opposed it? What arguments did they make? What do you think?

## Give Back

"Battling Bella" was never silent when she felt there was an injustice or something that must be changed. Causes she fought for included women's rights, gay rights, the environment, opposition to the Vietnam war, and opposition to the draft.

Bella's activism took many forms: aside from working within the government to effect change, she also helped organize and participated in demonstrations and marches. What causes do you feel strongly about? How can you stand up and demand change? What tools are at your disposal? Find a cause that you believe in and, inspired by Bella, work for change.

## See Something New

"This woman's place is in the house — the House of Representatives," Bella famously said.

How much do you know about governing bodies where you live? Where are the decisions made and how? Can you learn more about your local government or city hall and pay it a visit?

## Get Out of Your Comfort Zone

Bella Abzug had a lot in common with Shulamit Aloni (see chapter 4), despite the fact that one lived in Israel and one in America. Both were women who fought for what they believed in within government and outside of it. Both worked to secure equal rights for women and for other groups. Both were known to ruffle some feathers. How were they similar and how were they different? What influenced them? What other female Jewish politicians do you know of, and how do they compare to Bella Abzug and Shulamit Aloni? Are there other women you can think of who contributed similarly to society? Can you use a new medium to express your conclusions — a podcast, written post, poem, or a different creative form?

# 3

# GRACE AGUILAR

## *Groundbreaking Poet and Thinker*

Take a deep breath — off we go!

It's truly hard to follow Grace Aguilar's life story — in her thirty-one years, she managed to become a writer, poet, thinker, historian, and activist for Jewish rights and women's rights — but we'll try.

Grace Aguilar was the oldest child in a well-respected, intellectual family that came from the **Marranos**, or **crypto-Jews**, of Portugal and returned to the Jewish religion when they reached the shores of enlightened England. Her father was a *gabbai* and *parnas* in London's Spanish and Portuguese Synagogue.

From a young age, Grace was sickly. No one seemed able to diagnose her, but her disease made her vulnerable and sensitive. Still, it did not keep her from being an active child, from dancing, playing piano and harp, and spending time with friends her age.

Nor did it keep her from writing. Grace kept a journal from age seven until her death, and she wrote a play, about King Gustav of Sweden, at age twelve. When she was fifteen, Grace began to write a romance novel about the secret lives of Spain's Marranos; she called it *The Vale of Cedars*. Her book expressed the tension between romantic love and loyalty to the Jewish religion. The book's heroine ultimately abandoned her beloved and would not leave her religion:

"Tempt me no more, Arthur; it cannot be." She speaks of "a love, a duty stronger than that I bear to thee. I would resign all else, but not my father's God." Grace spent four years writing the book, but it was only published three years after her death.

Grace was educated at home. Her father Emanuel taught her about the heritage of Spain and Portugal's Jews; her mother Sarah told her about the traditions that Marrano women passed from mother to daughter and studied Bible with her as well. Aside from her Jewish education, Grace was very interested in Christian heritage, and visited many churches. She may have been seeking opportunities to read the Bible in her mother tongue, English. At the time, there was no **Tanakh** — Bible — in English. As an adult, Grace campaigned for a translation and, while she was able to bring it about, she did not get to use it; it was published after her death.

Grace's father contracted tuberculosis when she was twelve, and a few years later her mother fell ill as well. Grace joined her mother running a Hebrew school for boys and made her hobby of writing into a job, supporting the family.

Grace Aguilar was considered the most important Jewish writer of her generation. She published poems in Jewish and non-Jewish journals in England and the U.S. She wrote essential articles about Jewish history and the meaning of Judaism; she published books about Jewish women and the Jews who were expelled from Spain and Portugal.

Her most prominent work was a three-volume series called *The Women of Israel*, which told the stories of significant women in the **Torah, Talmud, Midrash**, and Jewish history. Her book emphasized the importance of the women's personal growth.

In books and articles that she wrote for Jews and Christians, Grace fought for the honor of the Jewish nation and its right to equality, and battled specifically for Jewish women and their rights. She was a feminist before the word was invented. About a year after her death, the first association for women's rights was founded in the U.S. Although Grace did not witness the women's rights movement in her own lifetime, she did receive a letter from one hundred Jewish women, who thanked her for teaching them to live proudly.

Grace Aguilar died far from her family, in Germany, where she had gone for healing waters. Newspapers in England and the United States declared national mourning. Her gravestone, in Frankfurt, bears words from the poem "Woman of Valor" (*Eshet Hayil*) that appears in the book of Proverbs: "Give her of the fruit of her hands; and let her own works praise her from the gates" (Proverbs 31:31).

# ADD YOUR VOICE

## *Explore*

Beginning in the fourteenth century, Jews living in Spain and Portugal were persecuted and threatened with death if they refused to convert to Christianity. Some Jews were sent to their deaths and some were expelled from their lands, but many Jews chose to convert publicly and continue to practice their religion in secret. These people — sometimes called crypto-Jews or Marranos — continued to pass their secret practices down from generation to generation.

You can study the history of crypto-Judaism, and give some thought to what it must have meant to conduct Jewish practice in secret. Where did the crypto-Jews practice? How could they recognize one another? What is their status today? Furthermore, you can take a closer look at how the role of women shifted in the age of crypto-Judaism: Grace Aguilar herself noted that it was the women who reinvented Jewish practice in a time when it moved from having an external character — in the synagogues and houses of study — to the home. And that was where the women took control of transmitting Jewish heritage to the next generations.

You may also want to learn more about Judith Montefiore, who joined Grace Aguilar's synagogue when she married Moses Montefiore. While she herself was not a crypto-Jew, her marriage was the first to blend the two communities, and her husband had the rule banning non-**Sephardim** from the synagogue changed to let her in. Judith Montefiore traveled with her husband and kept diaries about their life together. Another fascinating crypto-Jew was Doña Gracia Mendes Nasi, whom you can learn about later on in this book (chapter 35).

## Give Back

What women's organizations exist in your community? To honor Grace Aguilar and the difference she made in Jewish women's lives, look for volunteer opportunities around you. Organizations like the National Council of Jewish Women, the Union of Jewish Women, JOFA (Jewish **Orthodox** Feminist Alliance), and Jewish Women International may be looking for volunteers for various programs or, in Grace's spirit, teen writers.

## See Something New

One of the most beautiful spots in the Jerusalem Forest is called, much like Grace Aguilar's book, the Vale of Cedars, or Cedar Trail. The valley is full of signs of life from the past: rock steps and orchards mark ancient villages; hilly springs supplied water and made it possible for people to live here years ago. Forests have been planted by the JNF-Keren Kayemeth LeYisrael next to the natural thicket.

If you are a bike rider, you can bike the forest on a path that extends from the Mesila Park in southern Jerusalem to the heart of Emek HaArazim, a valley in Jerusalem's northwest. In one special area, a children's play space has been carved out of stone. It contains games, each enlarged so that a number of children or people can play at once: checkers, chutes and ladders, dominos, and more.

And if you're in London, you can see the synagogue where Grace Aguilar prayed, today called the Bevis Marks Synagogue. Built in 1701, it tells the story of the community throughout the ages; its **ark** was designed in Renaissance style, and Moses Montefiore's seat is reserved only for special visitors — King Charles (when he was Prince Charles) and Prime Minister Tony Blair both sat there on special occasions.

## Get Out of Your Comfort Zone

Grace Aguilar was ahead of her time. Her style, talent, output, **Zionism**, and feminism were all revolutionary. But somehow she is relatively unknown today. Perhaps you can take on a project: helping people learn more about her and recognize her brilliance. You can learn more about her to add to her Wikipedia entry or hold an essay contest in her honor.

# 4

# SHULAMIT ALONI

## *Social Justice Warrior*

"We grew up, my brother and I," Shulamit said, "like small wild animals. I cooked and cleaned... At age four, I was already teaching another girl, and later on I washed the school and worked cleaning." In seventh grade, she had to leave home.

Shulamit Adler was born in Poland to Yehudit and David, and her brother Mordechai was born after her. Her parents, who were **Zionists** and socialists, moved to the Land of Israel when she was small and settled in southern Tel Aviv.

Shulamit's father was a carpenter and her mother was a seamstress. They lived in abject poverty and their marriage was not a happy one. Shulamit's mother would often leave the house for long periods — always without warning, and always without saying goodbye to her children.

When the Second World War broke out, with Shulamit at bat-mitzvah age, both of her parents enlisted in the British army, and she moved to a dormitory school in Raanana. At the school she, like all of the students, had to work for her keep and collect food from the *moshava*'s farmers. It was at this time that her brother was found dead in a swimming pool; Shulamit believed that he had killed himself, overwhelmed by his life. His death shook her parents, and they decided to move Shulamit from her school to the Ben Shemen Youth Village. At Ben Shemen, Shulamit flourished. She joined the **HaShomer HaTzair** youth movement and the **Haganah**, and also met her partner, Motke Lipkin, a member of **Kibbutz** Alumot in the Lower Galilee. They built themselves a cabin and lived there for four wonderful years, until Motke was killed at the beginning of the **War of Independence**.

Shulamit also contributed to the war effort. She enlisted in the **Palmach** and defended Jerusalem's Jewish Quarter.

Shulamit trained as a teacher and was the first person to teach a new subject: civics. Good citizenship and preserving citizens' rights within the state would occupy her for her entire life. In the evenings, she studied law at the Tel Aviv School of Law and Economics, which later grew into Tel Aviv University.

These were the years when she met the man she would marry, the father of her three children, Reuven Aloni. The two bought a small bungalow on the edges of Kfar Shmaryahu, which was then an agricultural settlement, and there she lived for the rest of her life.

Shulamit was an editor and host of radio broadcasts, and became famous when she hosted a show on law in which people learned about their legal rights. In the early 1960s, she invented a new form of radio: discussions with people who felt they had been wronged by the state. The show, *HaNoseh BiTipul* ("The Issue Is Being Taken Care Of"), became one of the most popular in Israel; everyone knew who Shulamit Aloni was. She dealt with all issues great and small, turned to authorities and nagged them, and also taught people how to stand up for their rights. She primarily focused on issues such as **halakha** (Jewish law), marriage, and divorce. Shulamit believed that there was no crisis that could not be solved within halakha if the rabbis tried hard enough. Another issue she focused on was women's rights.

These two issues, women's rights and the relationship between religion and state, were her guiding light when she became a Member of **Knesset** as well. Her political activity began with the ruling party at the time, **Mapai**, but she was combative and scathing even towards members of her own party, which they did not like. The enmity between her and Prime Minister Golda Meir (see chapter 33)

43

was particularly noticeable. She left Mapai and established her own party, the Citizens Rights Movement (Ratz, which later united with other parties and was renamed Meretz).

Shulamit Aloni served as a Member of Knesset for thirty years, for the most part in the opposition party, because she could never agree with the majority and never compromised on her opinions. No one could remain apathetic to her. She was beloved by some segments of the population and hated and slandered by others. For a short time, during Yitzhak Rabin's term as prime minister, Aloni felt confident enough to join the government and was even appointed minister of education, but she was forced to give up her post due to objections on the part of the religious community.

Shulamit Aloni wrote six books about the relationship between citizens and the state. She founded important institutions, such as the Israel Consumer Council, meant to help citizens who were cheated in commerce and to fight large commercial bodies; it is hard to picture the state without these institutions today. She fought for the appointment of an ombudsman, whose job is to investigate the complaints made by citizens regarding public institutions.

On her grave, next to her name and the dates of her birth and death, one word is engraved: *Ezrahit*, Citizen.

# ADD YOUR VOICE

*"I tell the truth and the truth — nu, what can you do — is irritating."*

## *Explore*

---

What do you know about the idea of **tikkun olam**? The phrase means "repairing the world," but it has been used to mean different things at different times and for different communities. What does it mean to you? Do some research on the source of the phrase, its meaning, and how it is used today.

For some — like Shulamit Aloni — *tikkun olam* relates to granting equal rights to all. Does everyone where you live have equal rights today? If not, who is not yet equal? What rights are they refused? What rights were available or not available to your parents or grandparents? How has access to rights changed over time?

## Give Back

While rights are promised to everyone living in a democracy, oftentimes some people living in a country have trouble accessing those rights or using them fully. Which people in your community or city are having trouble accessing rights? Which rights can be harder to attain? Look around for an organization that tries to help people who are disenfranchised or underprivileged and ask how you can help.

## See Something New

Shulamit Aloni spent many years in the Ben Shemen Youth Village, located next to the Ben Shemen Forest, the largest forest to be planted in Israel. The youth village was founded nearly one hundred years ago in order educate youth about Zionism and working the land. It quickly became a warm and loving home for many young people who had escaped the Nazis and the horrors of the Holocaust.

Today the Ben Shemen Youth Village is one of fifty heritage sites in Israel, and it is open to visitors. You can arrange to tour the old residential buildings, one of which Shulamit Aloni lived in; you can look out at the green spaces, and imagine her shepherding the village's sheep. In the Museatar, the village's open museum, you can even see a telescope that was given to youth village director Siegfried Lehman by his friend Albert Einstein.

From the youth village, you can go to the nearby forest. Though there are many places to see in this huge forest, one beautiful spot in particular is worth seeing: a small park made accessible to the visually impaired (use GPS to search for "Ha-Ivrim Camping," or וינח ילקיזומה וגה-סירוויעה on Waze).

A metal railing to the left of the pathway leads the blind in the correct direction. The signage (at hand level) is embossed in Hebrew, English, and Braille. At the (wide) entrance there are samples of the forest's stones (which can be felt) and of the most common tree in the forest — the pine. The pathway winds between spices, which can be crushed and smelled and distinguished from one another. From there it continues to a fruit grove; you can feel the trees' texture (is it smooth? rough? round? extended?).

It's best if you and your guests close your eyes, at least for part of the time, and experience what blind people do: let your other senses lead you. The place's accessibility to the blind and visually impaired may even contain an echo of Shulamit Aloni's dream — equality for all.

## Get Out of Your Comfort Zone

The game suggested here is based on a concern for the rights of each and every person, and is quite complicated. Explain the game's goal and rules to your friends ahead of time, but let them know that you, as the game's leader, are permitted to break them. Tell them that if you break the rules, they are permitted to defend themselves in any way, except for violence.

Divide your friends into groups. Each group must build something. Give each of them the necessary items: cubes, clothespins, colored scarves, cardboard boxes, and so on. Do not give out the items evenly. Give some groups more, and some less.

You will be responsible for the items. When the representative of a team that has received less comes to you for more items, you can choose whether to give them more or to leave them at a disadvantage.

Pay attention to what happens: At what stage does a group re-alize that discrimination is taking place? When do different groups realize that they are more privileged than others? What do the un-derprivileged groups do in order to get what they need? What are others willing to do to help those who have less, if anything? Those who have received more, of course, have a better chance of winning if there are groups with less.

At the end of the game, try together to come to conclusions about what you have learned.

# 5

# ESTHER ARDITI

## *The First Woman to Receive Israel's Military Medal of Distinguished Service*

T he paratroopers who stormed toward the Western Wall in the early days of the **Six-Day War** thought they were seeing an angel. A small woman, in a white robe and with a helmet on her head, accompanied them through the alleyways of the Old City. She was with them day and night, never sleeping, taking care of each casualty quietly, stirring confidence, saving dozens. No one knew where she had come from and no one knew where she disappeared to.

But now we know: nurse Esther Arditi, who volunteered to accompany the soldiers in the Old City, simply went home, to her two children. And she was often known as the Angel in White.

In fact, Esther had been driving an ambulance and was instructed to take the injured soldiers to the hospital but she refused; she insisted that other people could drive but she, as a nurse, could treat the wounded in the field. The doctor she pleaded with agreed — he put a helmet on her head and she ran from injured soldier to injured soldier during the battle. After she disappeared, the soldiers searched for her, hoping to locate the angel who had saved their lives; her neighbor revealed her identity a few days later.

But this was not the first time that Esther had stood out for her courage and dedication.

Thirteen years earlier, as a young soldier of seventeen who had just completed the medics' course, she rescued injured people from a burning airplane and became the first woman in Israel to receive a commendation from the **IDF** chief of staff.

The night of November 29, 1954, was particularly stormy. The air force base at Hatzor was hit by lightning; electricity was lost and the lights on the landing strip went out. Up in the air above the base, Major Yaakov Shalmon lost control of his plane and it caught fire upon landing. Young Esther was driving an ambulance that became stuck in the mud. She raced barefoot toward the plane with the rescue team, but no one dared approach it. Hearing the navigator's cries of pain, Esther rushed inside, ignoring her friends' calls to stay out of danger. With a strength that came from nowhere (she was the size of a child, under five feet tall and only eight-five pounds), she dragged the navigator from the burning plane to a nearby ditch, and then returned to rescue the pilot, Major Shalmon, who was unconscious and still belted to his seat. She cut the burning seatbelt with scissors and rolled him from the burning plane to the ditch where the navigator lay. Then she leaned over the two, protecting them with her body as the plane erupted in a huge fireball.

The navigator, Shlomo Hertzman, died of his wounds. The pilot, Yaakov Shalmon, awoke two weeks later to find the small soldier who had saved him sitting beside him. Esther became part of his family, adopted by his parents; until then, she had lived on her own.

Esther was born in Bulgaria in 1937, and her family was expelled to Italy during the Second World War. In 1943, when Esther was six, the Germans conquered northern Italy, including Livorno, the city where they lived. The family — father, mother, and three children — was forced to hide in a bakery in one of the villages. Esther's baby brother died of typhus; her mother was killed in an accident, hit by a truck carrying soldiers; their house was destroyed (like most of the city's houses); and her father sank into depression.

Esther's father could not recover after the loss of so many family members during the Holocaust; Esther, at age ten, understood that she would have to take care of herself. She signed herself up for a Catholic school and tried to put her past behind her, along with the Judaism that she saw as the reason for her suffering.

But then the State of Israel was established. Esther, now eleven, heard about the new country and the **War of Independence** and grew excited. For the first time in her life, she was proud of her Jewish heritage. She asked her father to leave Italy and move to Israel, but he refused. Under the cover of night, she left the house on her own, headed for Naples, and boarded a ship. She was sure that the ship would take her to the Land of Israel. She had not taken into account that each ship had its own destination; she had boarded a Tunisian ship. But Esther was lucky — she was found by police who had been alerted by her father.

Father and daughter reached an agreement: when Esther finished school and completed her exams, she could move to Israel. With her burning desire for a new life in the Jewish homeland, Esther finished her exams at age sixteen, moved to Israel, and insisted on enlisting in the IDF early.

It was for that reason that she was only seventeen when she became a hero. For her dedication in 1954, Esther received the Medal of Distinguished Service; for her aid in later wars, she received another citation.

But we should also tell the rest of Esther's story, because not everything has been told.

We have not mentioned that she was the first female ambulance driver in the state, and a registered nurse, and that six years after the Six-Day War, when the **Yom Kippur War** broke out, Esther, now almost forty, once again appeared with her first aid kid at the Suez Canal to treat the wounded.

When Esther understood that she had had enough of working as a nurse, that she had "seen enough blood," she became a tour guide for Italian tourists, teaching them to see the beauty of the state and the land.

As fate would have it, Esther Arditi, who so loved the Land of Israel, passed away when she was on a roots trip to the home of her youth, Livorno, Italy, and that is where she is buried.

# ADD YOUR VOICE

*"I have never been religious. Quite the opposite, I am quite weak in the Jewish subjects... I had never even been near the Western Wall before, as I arrived in Israel when the Wall was in the hands of the Jordanians. Nonetheless, I was moved when I neared the Wall in the twisting alleys of the Old City... I saw the massive stones...and something pinched my heart. I jumped from the half-track vehicle, approached the Western Wall, and began to cry on the cold stones. I cried, and I don't know why. I cried because of all of the blood that I had seen in the recent days. I cried because of the great victory. I cried because of the fate of my mother in that village in northern Italy. I cried because of what we had suffered for generations. I cried with all my heart."*

## *Explore*

———

Esther Arditi loved her land, Israel, and especially Jerusalem, where she lived. She guided tourists around the city and the country, teaching them about the land's history and sites that were special to her. She loved showing Jews from around the world her beloved country.

Using today's technology, you can create your own virtual tour and see the path that Esther Arditi took during the war in 1967. Begin on Bar-Ilan Street, move toward Ammunition Hill, and from there travel to Mount Scopus, the Mount of Olives, the Old City, and, finally, the Temple Mount. You can also visit the road named for her after her death, located in the Abu Tor neighborhood.

## Give Back

---

In the spirit of Esther Arditi's work with the sick and injured, you can visit children in pediatric wards in hospitals. You may connect with a child whom you could have befriended even if they were not sick; you can even hold a celebration there. (Most hospitals have community relations departments that you can contact to arrange a visit.) You can organize an activity for the children in the hospital — a craft, imagination game, contest, singalong, computer game, and more. You can also ask some or all of your guests to donate money to the children's ward instead of giving you a gift, or you can choose to donate some of your gifts.

## See Something New

---

A lookout point named for Esther Arditi stands on the banks of the Jordan River at "Old Gesher," the original site of **Kibbutz** Gesher in the Jordan Valley. The kibbutz, founded in 1939, was evacuated in 1948, and rebuilt to the west of the initial location. From "Old Gesher" you can look out over four ancient bridges on the Jordan.

And if you've come as far as the Jordan Valley, you can enjoy the audio-visual presentation at Old Gesher, which tells the story of the first power plant in the land, and take note of the way in which they built the first **children's house** (and other houses) of mudbrick at Kibbutz Gesher. You can reserve a guided tour.

Or you may want to take another path: Esther Arditi's story is interwoven with the story of Jerusalem, and it is a story of military heritage. One of the sites most commonly associated with the 1967 war is Ammunition Hill, where Esther joined the soldiers at her own initiative in order to care for the wounded in the Six-Day War.

Walk around and inside of the trenches at the memorial site. Try to imagine the battle, a battle of trenches and ditches, and the kind-hearted nurse answering the cries of the injured. Visit the museum and watch the audiovisual program with its descriptions of the war.

## Get Out of Your Comfort Zone

In Esther Arditi's spirit, you can invite friends to a first-aid workshop. Dressing wounds, saving infants from choking, knowing when not to move a patient, and how to call for professional help are invaluable skills that perpetuate the legacy of Esther Arditi, who saved so many from death.

# 6

# RUTH BADER GINSBURG

## *Supreme Court Justice and Defender of Equal Rights*

On the wall of Supreme Court Justice Ruth Bader Ginsburg's office hung the biblical verse "Justice, justice shall you pursue" (Deuteronomy 17:20), a verse she saw as a value that had guided Jewish tradition from time immemorial.

Ruth Bader Ginsburg was born to a working-class family in Brooklyn, New York. Her father, Nathan, had immigrated from Russia as a youth, and her mother, Cecilia, was born just months after her parents arrived in New York from Poland. When Ruth was a year old, her only sister died of meningitis.

The Bader family belonged to a traditional congregation in the city, and Ruth was active; she took part in its summer camps from age four, and at age thirteen she became a camp counselor. But there was a moment of crisis between her and her community, when she was not allowed to read from the **Torah** for her bat mitzvah.

Ruth tied for first place at Columbia University's law school in New York. But when she searched for work as a law clerk or lawyer, no one would accept her. Why? Because she was a woman. This may have been the moment when she decided to fight for women's rights.

But that moment may also have come years earlier, when she saw her mother Cecelia, who was an outstanding student herself, working long hours at a factory. Cecelia, who was not able to go to college, worked to support her family and her brother, who was selected by her parents for higher education.

Ruth's mother, who closely guided her education, died of cancer a day before Ruth finished high school. Her daughter continued to worship her until her last day. When she was sworn in as Supreme Court justice, she spoke about her mother, who had had to give up on her education because she was a woman.

Ruth was a pioneer. At Harvard, she was one of nine female students of the total five hundred in her graduating class. Her husband, Martin Ginsburg, was also in her department. When they completed their studies, Martin's career took off, but Ruth — despite warm recommendations from the best of teachers — had trouble finding work. "In the fifties," she later explained, "the traditional law offices were only just beginning to turn around on hiring Jews. But to be a woman, a Jew, and a mother to boot — that combination was a bit too much."

A few years later, working at the American Civil Liberties Union (ACLU), she was part of a team that formulated a law stating that employers may not discriminate against employees based on their gender.

She was the first woman to receive tenure as a law professor at Columbia University. And, in fact, she was the first in many fields throughout her life. She was the first female Jewish Supreme Court justice (and the second woman), and, when she got older, the oldest person to serve on the Supreme Court.

Three stories tell the story of how she worked for gender equality; in two, she was a lawyer; in the other, she was in her early years on the Supreme Court.

In a 1975 case, Ruth helped a widower sue for social security benefits when he was left the sole provider for his son. Finding that he was not eligible to receive benefits as a single parent because he was male, he felt that the Social Security Act was guilty of gender discrimination. Ruth argued that the act discriminated against widowers and also denied them the opportunities to care for their children; she also argued that the same act discriminated against women — including her client's wife — because they earned less family benefits for their contributions to Social Security than men did.

In her final case as a lawyer, before she was appointed a judge, Ruth defended a man who had been accused of murder and robbery. She made a motion for a new trial, claiming that the state of Missouri, in making jury duty optional for women, made it impossible for him to have an impartial jury. Ruth had his conviction overturned.

In "United States v. Virginia," Ruth served as a judge. The Virginia Military Institute at the time did not accept women, and the federal government challenged its admissions rules, saying it violated the Fourteenth Amendment's Equal Protection Clause. Virginia's authorities claimed that there was another military academy for women; Ruth and her colleagues ruled that the military academy for women paled in comparison to the men's academy and therefore could not serve as a justification for gender segregation. The case broke a tradition more than 150 years old, and the academy in Virginia was forced to accept women.

Ruth Bader Ginsburg served as a Supreme Court justice for forty years, until her last day; over the years, she became an influential figure for young and old alike. She was affectionately known as RBG, and two films — one a documentary, one a drama — were made about her life.

# ADD YOUR VOICE

## Explore

What do you know about America's Supreme Court? When was it founded? How are justices selected? How long do they serve? Why do you think the court was designed this way? Can you compare it to Israel's Supreme Court? Which of the two systems do you think is better and why?

## Give Back

Ruth Bader Ginsburg's first leadership role was as a camp counselor. Do you go to a summer camp or belong to a youth movement? Both summer camp and youth movements constitute special communities, places in which groups band together and learn about their own identity and world. Jewish summer camps and youth movements give kids an opportunity to make new friends, to learn more about their heritage, to experience Jewish traditions and activities, and more. Can you hold a bat mitzvah celebration with a youth movement or summer camp? How can you contribute to your summer camp or youth group? Can you run programs for other kids or create a new program?

## See Something New

Have you ever visited a courthouse? America, for example, has a dual court system, with district courts and state trial courts, and judgments in both can be appealed and eventually reach the Supreme Court. Why are different levels of courts important in all countries? What happens in the appeals process? Visit a courthouse and learn more about the system.

## Get Out of Your Comfort Zone

Miriam Ben-Porat, the first woman on Israel's Supreme Court (see chapter 8), once said: "I do not see myself as the representative of women on the Supreme Court. We all serve justice, serve the public, and it is a joint task." Esther Hayut, Chief Justice of Israel's Supreme Court since 2017, has quoted Miriam Ben-Porat, and added: "If we think about this statement in depth, it in fact reflects gender equality at its best." Would Ruth Bader Ginsburg agree? Why or why not? Can you write your own legal statement on the subject?

# 7

# OSNAT BARZANI

## *The First Female* **Rosh Yeshiva**

O snat was clever and pleasant, the only child of Rabbi Shmuel
Halevi Barzani, and her story is unique in the history of Jewish
communities. Few women at her time, in the sixteenth and seventeenth centuries, held influence within their communities, and certainly none stood at the head of a **yeshiva**. Her story is a surprising
one for many reasons — but it also gives us pause: we think of the
women who serve in roles of Jewish religious leadership today as
pioneers, but Osnat did the same almost four hundred years ago.

Osnat's father taught her only **Torah**; he did not want her to waste
her time on anything else. "I was like a princess of Israel," Osnat
wrote. "I grew up on the laps of scholars, anchored to my father of
blessed memory. I was never taught any word but sacred study." Her
husband, her father's beloved student Rabbi Yaakov Mizrachi, promised her father that he would not let her do any housework. Her father directed him to allow her to continue learning Torah as he had:
"He made my husband swear that he would not make me perform
work, and he [my husband] did as he [my father] had commanded
him." Perhaps her father did this because he had no sons, but he may
simply have recognized his daughter's superior wisdom.

Rabbi Shmuel established four yeshivas throughout Kurdistan, an
area made up of what is today southeastern Turkey, northern Iraq,

northwestern Iran, and northern Syria. When he died in 1630, he left the yeshiva in the city of Mosul to his son-in-law. But the young couple decided that, although Yaakov would hold the title of **Rosh Yeshiva**, he would continue to learn Torah, and Osnat would teach — and so it was. When Yaakov passed away a few years later, Osnat naturally took on the role of *Rosh Yeshiva*. Her community accepted her authority and recognized her ability to hold the honored position, giving her the title "tanna'it." **Tanna** was the designation given to sages from the **mishnaic** period and the term had, until that time, only referred to men; the word "tanna'it," using the feminine form, had never before been used. Within Osnat's community, it was said that the tanna'it used God's names to effect miracles. Many generations of people would write her name in amulets for luck and health.

Nonetheless, Osnat's yeshiva faced a challenge: it was in danger of closing. The Barzani-Mizrachi family had put all of its money into the yeshiva and left little for themselves. Ultimately, Osnat remained with nothing. In a pained, tempestuous letter, she describes how the authorities came into her home with a judge's order and took everything: "And they seized the house and took [the] key, the unbelievers, and sold all of my clothes and the clothes of my daughters, may they be blessed by their maker. Even my books that I had before me."

Osnat could not let her yeshiva go down without a fight; she chose to ask for help, and wrote to Jews in communities around the world asking for assistance. Her letters were written in Hebrew and sprinkled with verses from the **Tanakh** (Bible) and the words of the sages, and contained brilliant rhymes. In them, one gets a sense of her comprehensive knowledge of Torah, learned from her father and taught to her students:

Hear, o sages, my words and wise ones listen to me...
For Torah do I cry, do I groan because it is vanished from all of my borders...
I am presented empty, my coat and my robe of glory are removed
I cried: Have mercy, my friends, for woe, alas, alas...

This type of campaign may have been unusual at the time, especially given Osnat's singularity as a woman in a man's world. Did Osnat succeed in her mission? Did philanthropists respond to the request of the only known female *Rosh Yeshiva* and lend support? It appears so, because only a few years later, her son Shmuel continued her path and became the *Rosh Yeshiva*.

Osnat was buried in Amadiya, the city of her birth, and for many years the women of the community would make pilgrimages to her grave to remember her and be blessed by her memory. But if the Jewish women of Kurdistan had not kept telling the story of the tanna'it who was a *Rosh Yeshiva*, no one would believe it. Moreover, no site, neighborhood, or street has been named for her until today. It is only in the past few years that people have begun to tell her story again.

# ADD YOUR VOICE

*"I was never taught any word but sacred study."*

## Explore

More than 350 years have passed since Tanna'it Osnat Barzani served as a *Rosh Yeshiva*, but it is only in recent years that women have begun to find their paths to Jewish religious leadership once again. More and more women learn on special tracks for rabbinical studies. Some are **halakhic** leaders, some are advisors, some serve as rabbis or **rabbaniot** in synagogues or temples. These are women who are following in the footsteps of Osnat Barzani, a true revolutionary.

Do you want to learn more about these groundbreaking women? Look into their history: When did different streams of Jewry first welcome women as leaders? What were their titles? What were their responsibilities? What programs today train women to hold religious leadership roles in your community? How were Osnat's community and students different from yours today?

## Give Back

The website 929 encourages learning the entire Tanakh, all 929 chapters of it, in daily or weekly study. It has resources in English and Hebrew for each chapter, written by figures from a variety of different Jewish communities. You can form a 929 group to study on a weekly basis (instructions are given on the site).

## See Something New

---

The Jewish community of Kurdistan — Osnat Barzani's community — celebrates a "Seharane" festival every year. The Seharane was originally a celebration of springtime; today it is held on the **Sukkot** holiday. The holiday includes going to nature, singing and dancing, and a feast of special Kurdish foods.

One truly Israeli way to celebrate nature is the Israel National Trail (known in Hebrew as *Shvil Yisrael*). The trail stretches the length of the country, running over 600 miles (or more than 1,000 kilometers), and can take up to two months to complete. It winds its way through national reserves with unequalled views. Many Israelis and tourists challenge themselves to hike the trail all at once or a little at a time. You can choose one part of the trail — or more — and plan a hike, in the spirit of the Seharane festival's celebration of nature.

## Get Out of Your Comfort Zone

---

Even if you can't hike the Israel Trail in person, you can visit it online. Use tools like Google Maps to find different segments of the trail and "hike" them, or even search for online games and quests that lead you to parts of the trail and challenge you to learn more. Many parts of the trail relate to biblical stories or the history of the land. Can you focus on one part of the trail, learn about its history, and visit it virtually?

January 1, 1918–July 26, 2012
12 Shvat 5678–7 Av 5772

# 8

# MIRIAM BEN-PORAT

## *The First Female Judge on Israel's Supreme Court*

T he path of Miriam Ben-Porat, who broke the glass ceiling in almost every role she took on, was rife with difficulties and challenges.

Miriam's family — the Sheinson family — left Russia shortly
before she was born. They were wealthy and well-respected mer-
chants, but the Russian Revolution that began in 1917 had changed
life for tradesmen; they were now seen as enemies of the people.
When the family reached Kovno, Lithuania's capital city, they had
nothing. It was there that Miriam was raised, the youngest of seven
brothers and sisters. At age eighteen, when she finished high school,
she left her parents' home and moved to the Land of Israel on her
own. Her parents, who remained in Lithuania, were later killed in
the Holocaust.

Miriam registered as a law student at the Hebrew University in Jerusalem, and stood out from the very beginning. After the establishment of the State of Israel, Miriam worked in the State Attorney's
Office, the body that represents the state in court.

Miriam was a spirited prosecutor, and at times made waves. One
such incident, which went down in the law books and influences

rulings still today, took place when instead of demanding a stringent punishment for a defendant, she requested, as prosecutor, that he receive a lighter sentence. The defendant, who had been accused of assault, suffered from mental illness. Miriam made it clear to the court that it was his illness that had made it difficult for him to control himself, and she felt that his sentence should be light. The judges adopted her opinion that illnesses that can hinder restraint should be taken into account, and courts rule similarly today.

Miriam Ben-Porat was sharp; she expressed herself well, and as a jurist had vast knowledge and the ability to use it. But when she was appointed a judge in the regional courts after ten years as a prosecutor, not everyone was happy. Some claimed that it was a political appointment, that more experienced lawyers than she were still waiting to become judges. The Israeli Bar Association boycotted her swearing-in ceremony.

But these claims were short-lived. She was appointed, only a few years later, as the first woman to serve as president of the Jerusalem District Court, and, later, she was selected to serve in the country's most prominent legal institution — the Supreme Court. There, too, she was the first woman, opening the door for many after her.

Often, as a judge, Miriam was lenient in the sentences she gave younger people, because she did not want them to be exposed to prison and criminals, which would have an effect on their lives; she was also lenient with the elderly, trying to make sure that they did not spend their last days in jail. "The judge must hate the sin," she explained, "not the sinner."

The Supreme Court is occupied with appeals regarding sentences that have already been handed down and defending civilians from injustice on the part of authorities. Miriam Ben-Porat's transition to her next role, as state comptroller and ombudsman, was natural. As comptroller, her job was to stand guard to ensure that civil servants did not abuse their power.

At age seventy, then, after twelve years in the Supreme Court, Miriam Ben-Porat once again was a pioneer, attaining yet another position that no woman had before. All comptrollers before her had fought for good governance, but Miriam worked tirelessly to combat government corruption and to maintain public integrity, making the State Comptroller's Office a body that civil servants feared. She made sure that all donations, any benefits that public servants received, would be known to the public. Twelve years later, when she exited the Comptroller's Office, she left behind an agency that was more committed to safeguarding moral integrity and the purity of the state's institutions and far more accessible to citizens.

At age eighty-two, Miriam Ben-Porat, the spirited judge who left a magnificent legacy, stepped down to enjoy her family, her daughter and her grandchildren, who surrounded her with love.

# ADD YOUR VOICE

*"A judge must not forget that the great power held in the pen in his hand is only a trust to be used with awe for the members of the public knocking at the gates of the court."*

## *Explore*

The Supreme Court of Israel was founded in July of 1948, right after the establishment of the state. Its shape and function have changed over time. Look into Israel's Supreme Court and learn more about it. How many justices serve on the Supreme Court? How are they appointed? How long do they serve? What are the court's primary tasks? What is the High Court of Justice, and how does it differ from the Supreme Court? How is Israel's legal system different from that of your country?

You can also look into the history of courts in the Land of Israel. What was the court system like when the British ran the country? And before that, under the **Ottoman Empire**?

## Give Back

Miriam Ben-Porat took special care to ensure that mistakes made in a defendant's youth did not affect his or her whole life. She was careful to give sentences that would help rehabilitate young people and give them a second chance at making a good life for themselves.

Another way to give youth a chance is to prevent criminal behaviors before they start. Many communities have anti-bullying programs, where you can become an ambassador. You can learn about different forms of bullying, how to identify bullying around you, and how to support people around you who may be facing bullying behaviors. Being an ambassador means being part of creating a safe space for others at your school or in your community.

## See Something New

In Miriam Ben-Porat's spirit, you can visit the Supreme Court, which is one of Jerusalem's — and perhaps Israel's — most beautiful buildings.

Regular tours are held at the Supreme Court, with a variety of elements emphasized. If you are interested in architecture, you can learn about the building and the way it fits in with its surroundings. If it is the legal system that interests you (if you dream of following in Miriam Ben-Porat's footsteps), you can arrange a tour that focuses on the history of law in Israel or around the world.

The **Knesset**, government offices, and the Supreme Court all sit on Eliezer Kaplan Street in Jerusalem. On the same road is one of the most interesting gardens in the city — the Rose Garden. This is a place where people who want to influence Knesset decisions meet, where demonstrations are held by people who want to be heard by the decision-makers. Fifteen thousand rose bushes, comprising four hundred different species, are planted in the garden and arranged according to their land of origin; a lake stands at their center.

# Get Out of Your Comfort Zone

Ruth Bader Ginsburg (see chapter 6) and Miriam Ben-Porat were both elected to their Supreme Courts (Miriam Ben-Porat in 1976, Ruth Bader Ginsburg in 1993). Both were named for strong women from the Bible; both had families that hailed from Eastern Europe. Both broke glass ceilings throughout their lives, oftentimes while also navigating society's expectations of them as women. Ruth Bader Ginsburg recounted how the women at her university were asked how they could justify taking the place of a man in the program; Miriam Ben-Porat remembered her landlord telling her that she could still reconsider her law program: "It's hard to be a nice girl and a lawyer. You have to choose between the two."

Imagine a discussion between the two women. What would they have agreed or disagreed on? What else did they have in common? What were their attitudes toward equality? What did they say about community involvement? What causes were important to them? You can write up or act out your imagined conversation.

# 9

# RACHEL BLUWSTEIN

## *Famed Mother of Modern Hebrew Poetry*

Rachel Bluwstein was part of a wealthy and distinguished family in Russia. Her grandfathers and uncles were important rabbis, lawyers, poets, and even revolutionaries. Her home hosted the best artists of the time, famed Russian writer Leo Tolstoy was a friend of the family, and Rachel and her eleven siblings were expected to have futures as independent, enlightened people.

In her youth, Rachel suffered from a lung disease, most likely tuberculosis; her mother died of it when Rachel was only sixteen. When her father married a woman who was neither loving nor loved, Rachel and her sister Shoshana left home and traveled to the big city, Kyiv. Rachel, whose artistic talent had stood out ever since she was a child, studied painting and art. But the two were not satisfied; they wanted to learn more. And because women in Russia at the time could not go to university, they decided to travel to Italy. On the way, they stopped on the shores of Jaffa to take a peek at the Land of Israel; they had no intention of staying. They were far from being fervent **Zionists**, although they had been part of a Zionist youth movement and the land intrigued them. Many of their friends already lived there, as did their older brother.

Rachel and her sister saw the Land of Israel and were enchanted; they fell in love with the people, too. Instead of continuing to Italy, they settled in the *moshava* of Rehovot.

Rachel learned the Hebrew language from the preschool children in Rehovot — she went to the nursery each day and listened to them speaking. The workers in the *moshava* exposed her to the dreams of the youth of the **Second Aliyah**: an egalitarian society that lived from its own work, from agriculture.

Rachel abandoned her artistic dreams to focus on agriculture and the vision of building a new land. She went north to search for a mentor, and met Dr. Hannah Maisel, a teacher of agriculture (later called Hannah Maisel-Shohat; see chapter 31). Rachel became the first student at Dr. Maisel's Young Women's Farm overlooking the **Kinneret**, or Sea of Galilee.

These were happy days. Rachel loved the Kinneret, and the people who lived around the Kinneret loved the joyful, tempestuous Rachel. Zalman Shazar — later the president of the State of Israel — remembered falling in love with the "lithe goose shepherdess with blue eyes and a white dress." Everyone in the valley recalled how she led the people of the Kinneret Farm in a raging dance to Degania, the neighboring **kibbutz**, along the Jordan River.

When Rachel left the farm two years later to travel to the University of Toulouse in France to study agriculture, no one knew that within the year the First World War would break out. The war ultimately kept Rachel away from her land, from her family and friends, for many long years; she couldn't have known that this period of time would change her life.

During the war Rachel returned to Russia, but without proper means to live; she wore spare, light clothes in the freezing weather and unsuitable shoes. Rachel volunteered with Jewish homeless children and was reinfected with tuberculosis, which at the time was contagious and often fatal. At the end of the war, when she returned to the Land of Israel, her friends did not recognize her. She was not yet thirty years old, but nothing remained of her youthful beauty. Her svelte body was bent under the weight of the disease; her hair was thin and sparse.

She had dreamt for years of her return to the Kinneret; however, when she returned, she discovered that her small group from the Kinneret Farm had disbanded. The members of the neighboring kibbutz, Degania, remembered her from her youth and invited her to live with them — but when they discovered that she had an infectious illness, they banished her. She carried the pain of that exile for the rest of her life.

The insult and sting, it seems, opened wells of poetry within her. The crisis, the abandonment, and the loneliness became Hebrew words that touch people's hearts still today.

Every week, on Friday, a new poem of Rachel's would be published in the newspaper *Davar*, in clear and simple language that was easy to identify with; readers waited with bated breath for her new composition. Despite the difficult times and the isolation she felt, her poems inspired happiness and hope; moreover, they brought a woman's voice to the world of Israeli poetry which had been, until that point, primarily male. Today her poetry is an indisputable part of Israeli heritage and the Zionist story — Rachel built the new state with words.

But Rachel was ill; her condition continued to deteriorate until her death at age forty-one. She was buried in the Kinneret cemetery. Two books of her poetry were published during her lifetime, and even then students studied her work in Israeli schools and overseas. Her third book was published after her death.

# ADD YOUR VOICE

## *Explore*

Today, the Kinneret is Israel's only freshwater lake and is closely watched by Israelis; when it rains and the water level rises, Israelis are overjoyed. But the Kinneret and the area around it have also been home to many poets, agronomists, and Zionist leaders. The cemetery holds gravestones of fascinating artists and early founders of the land. What drew people to the Kinneret? Look into the history of the lake. Learn its story and the stories of the Jews who were tied to it so closely. Was the Kinneret similar to the lands they had come from or different? What do you think it is about the Kinneret that makes it a source of inspiration for so many?

## Give Back

As Rachel lay ill in her Tel Aviv apartment, dreaming of the outdoors and the children she would never have, she was asked to write poems to go with a series of illustrations of animals. She had never written for children before, but her book, *Inside and Outside*, quickly sold out.

In Rachel's spirit, and in the spirit of her final book, you may want to lend a hand reading to children. Reading books aloud with children helps them develop a good imagination and preparedness for reading; however, not all children are lucky enough to have people read with them on a regular basis. Perhaps you can offer to read to children in an after-school program, or you can spend some time with children whose parents are not able to put aside time to read. You may also want to offer to read books to elderly people whose eyesight is failing. A weekly commitment to reading with others is a great way to give back to the people around you.

## See Something New

The Kinneret was Rachel's favorite place, and her happiest days were spent at the Young Women's Farm, part of what was called the Kinneret Farm or the Kinneret Courtyard. The courtyard has been restored, and now appears as it did in the days when Rachel was a student there. You can take a guided tour, watch a movie about Rachel, see the stunning views, and learn about the way in which people once lived, including seeing the clothing of the time. There are also plenty of water sports and activities at the Kinneret if you're so inclined. A few miles away is Kibbutz Degania, where Rachel lived after she returned from Russia. In Degania Aleph, at the Beit Gordon Museum, you can watch a movie about her life.

## Get Out of Your Comfort Zone

How familiar are you with spoken-word poetry? You may have seen the poetry of Amanda Gorman, American's National Youth Poet Laureate, at President Biden's inauguration in 2021 ("The Hill We Climb"). Spoken-word poetry is a performance art; poems often incorporate alliteration, repetition, and rhyme and can evoke elements of hip-hop, folk music, or jazz.

Create a spoken-word poem to perform in front of your family and friends, perhaps even at your bat mitzvah celebration. You can take a theme from one of Rachel's poems, look into a topic that interests you during your bat mitzvah year, or relate to a subject that is personal and meaningful. Watch spoken-word poems being performed online for inspiration before diving in.

# 10

# BRURIAH

## *A Sage Woman
in the Talmud*

Bruriah, the most learned woman of her time, was born in Tiberias, on the shores of the **Kinneret**, nearly two thousand years ago.

In contrast with other women, Bruriah learned in the **Beit Midrash**, the center of Jewish learning. Her way of life was more similar to that of her father, brother, and husband than it was to that of the women of her time.

Bruriah was a brilliant student. The **Talmud** notes in wonder that she taught three hundred **halakhot** in one day; she was known to be learned, knowledgeable, and the only woman who also gave halakhic opinions. She and her brother were once asked a question about purity and impurity. Rabbi Yehuda ben Baba heard their two answers and stated that Bruriah was right: "Bruriah spoke well." In another instance, she settled a debate between Rabbi Tarfon and the sages, and, once again, Rabbi Yehuda (it appears to have been the same Rabbi Yehuda) stated, "She spoke well."

Bruriah's behavior toward her peers, the sages, was at time harsh: Rabbi Yose HaGlili, one of the most important men of the generation, was once on his way to the city of Lod, and saw Bruriah sitting by the road. He asked her: "By which road should we go to Lod?" and she answered "Foolish Galilean, did not the sages say: 'Do not talk much with women'? You should have said: 'Which way to Lod?'" The Talmud tells us, with the same amazement, that she once kicked a student who was learning quietly; she believed that only **Torah** learned out loud would be retained in one's memory.

These were hard days for the people of Israel. The Romans who ruled the land made severe decrees: the Jews were not permitted to learn Torah or circumcise their sons. Bruriah's father, Rabbi Hanania ben Tradion, who was one of the most important rabbis — or **tannaim** — of the time, was executed because he insisted on learning Torah. But he was not the only one; her mother was also sentenced to death, and her sister was forced into sexual slavery. We may assume Bruriah was saved because she was already married to Rabbi Meir, who not only held a special status but was also known to experience miracles.

Bruriah's life was full of sadness and loss. One particularly striking story about Bruriah and her husband, Rabbi Meir, attests to Bruriah's faith and self-control. The couple had two sons who died tragically on **Shabbat** (the Sabbath). But Bruriah did not tell her husband about the calamity for the entire day, because one is not permitted to mourn on Shabbat. It was only with the end of the day that Bruriah described a halakhic issue to Rabbi Meir, and asked for his opinion: Someone has given me something in trust, she said, and now has asked for it back. Must I return it? Of course, Rabbi Meir replied. She then led him to the room where the two boys lay, and said: "God gave and God took away."

The first *midrasha*, women's seminary, in Israel to cater to young women and teach Jewish religious subjects on a high level — primarily Talmud — opened in the late 1970s and was named for Bruriah. Many similar ones have opened since, and Bruriah still serves as a model and inspiration for girls and women.

# ADD YOUR VOICE

## *Explore*

———

Women's Talmud study was uncommon for centuries, but there were certainly precedents among women like Bruriah and Osnat Barzani (see chapter 7). Today many women's learning programs exist, including the one named for Bruriah in Jerusalem. You can seek out a Beit Midrash to learn in — whether mixed or separate — and dive into religious study. You can also look at Beit Midrash programs online and study virtually. Beit Midrash learning typically involves learning in a *havruta*, with a partner, and regrouping with a teacher to sum up what was studied. Pick an idea or book that interests you and put aside time to study it. If you create your own source sheet, you can also upload it to the Sefaria website, which offers free access to Jewish texts in Hebrew and in English translation.

If you're interested, you can visit the Bruriah learning program (today called Midreshet Lindenbaum, located in Jerusalem) if you arrange it in advance, or, for that matter, arrange a visit to any *midrasha* or learning center. If you're not near a women's learning center, see what virtual opportunities you might have to experience religious study.

The world of Talmud, once closed to women and studied only by men, has opened up over the last half a century. In fact, today's women take part — whether in groups or alone — in the **Daf Yomi** (one page a day) study cycle; the entire Talmud is studied, one page (both sides) per day, over the course of roughly seven and a half years. Plenty of tools and programs exist for people who would like to put daily study into their schedules — from podcasts to study groups to websites. Look, for example, at the Hadran website, which supports women who are studying Daf Yomi in a variety of ways, providing resources, insights, and learning communities.

## Give Back

If you'd like to study halakha like Bruriah, pick one halakha that you can teach others. Many online platforms have materials that you can read to learn more about a specific issue that interests you (check out Sefaria for source sheets and primary sources). Whether you'd like to prepare a lesson to teach others, create a comic or cartoon, or even make a video clip that you can upload to social media, you can be part of bringing more Jewish learning to the world.

## See Something New

The Talmudic Village in Katzrin is located in the Golan, in a place where the sages of the Talmud lived. The village turns the clock back hundreds of years. A tour will take you to a "Talmudic House" with all sorts of ancient items, an attic, the ovens of ages past, a spectacular reconstructed olive press, and more. The highlight of the tour is the magnificent ancient synagogue — a hall built in the form of a huge amphitheater, where a presentation runs on screens along the length of the four walls.

Between Beit She'arim, where dozens of **mishnaic** sages are buried, and Tiberias, where the greatest concentration of Jews lived beginning in the second century, there are about forty-five miles, or seventy kilometers, that Israel's Antiquities Authority is developing as the "**Sanhedrin** Trail." The trail winds through many archaeological sites from around Bruriah's time, some which have already been excavated and some that youth and adults alike can take part in excavating. If Bruriah and others like her speak to you, you can arrange to take part in an archaeological dig, to help prepare the Sanhedrin Trail, or to walk along it.

# Get Out of Your Comfort Zone

Bruriah was never shy about disagreeing with those around her, and the Talmud even tells the story of her disagreeing with her husband on halakha; Rabbi Meir was praying for violent men to die, and she used a biblical verse to prove him wrong.

The world of debate is a fascinating one. Debate clubs help develop speaking skills, critical thinking, and self-confidence. Members of debate clubs train for competitions that are often held around the world; you can find them in high schools or universities.

In the spirit of Bruriah, hold a debate. You can search for a topic she discussed in the Talmud or research an issue from your world that you believe has many sides. Divide your friends or family into two teams to argue both sides, known as proposition and opposition or as supporting and opposing a resolution. Find online resources that describe what the different stages of a debate are and how much time is given for each.

# 11

# GEULAH COHEN

## *The Story of a Fierce Fighter*

" **F**rom my father, I got the dream; from my mother, I got the war," said Geulah Cohen, and indeed, throughout her life, she was both a warrior and a dreamer.

Geulah's father moved to Israel from Yemen in 1908; he was a community activist who worked within the Yemenite community. Her mother — whose roots were in Morocco and Turkey — came from a family that had lived in Jerusalem's Old City for eight generations. Geulah's mother, Miriam, was a nurse, and treated the wounded in the Tel Hai courtyard on the day of fighting when Joseph Trumpeldor was killed in 1920.

Geulah, one of ten siblings, grew up in the Kerem HaTeimanim (Yemenites' vineyard) neighborhood in Tel Aviv, and joined the underground to fight the British when she was seventeen — first the **Etzel** and then the more extreme **Lehi**. Because of her activity, she was expelled from the Levinsky College of Education, where she was training to be a teacher, right before her final exams.

Geulah, known also by her underground name, "Ilana," had a strong Hebrew accent, and was chosen to be the announcer on the "Voice of the Jewish Underground" radio station. But on February 18, 1946, she was caught by the British in the middle of a broadcast and sentenced to nine years in jail. She was first held in the "Kishle"

(Turkish prison) in Jaffa, and then, when she tried to escape, sent to the women's prison in Bethlehem. When she attempted to break out of the Bethlehem prison, climbing from a tree to the prison wall, she was shot in the leg.

One year later, with the help of three other underground connections — one of whom was Arab — she was smuggled out of prison wearing the clothes of an Arab woman. Her hair was then dyed blond, and no one recognized her when she rode on the bus. She hid in Haifa for a while, and then returned to her underground activities. Among other things, she edited the Lehi newspaper, *The Youth Front*.

When Geulah fell in love, Yitzhak Shamir, her commander in the Lehi, forbade her from marrying, even though her intended was one of the Lehi's commanders himself. Later on, the ban was lifted, and in 1947 Geulah married Emmanuel Hanegbi. Their son, Tzahi Hanegbi, is a politician who has served as a minister in many of Israel's governments.

With the establishment of the State of Israel, Geulah Cohen tried to be elected to **Knesset**; when she was unsuccessful, she chose a very different path: she became a journalist and writer. Geulah Cohen's language was rich and multilayered, and even when angry or when passionately defending her principles — which she did for all ninety-four years of her life — the language she used was powerful and meticulous.

For more than twenty years she wrote, but in her fifth decade, she returned to politics and was elected a Member of Knesset in the Likud. When Menachem Begin signed a peace treaty with Egypt, Geulah declared war on him, left the Likud, and founded a new party — Tehiya, or Resurrection — with author Moshe Shamir.

Geulah Cohen served as a Member of Knesset for nineteen years. The most important law that she initiated was the **Basic Law**: Jerusalem, Capital of Israel. As chairperson of the Knesset's Immigration and Absorption Committee, she fought the war of the Soviet Jews who wished to move to Israel and were denied. Years later, when she once again served in the same position, she traveled to Ethiopia to check on the conditions of the Jews who were waiting to come to Israel.

At the same time, Geulah continued to fight for her principles: she was the most stubborn warrior in all the peace initiatives adopted by Israel's government, refusing to recognize agreements that involved the transfer of even a sliver of land to Arab countries. She fought the Arab Israeli parties, too, hoping to deny them the right to organize. Until the end of her days, she was a passionate revolutionary who refused to compromise on her political beliefs.

When Geulah Cohen, at age ninety-two, was asked how old she was, she said: "I am four thousand years old, like this nation; seventy like the state; ninety-two like my biological age — but I am always eighteen."

# ADD YOUR VOICE

*"The moment I stop being inspired and believing that I can change the world — that is the moment that old age will pounce on me."*

## *Explore*

Geulah Cohen's activities as a radio broadcaster were crucial for those she worked with. But radio has many uses, as do broadcasts on other media today. Podcasts, for example, serve many of the same functions that radio did in the past. What are media's most important roles? What are its benefits? What are its drawbacks? What are the rules of media? What talents and skills are necessary in the world of media generally and social media today? Give some thought to how media influences your life and how you might be able to use it to achieve personal goals.

## Give Back

The world of social media is a complex one. Whether it's Instagram, Snapchat, TikTok, or something else, every app has tremendous potential to connect people with each other — but also potential for harm. How can you help ensure that you and your friends are safe on social media? Make sure you know the basic rules about online safety. How can you create safer social media communities? Take social media safety on as a project; come up with a list of rules and find a creative way to educate others on the subject. You can help protect your community.

## See Something New

You cannot visit the women's prison in Bethlehem that Geulah Cohen was held in for more than a year, but you can see another prison that was felt to be far more frightening at the time, where the male underground prisoners were held — the Akko (or Acre, as it is sometimes spelled) Prison.

The gallows room in the Akko Prison served the British for executions, and nine underground fighters lost their lives there. Today, the site is known as the Underground Prisoners Museum, and it reconstructs the experience at the prison in those days through interactive media. You can reserve a guided tour by calling ahead.

Akko is one of the oldest port cities in the world, and was formed thousands of years ago, but it reached the peak of its importance when it became a **Crusader** capital some eight hundred years ago. Most of the large and impressive reconstructed buildings that you can visit belong to the Crusader period. And, once there, you can also visit Akko's Knights' Hall, the city walls, and the beach.

## Get Out of Your Comfort Zone

On May 4, 1947, one year before the founding of the State of Israel, Etzel's fighters broke into the Akko prison walls and made it possible for the prisoners to escape. The operation was clearly a dangerous one; the prison was secure and well-protected. Still, Etzel's members felt that they must do everything possible to save their comrades. Can you create a computer game simulating the escape from Akko prison? Look for software that you can use or ask someone in the field for a little help to get you started.

# 12

# DEBORAH

## *Prophetess, Judge, Military Strategist, Leader, and Poet*

D eborah the Prophetess was the lone woman among the judges who led the Israelites. She was a leader, judge, seer, military strategist, commander, poet, and "mother in Israel" (Judges 5:7). Deborah was the first woman in the Israelite nation to serve in these roles; for many long years after her, no other woman held the same position.

Nonetheless, we know very little about her. We do not know about her family, where she learned, where she lived, and how she became a leader. The biblical text focuses on her military wisdom and great victory. But between the lines we catch glimpses of her decisive character, her leadership abilities, and the way she drew the dispersed tribes together to go into battle.

For most of her life, Deborah lived between the cities of Ramah and Beit El, in the territory of Benjamin, under a tall, broad palm tree. The entire nation knew the tree; in its shade, they would come lay out their sorrows before Deborah and ask for justice.

These were difficult days for the Israelites. God had placed the sinning nation in the hands of the Canaanites, a large and strong nation, which had nine hundred "tanks" — iron chariots. The nation was dispersed and weak, and had no weapons.

The Canaanite capital was in the north, in Hazor, and the tribes of Zebulun and Naphtali, who lived in that area, suffered from oppression. Wishing to put an end to the subjugation, Deborah sent messengers to the area of the **Kinneret**, in Naphtali's land, to bring Barak the son of Avinoam, a military leader, to her. She charged him, in God's name, with a military mission: to bring ten thousand men from his tribe and the neighboring tribe of Zebulun to Mount Tabor, "And I will draw Sisera, Jabin's army commander, with his chariots and his troops, toward you up to the Wadi Kishon; and I will deliver him into your hands" (Judges 4:7).

Mount Tabor is steep and high; underneath it, in the valley, snakes the Kishon River. Not far away, in Haroshet-HaGoyim, was the base of Jabin's army, under the commander, Sisera.

Barak was concerned about a battle that would be conducted against an armed, skilled army, and conditioned his agreement on Deborah joining him. Deborah's answer reveals to us, for the first time, her biting, mocking language. "I will go with you," she promised, but you should be ashamed: "There will be no glory for you in the course you are taking, for then the Lord will deliver Sisera into the hands of a woman" (Judges 4:9). And so Deborah and Barak went north, and, with the ten thousand soldiers that Barak had assembled, ascended Mount Tabor.

Deborah also called the other tribes to join the battle. Ephraim and Benjamin (Deborah's tribe and the neighboring one) responded and were praised — but those who did not join were mocked by Deborah in the thankful song she sang with the battle's end: She describes the tribe of Reuben sitting on the road to see who will win and then join them, the tribe of Dan poised to escape to sea on its ships.

At the end of the draft, the Israelite army stood atop the high mountain looking out at the great army of Jabin king of Canaan and its armored chariots spread out across the Jezreel Valley.

No wise military leader would place chariots and horses in the valley during the winter, because the valley's soil was — and still is — heavy and muddy. But these were, it appears, days of spring; no one expected rain, and the river was at its highest.

Suddenly, a powerful storm poured down from the skies, and the river overflowed and swept away the armored vehicles. In Deborah's later words,

The stars fought from heaven
From their courses they fought against Sisera.
The torrent Kishon swept them away
The raging torrent, the torrent Kishon.

(Judges 5:20–21)

Barak the son of Avinoam, at Deborah's command, led his light infantry directly at the enemy, which was already confused and bogged down in the mud. "And the Lord threw Sisera and all his chariots and army into a panic before the onslaught of Barak" (Judges 4:15).

Sisera himself left his chariot and fled to the camp. On his way, he stopped at the tent of his friends from the Kenite tribe. There, tired and thirsty, he asked Yael, one of the tribe's women, for a little water. She served him milk and put him to sleep in her bed; when he fell, "destroyed" (Judges 5:27), she took the tent peg, stuck it through his temple, and killed him. That was how Barak found him. "On that day God subdued Jabin the king of Canaan before the Israelites" (Judges 4:23).

And Deborah?

In exquisite language, she wrote the story of the miraculous battle (known to us as "the Song of Deborah"), and then returned, it appears, to judging Israel under the palm tree, "And the land was tranquil for forty years" (Judges 5:31).

In the mid-nineteenth century, when Jewish communities in Italy decided to hold joint bat mitzvah ceremonies for their girls, Deborah was chosen to stand at the center of the ritual celebrated on the **Shavuot** holiday. Thus three thousand years after her time, the girls of the community read the song she wrote, the Song of Deborah.

# ADD YOUR VOICE

*Hear, O kings; give ear, O princes!*
*I, unto the Lord will I sing,*
*I will sing praise to the Lord, the God of Israel.*

*(Judges 5:3)*

## *Explore*

Deborah served and still serves as a role model for girls celebrating their bat mitzvah in the Italian community and in other communities that have adopted the custom. The girls stand before the open **ark** with its **Torah** scrolls. Each girl reads verses of prayer and, after the prayer, the chief rabbi speaks to the girls and their families, and with the end of the ceremony the girls hold festive meals at their homes.

Learn more about the Italian ceremony for bat mitzvah girls. When did it begin? What types of foods were served at festive meals? Look into similar bat mitzvah ceremonies in other cultures: Were they tied to other biblical women? What did they look like? Read "The Wide World of Bat Mitzvah Ceremonies" at the end of this book for more information.

## *Give Back*

While other biblical women are described in later commentary and **Midrash**, Deborah alone has had very little told about her. It is only in recent generations that she has once again been recognized. In fact, I was privileged to read her song when I was sworn in as a Member of **Knesset** in 2013, and the women from my party did the same. More-over, at my suggestion, the opening ceremony of the **Yom HaAtzmaut**

(Independence Day) celebrations in 2014, whose theme was women, opened with the Song of Deborah set to music. Deborah — a war hero, a judge, a leader, a poet — is finally being recognized.

What can you do to teach others about Deborah? What means can you use? Look for a creative way to tell her story — perhaps in song, perhaps online, perhaps in a celebration or activity within your community.

## See Something New

Deborah's impressive strategic military story took place in the area of Mount Tabor. At the top of the mountain today there is a Franciscan monastery, but the mountain's history is also extensive, including the gathering of Israel's tribes at atop the mountain before they descended to the west, toward the Canaanite army, with Deborah and Barak in the lead.

While on the mountain, you can read the passages from the book of Judges about the battle, or read Deborah's song. Look from the top of the mountain toward the valley. Picture the armed Canaanite battalions and the array of forces. Imagine the thunder and lightning spooking the Canaanites' horses and the water filling the riverbed, creating a flood and sweeping away horses and riders.

## Get Out of Your Comfort Zone

If you are a writer, you can hold a women's writing workshop. You can recreate the story of Deborah — prophetess, judge, military leader. Can you imagine Deborah in all her glory, write her story in detail, and read it to your guests?

# 13

# ESTHER

## *From Beauty Queen
to Leader*

"**G**o, assemble all the Jews…" (Esther 4:16)
Everyone thinks they know about Esther, the beautiful queen. But who was she really?

When she first appears in the *megillah*, Esther is an orphan with no mother or father, whose cousin has taken her in, a beautiful girl, obedient and shy. Over the course of the *megillah*, she evolves from a young girl into a woman, and her obedience and shyness are replaced with the decisiveness of a leader.

Esther was brought to the Persian palace in Shushan (Susa); King Ahasuerus, regretting having his pretty wife Vashti killed, had asked his ministers to bring all of the beautiful women in the kingdom to him. When Esther arrived at the palace, she was transferred to Hegai, guardian of the women, and he liked her immediately. He gave her seven maids, and **Midrash** tells us that she named each of them for one day of the week so that she would not forget when it was **Shabbat**. Esther had promised Mordechai, her uncle, that she would not tell a soul that she was a Jew, and she was forced to keep Shabbat in secret.

When Ahasuerus met Esther he fell in love with her, put a crown on her head, and named her queen in Vashti's place.

And Mordechai, her foster father, sat in the palace gates to watch her from nearby. When Mordechai and Esther wanted to pass messages to one another, they used Hathach, the personal servant that the king had given Esther.

One day Hathach reported to Esther that Mordechai was wearing sackcloth and ash. Esther was horrified: Had Mordechai lost his money? Perhaps he had no clothes? She sent him clothes, but he refused to accept them.

It was not poverty, Esther learned, that had made Mordechai wear sackcloth; he was wearing them as a sign of mourning. Haman, head of the king's ministers, had decreed that the Jews in all of the king's lands would be destroyed, massacred, and exterminated.

Go to the king, Mordechai commanded Esther, and ask him to have mercy on us.

It's too dangerous, she answered. People who come to the king without being called are executed, unless the king extends his scepter, and "I have not been summoned to visit the king for the last thirty days" (Esther 4:11).

But Mordechai took no pity on Esther; he would not leave her alone. Do not worry, he told her in a message that Hathach relayed. Even if you do not help, he told her, "relief and deliverance will come to the Jews from another quarter" (Esther 4:14). But if you do not step up as part of the struggle, he stated, you and your family will disappear from Jewish history forever.

Suddenly, the roles were reversed: Esther, the young girl who was always controlled by those around her, became a leader, taking on responsibility and choosing the next steps in the struggle.

"Go, assemble all the Jews," she commanded Mordechai, who until that point had instructed her, "and fast on my behalf... My maidens and I will fast as well" (Esther 5:16). Mordechai internalized the change immediately: "And Mordechai...did just as Esther had commanded him" (Esther 5:17).

For three days, the Jews in Shushan fasted and prayed for her mission to succeed, and on the third day, Esther rose, put on her royal clothing, and went to meet the king. He was very happy to see her, extended his golden scepter, and asked her to tell him what was bothering her. But she — diplomatically — did not tell him right away; instead, she invited him and Haman to a feast, and then to a second feast. It was only at their third meeting that Esther told the king about the evil that Haman was plotting against her people.

When he heard about the catastrophe that could take away his beloved queen, the king was enraged and gave Esther permission to do anything she felt necessary to rectify the situation. He instructed that Haman be hung along with his family members, reversed the decrees to kill the Jews, and demanded the annulment of the decrees in all of the king's lands; the Jews were permitted to fight back against their attackers. A day of celebration was established by Esther and Mordechai, Purim — and the two of them, many believe, wrote the *megillah*, or scroll, of Esther.

The **Talmud** states that Esther's greatest enterprise was writing the book of Esther. Esther, who was given the gift of prophecy, saw that the nation would be in a lengthy exile with no end in sight. Much like a person drowning at sea, the nation would need a life raft that it could hold onto, and the scroll was meant to be just that life raft. Esther wished to draw on her experience to teach her nation that even in the terrible event of a decree to "destroy and massacre" they must not give up, because the decree can be changed overnight.

Indeed, over the course of history, women have relied on Esther's character and drawn strength from it. There are a fair number of testimonies about the **crypto-Jews** from Spain and Portugal who identified with Esther deeply; she, too, was made to hide her faith. These women would fast for three days on the Fast of Esther, endangering their lives, with the hopes that their fate would change, too.

# ADD YOUR VOICE

*The Talmud tells us that the sages debated whether to include the book of Esther in the Bible. Esther was the one who had said "Write me for generations" (Megillah 7a) — and she won.*

## Explore

The story of Esther's rise to power begins with her invitation to the palace, an invitation that relates solely to her outward appearance. Beauty pageants have a long and problematic history, but many women have used the competitions — much like Queen Esther — as a springboard to greater careers, employing whatever means they had to move forward. Esther is chosen based on her looks but transforms over the course of the story from passive to active, from a follower to a leader.

Look into the history of beauty pageants. When did they begin? How have they changed over time? Which women began their careers in beauty pageants, and how did they use those beginnings to achieve their goals? What are your feelings on the subject?

## Give Back

Mishloach Manot — sending packages of food — is a special commandment referred to in the book of Esther. On the Purim holiday, people are meant to deliver gifts of food to their friends. And, still today, many Jews go from house to house on Purim, delivering goodies to their friends and extended family.

Some charities and organizations organize virtual Mishloach Manot. This can take a number of forms: With some, a virtual Purim card goes out to your list of friends with a note explaining that instead of bringing them food, you have given money in their honor to a cause that is meaningful to you. With others, physical food packages are given to people who are sick or in need with the money you donate.

Some communities choose to raise money for a cause by agreeing not to give each other extravagant Mishloach Manot. Instead, all members put in some money and each member receives an identical package; this can involve an element of giving as well, with enough money collected to also give to charity or by involving an organization for people with disabilities who can prepare and package the items.

You can look for an organization or cause that you would like to support and join in their campaign, or perhaps begin a Mishloach Manot campaign of your own.

## See Something New

According to the tradition of Persia's Jews, the place of Esther and Mordechai's burial is in the city of Hamedan in the country's north. In contrast, Rabbi Menachem HaChevroni identified Queen Esther's bones (without Mordechai's) in the Galilee during the thirteenth century: "I went to the land of Arabia, and I saw a boulder, and inside the boulder the tomb of Queen Esther, who commanded during her life to her son Cyrus to bring her there. And near there, a short distance away, the tomb of Rabbi Pinhas ben Yair and Obadiah the Prophet." HaChevroni's description brings us to the entrance to Kfar Baram.

You can hike in the Baram Forest. The path is pretty and the hike spectacular, especially during the Purim season, when everything is blossoming. Between the Hiram intersection and Baram, find the brown sign that leads to "the burial place of Mordechai and Esther." A path leads north from there, marked in black. The enchanted pathway winds between the densely positioned trees — oaks — of the Baram Forest, and on its sides are boulders that an anonymous hand has marked with blue dots to indicate the path leading to the tomb.

## Get Out of Your Comfort Zone

While in some religious communities, the question of women reading from the **Torah** for ritual purposes is a complicated one, most rabbis — even in the **Orthodox** community — agree that women may read *Megillat Esther*. You can prepare to read the *megillah* on Purim, learning to read the special cantillation symbols that indicate how a word should be chanted.

If you would like, you can even combine your *megillah* reading with a costume party in honor of the holiday. Our traditional foods are part of telling our story, too: make sure to prepare special Purim pastries — called *hamantashen* (Haman pockets) in Yiddish and *oznei Haman* (Haman's ears) in Hebrew — triangular cookies with a filling of your choice.

# 14

# ADA FISHMAN MAIMON

## *Revolutionary Founder of a Women's Labor Movement*

S ometimes one childhood memory dictates the rest of someone's life. As a young girl, Ada was taught that women were exempt from time-bound commandments (*mitzvot aseh shehazman graman*), but she could not accept her father's explanation. A woman is simply too busy, he said, and cannot at a given time be available for prayer or ritual. Ada's understanding was that **halakha** views the woman as inferior, someone who does not have the skills necessary to keep the commandments. This stinging insult filled her, and she swore to fight against the oppression of women.

And that was exactly what she did.

After she gained a broad general and Jewish education in her father's house, Ada moved to the land of Israel at age nineteen, in the year 1912, from Romania. Her beloved eldest brother, nearly twenty years her senior and already **ordained** as a rabbi, Rabbi Juda Leib, moved with her. The two would both eventually become part of public life in the land, but as adversaries: he was the State of Israel's first Minister of Religions; she, who was no less observant than he, fought the religious establishment for women's rights her whole life.

Ada's first fight began almost immediately after she arrived in the Land of Israel, when she began to work as a teacher at a small Hebrew school in Tzfat. Ada waited with excitement for **Lag BaOmer**, the day of pilgrimage to Meron and the tomb of Rabbi Shimon bar Yohai. But when that day arrived, she was astonished to discover that Tzfat's rabbis would not allow women to come to the tomb. Ada decided to disregard the ban. She and another teacher went to Meron on their own, two women among thousands of men. The people at Meron were shocked by their audacity and refused to let them stay there overnight, but they rented a mud hut from local Arabs.

A year later, many women went to Meron.

An unofficial ban was placed on Ada when she became the first woman in the history of the Land of Israel to be selected as a member of a local council. It was 1919, and Ada was chosen for the central council of Jews in Jaffa. Members of **ultra-Orthodox** parties were selected as well. Every time the ultra-Orthodox representatives came to a council meeting and saw Ada, they would turn and leave.

Three years later, four women were selected for various local councils, and the ultra-Orthodox community grew used to the idea.

And Ada? She was already on to another struggle — the struggle for working women. The Women's Workers' Council that she established was the first institution in the land — and one of the first in the world — in which women could vote, be elected, and fight for equal rights in work. And Ada still had not realized her truly great dream.

Ada dreamed of a great farm, "a women's farm," that would train hundreds of young women in agriculture. She fulfilled this vision, too, in her characteristic style: on **Tu BeShvat** 1932 she and ten other women went, after great effort, to the farm that had been named Ayanot, south of Nes Tziona. There she was forced to fight a fever that mosquitos brought from the nearby swamp, and to face the destruction that took place at the farm each time rioting broke out, as well as financial problems (it took time for the farm's crops to support the women).

Hitler's rise to power in Germany, and, later on, the Second World War, transformed Ayanot from a farm for young women to a school that took in young men and women, saving them from the Holocaust in Europe.

Here, for example, is the testimony of one of the girls who was saved by Ada, Leah Fisher:

> I received a message that I must come see Ada Maimon-Fishman, and she will choose who is moving to the Land of Israel to be a student in the women's workers' farm Ayanot... When Ada spoke to me, she asked: "And what will you do in the Land of Israel with your delicate, silken hands?" I answered that they would get stronger and do the work I was given... "Start preparing to travel to the Land of Israel." I was lucky... (Only) later did I understand that I was saved from the Holocaust.

Over the years, thousands of young women (and men) were trained in agricultural work as well as general studies at Ayanot. Ada Fishman Maimon lived at Ayanot for forty years, and left there, in the early years of the State of Israel, to serve as a Member of **Knesset**.

It is not hard to guess what laws Ada tried to pass as a Member of Knesset: a law for women's equality, a law for women's work, and, no less important, a law determining the age of marriage. In the years that followed the establishment of the state, no small number of parents tried to marry off their children at age twelve and thirteen; Ada fought like a lioness to pass a law that would prevent young girls from getting married. All of the ultra-Orthodox parties were against her.

Ada sufficed with little, and fought for the right not to make more money than she thought was correct and just. When Members of Knesset wished to raise their salaries, Ada opposed them. We are a country in *tzena* (austerity measures), she explained to her colleagues the Knesset Members; we must serve as an example. In a letter to the minister of finance, she demanded that he pay her no more than 60 pounds a month.

Ada also sufficed with little in her personal life; she chose not to marry and not to have a family, and asked that no one eulogize her after her death.

# ADD YOUR VOICE

*"Girls of Israel, prepare for the election day. Justice is with us and it holds the power. The Hebrew woman will no longer serve as a sculpture to be liberated by artists, but rather the symbol of her own liberation." (Ada Fishman Maimon, To the Hebrew Woman: In Advance of the Founding Meeting, 1918)*

## *Explore*

Ada Fishman Maimon was tied closely to her land, and felt strongly about agriculture. Judaism is a religion that preserves nature and converses with nature. Check how the Jewish sources relate to the land, to vegetation, and to individuals' responsibility to them. Look into rules like the land's Sabbatical and Jubilee years. The Sabbatical Year, or *Shemitta*, is still observed today in Israel; every seventh year, agricultural land must lie fallow and may not be planted or harvested. The Jubilee Year follows every seventh Sabbatical Year.

What other rules apply to the Sabbatical Year? Why, in your opinion, were the laws of the Sabbatical Year instituted? What benefit do they have for the land? What benefit do they have for us as people? What important messages do the rules of the Sabbatical Year express? You can also look into similar agricultural laws in the Bible — *ma'aser* (tithing), *pe'ah* (the corners of the fields), and *orla* (fruit from young trees), for example — and consider what benefits they have for the land and for communities.

## Give Back

Agricultural sustainability and social justice often go hand in hand. Jewish organizations — for example, Leichtag Commons and the Coastal Roots Farm in California — base their understanding of that connection on Jewish religious sources, which have requirements for farming methods and time frames. Look for organizations and initiatives in your area that use techniques that aim to preserve the land and work toward a healthier environment. Can you volunteer with them? Or perhaps bring some of their techniques and ideology into your home or community?

## See Something New

Ada Fishman Maimon's life's work was the farm. She saw in agriculture the very essence of **Zionism**, and demanded from all of her students that they find work with the land.

Mikveh Yisrael was the first agricultural school in the Land of Israel, and was founded in the nineteenth century by young people from the Alliance Israélite Universelle, an international Jewish human rights organization known in Hebrew as Kol Yisrael Haverim. Theodor Herzl, Zionism's founding father, made a point of visit the school on a trip to the land in 1898.

Mikveh Yisrael still exists today near Tel Aviv and is maintained by the Council for Conservation of Heritage Sites in Israel. There you can see the first botanical garden, the farm buildings, the vineyard that made wine, and the impressive synagogue built more than 120 years ago; follow the boulevard of palm trees to the two-story building.

# Get Out of Your Comfort Zone

Do you want to get close to the earth, like Ada? Hold an event with your friends or family that celebrates land and soil. Explore traditional Jewish sources and discover how they relate to the land; look for poetry and music that relate to the earth. You can also ask your guests to bring passages or songs about land that are meaningful to them. Moreover, you can experience soil hands-on in a workshop dedicated to building with soil and experimenting with soil. You can even try to build an oven out of mud and cook for your guests!

# 15

# ANNE FRANK

## A Young Jewish Diarist
## in the Holocaust

Saturday, June 20, 1942

Writing in a diary is a really strange experience for someone like me...
It seems to me that later on neither I nor anyone else will be interested
in the musings of a thirteen-year-old schoolgirl. Oh well, it doesn't
matter. I feel like writing, and I have an even greater need to get all
kinds of things off my chest...

I have loving parents and a sixteen-year-old sister, and there are
about thirty people I can call friends. I have a throng of admirers
who can't keep their adoring eyes off me and who sometimes have
to resort to using a broken pocket mirror to try and catch a glimpse
of me in the classroom... On the surface I seem to have everything,
except my one true friend.

Imagine a thirteen-year-old girl, sociable and popular, full of spirit,
inventions, and humor, suddenly having to enter a hidden apartment. And in the hidden apartment — a "Secret Annex," as the girl
calls it — she is only permitted to whisper. For nine hours a day, she
cannot speak at all, nor open a faucet, nor move objects.

She is not alone there. She shares the apartment with seven other people. These include her parents and sister, but also complete
strangers: another family — father, mother, and son — and another

adult, a dentist, who shares a room with her. This is not an easy life; spending twenty-four hours a day with strangers demands endless patience and good will.

But the girl is lucky; she is keeping a diary, and she loves to write and is good at expressing herself. When things become unbearable, she turns to her diary to unburden herself. We are lucky, too; her diary gives us a window into her world, telling the story of just one of the many children who were lost in the Holocaust.

The girl's name is Anne, Anne Frank, and her diary is written in the form of letters to an imaginary friend, "Kitty"; she yearns for Kitty, to tell her "everything...as I have never been able to confide in anyone."

These were the days of the Holocaust in Europe, and were it not for her diary we would not know that a young girl named Anne was born in Germany and grew up in Holland, a girl who experienced small joys and great anger and emotions and terrible fears, who lived for two years hidden in the very center of the great city of Amsterdam and was caught with her family and taken to her death — one girl out of more than a million children who were killed.

Anne insisted on writing almost every day, sometimes with humor and sometimes with a sense of suffocation:

Monday evening, November 8, 1943

Dearest Kitty,

...I see the eight of us in the Annex as if we were a patch of blue sky surrounded by menacing black clouds. The perfectly round spot on which we're standing is still safe, but the clouds are moving in on us, and the ring between us and the approaching danger is being pulled tighter and tighter. We're surrounded by darkness and danger, and in our desperate search for a way out we keep bumping into each other... I can only cry out and implore, "Oh, ring, ring, open wide and let us out!"

The Secret Annex was a whole world. Loyal Dutch friends helped the families in hiding, buying them food and clothing, exchanging books for them at the library, registering them for correspondence courses (under assumed names), and making sure to mark each holiday, special date, and birthday with them.

Anne continued to be amusing and full of ideas. She created **Hanukah** presents for all of the members of the Secret Annex from scraps and added original poems, and when there were no scraps left to use, she hid rhyming greetings in each person's shoes. Even in hiding, she wanted to live a full life.

But even though they tried to keep a healthy lifestyle when possible, and even though they had loyal friends on their side, they could not avoid the terrible reality: their hunger grew, their Jewish friends disappeared in the camps, and mostly, they lived with the fear of the unknown awaiting them:

Thursday, September 16, 1943

Dearest Kitty,
...I've been taking valerian every day to fight the anxiety and depression, but it doesn't stop me from being even more miserable the next day. A good, hearty laugh would help better than ten valerian drops, but we've almost forgotten how to laugh. Sometimes I'm afraid my face is going to sag with all this sorrow and that my mouth is going to permanently droop at the corners.

No one knows who informed on the Frank family — many theories exist and people speculate on the question even today — but when the police came to take the eight people in hiding, they knew exactly where to enter from and how to open the revolving bookcase that led to the hideaway. Anne did not have enough time to write about it, but her diary fell to the floor during the search and a neighbor who was also one of the trusted helpers, Miep Gies, kept it until Otto Frank, Anne's father, returned — the lone survivor of the eight. Anne, age fifteen, died of neglect and disease in the Bergen-Belsen concentration camp two months before the war ended.

Since then, the diary has been translated into seventy-five languages; in the end, Anne, who never got to grow up, became a beloved and famous author, and children and teens around the world are her trusted friends.

# ADD YOUR VOICE

## *Explore*

Monuments and museums about the Holocaust, and about Anne Frank in particular, can be found in many countries. You can see some of these places online or visit them in person — in Washington, Jerusalem, Los Angeles, Poland, Berlin, and Idaho, to name a few. Children who were killed in the Holocaust are memorialized specifically at Yad Vashem's Children's Memorial and Beit Lohamei HaGhetaot's "Yad LaYeled" (children's monument).

Learn more about Holocaust museums and memorials around the world. What countries are you surprised to find commemorating the memory of those who were killed? What do you think it is about the Holocaust that resonates so deeply that it crosses borders?

## *Give Back*

Many Holocaust museums keep records of the names of those who perished, including the more than a million children who were killed. Yad Vashem's Children's Memorial is a dark hall with memorial candles reflected seemingly endlessly as the names of the lost children are read aloud.

You can find information about one child and bring them to life. Mark their birthday and light a candle in their memory on the date of their death. Can you find a way to tell their story to ensure that they are never forgotten? Yad Vashem offers a bar/bat mitzvah twinning program, which lets you learn about one person who died in the Holocaust and share your bat mitzvah with them symbolically.

## See Something New

*"I go to the attic almost every morning to get the stale air out of my lungs... The two of us looked out at the blue sky, the bare chestnut tree... 'As long as this exists...this sunshine and this cloudless sky...how can I be sad?'"*

The tree Anne saw was already a few decades old then; it fell a few years ago, but people took cuttings from the tree, grew them, and sent them around the world. Each school named for Anne has a cutting, and two were sent to Israel. (For more information, look up the Sapling Project.) One of the cuttings was planted in Ramot Naftali, in the Upper Galilee, near the monument for Major Eitan Balhassan, a paratrooper commander from the *moshav* who fell in operational activities. The *moshav* of Ramot Naftali is located in one of Israel's most beautiful areas. You can also tour the forest and the nearby Hula Valley. The forest is densely planted in places, but, in others, there is a scenic outlook over the Hula Valley, a few hundred meters below.

You can also visit the Martyrs' Forest on the outskirts of Jerusalem, with its Anne Frank Memorial. Along the pathways, signs hold quotes from her diary.

If you ever have a chance to go to Holland, you can tour Anne Frank's Secret Annex in Amsterdam. It can also be visited virtually; you can "walk" through the rooms where Anne lived online.

## Get Out of Your Comfort Zone

A 2021 animated movie about Anne Frank, called *Where Is Anne Frank*, documents her story for younger audiences. In 2019, a project called "Eva.Stories" was uploaded to Instagram, telling the story of a fictional girl in the Holocaust as if she herself were documenting it.

Can you tell a Holocaust story in a new and different way? Other diaries have been found and published (see "Children's Art and Writings" on the United States Holocaust Memorial Museum's website); can you find a way to tell the story of one child who was lost?

# 16

# RACHEL "RUCHIE" FREIER

## *Hasidic Judge and Community Organizer*

"First and foremost," Ruchie Freier says, "I'm a girl from Borough Park." When she defines herself, she notes that she is a daughter, a wife, a mother, "and what I do in addition to that is I work in the legal profession."

"I started out as a legal secretary," she explains. "My dream always was to become a judge. So now I am a judge." Nevertheless, "My priority always was that I didn't want to compromise. I wanted to bake **challah** for **Shabbat**, I wanted to still *daven* (pray) three times a day, I wanted to still be the mother for my children. I wanted nothing to change, even though I wanted to do something else."

So Rachel — "Ruchie" — Freier describes herself. Let us look together at the different elements of who she is.

## *A Daughter*

Ruchie was born to a **Hasidic** family in Borough Park, New York. Her father, Hersch, owned a jewelry store and her mother, Sarah, was a wigmaker. At age sixty, when her children had grown and left home, Ruchie's mother studied interior design; she still works in the field today.

Like most of her friends in her Hasidic community, Ruchie studied at Bais Yaakov (see chapter 49 on Sarah Schenirer, the founder of Bais Yaakov). In her final year in school, she studied legal shorthand.

## A Wife

With the end of high school, Ruchie married David Freier, a **Bobov** Hasid. He studied in yeshiva and she supported their small family, first as a stenographer and later as a legal secretary. David went on to learn accounting at Touro College. With time, when her husband finished his studies and began working, Ruchie felt frustrated by serving people who were younger and less talented than she, and at age thirty she decided to further her studies; she went to college and then on to law school. She was in school for more than ten years, with her husband supporting her the entire way. Later on, when she had received her license to practice law, the two opened a joint office; he worked in commercial financing, and she, law.

## A Mother

Ruchie grew up as one of four sisters. When she was expecting her first child, her mother was also pregnant, with her only brother. Ruchie was already mother to four children when she began her studies; when she finished, ten years later, she had six. During her campaign to become a judge, all of her children who lived nearby (two of her daughters live in Israel) helped organize her campaign.

## A Lawyer and Judge

Ruchie passed the bar exam in 2006 and interned under Senator Hillary Clinton. Upon completing her studies, Ruchie opened her first office in Kiryas Joel, a village whose residents are primarily **Satmar** Hasidim. In addition to giving legal counsel to residents, Ruchie helped them explain their way of life to others. In parallel, she worked with her husband, David.

Ten years later, her beloved uncle and mentor, a judge in the district in which she lived and worked, vacated his seat and suggested that she vie for it. She ran for the democratic party and won the primary; however, the party's leaders did not wish to support her because the district, Kings County, has a large **ultra-Orthodox** population and the party heads did not believe that the community would vote for a woman. But Ruchie did not give up; she and her family went door to door to garner support. She convinced rabbis to endorse her as well, and was able to win the spot even without the support of the party. She thus became the first Hasidic woman to hold public office in America.

Her inauguration was unique, with Hasidic singer Lipa Schmeltzer singing the American national anthem partly in Yiddish and the song "God Bless America" entirely in Yiddish. Ruchie had once again broken a glass ceiling, becoming the first female ultra-Orthodox judge in America.

## An Activist

Ruchie Freier does not call herself a feminist, but she is a great believer in women's abilities to achieve anything. She often quotes her mother, who she says taught her that, as women, "we could do anything we wanted to do, so long as it wasn't illegal, immoral, or against the **Torah**." So when she heard, in 2011, that Hatzolah, the

Jewish volunteer emergency medical services in New York, would not accept women as volunteers, she founded a new organization, Ezras Nashim (meaning "aid to women"). She even took an EMT course. With this training, she was able to save a man who collapsed on a flight from Budapest to Frankfurt that she happened to be on.

Aside from Ezras Nashim, Ruchie has also established Chasdei Devorah, an organization that provides aid to underprivileged Jewish families, and B'Derech, a program that helps at-risk teens in the Hasidic community.

When she feels spurred to action, it seems, she cannot sit still: "They provoked me. Because they said that Jewish women weren't strong enough, fast enough, or smart enough. And I don't believe that's what God's Torah says."

Today, she does not hide her dreams to go further — maybe even to the United States' Supreme Court.

# ADD YOUR VOICE

## *Explore*

What do you know about the Hasidic community? What is its history? How has it evolved over time? What does the community look like today? What are its beliefs and practices? Ruchie Freier is a pioneer for women in the Hasidic world; what can you learn about women in the community? What are their roles and responsibilities?

On a broader level, how do you define community? Give a little thought to what communities you belong to, how they are defined, and what your roles and responsibilities are within them. How do you connect to your community? What other ways are there for people to connect to their communities?

## Give Back

Ruchie Freier's B'Derech organization aims to help Hasidic youth reach their potential, especially those for whom the school framework is a constant source of difficulty. She founded it seeing that students who struggle with academics often feel rejected and can ultimately leave a community because they cannot find their place.

Can you offer to tutor a younger student who can use a leg up? Look within your community or in neighborhood programs — after-school projects, JCCs, synagogues, or temples — for volunteer opportunities.

## See Something New

Are you interested in seeing the Hasidic community up close? If you live near such a community, whether in America, England, or elsewhere — or if you're visiting Israel — you may be able to find a walking tour given by a guide, ideally one who is respectful of the community and can help you see it from the inside.

## Get Out of Your Comfort Zone

In honor of Ruchie Freier, perhaps you want to stage a mock trial. You can ask friends or guests to play different roles — defendants, defense lawyers, prosecutors, witnesses, and so on — and come up with a case that you can act out. Make sure everyone knows what their job is and prepares what is necessary in advance. You can search online for tips and ideas.

# 17

# GLIKL OF HAMELN

## *Astute Merchant Who*
## *Left behind a Treasure*

F ew women knew how to read and write more than three hundred years ago; almost no women from the time kept a diary for
decades.

Except Glikl of Hameln.

Glikl wrote her diaries for her children, and the texts she left behind give us a rare window into the life of a Jewish woman at the
time and the people around her.

Glikl was fourteen when she married Chayim, and he was not
much older. She came from the big city of Hamburg in Germany and
he, from a small town, Hameln. At first, the two lived for a year in his
parents' house and for a year with her parents, like many couples at
the time, which Glikl did not always enjoy: "Hameln...taken by itself...
is a dull shabby hole. And there I was — a carefree child whisked in
the flush of youth from parents, friends and everyone I knew, from a
city like Hamburg... Yet I thought nothing of it, so much I delighted in
the piety of my father-in-law."

Glikl and her husband lived lives of love and mutual respect.
Chayim began to work trading gold and pearls, and Glikl was a full
partner in the business. Chayim would travel from town to town
and land to land for his business. He journeyed with a horse and

carriage, oftentimes staying away for days or weeks. Glikl would run the household and raise their fourteen children, but she also managed the "office" courageously and creatively: bills, contracts, letters, balances, hiring employees and helpers — she was responsible for it all.

"I do not think," she wrote later on, "there would have been a happier or more loving couple in all the world!"

This charmed life was cut short after thirty years, when Chayim was killed in an accident, leaving Glikl to deal with the business — spread out as it was over cities and countries — and their many children.

After Chayim's death, Glikl could not stay at her home and run her affairs from afar. She began to travel from city to city, to large business fairs in Berlin and Amsterdam, in Frankfurt and Hanover, negotiating with Jews and non-Jews, with clients who were honest and dishonest, gaining money and losing, falling and getting back up.

Glikl experienced a lot of sleepless nights, nights of tears, nights of missing the husband of her youth, and these were the nights when she began to write her memories, both the pleasant and amusing ones and the difficult and painful ones. Her writing was not only for her; her hope was to tell her story for her children, and give them the benefit of her experience and wisdom.

For twenty-eight years, Glikl wrote a meticulous journal, leaving us one of the rarest, most moving, and most important books from that time, a book that documents the story of a Jewish woman in Hamburg, northern Germany, three hundred years ago. Of course, Glikl does not represent all Jewish women. She was raised in a wealthy family, while many of the Jews of her city were poor. She was privileged to receive an education, and learned at a *cheder* — a kind of elementary school usually meant for boys — while many of the women of her generation were illiterate.

Glikl wrote about many subjects: about her family and her husband's family, about the years of raising her children, about the early days of the business, about financial difficulties and successes. She recorded humorous and poignant stories that she had read in

Jewish traditional sources, stories of the sages, legends, parables, and writings from the greater world, and she gave her children advice about the way to live lives of faith and honor. She also wrote about important events that took place during her times, and there were many: wars and terrible plagues that had people fleeing from the cities; **anti-Semitism**; and even a false messiah who shook the foundations of the Jewish nation.

After her husband's death, Glikl lived independently for more than ten years, but she was eventually persuaded to remarry. "I believed I was marrying a man who with his means and distinguished station could have aided my children and put them in the way of great wealth. But the very contrary happened." Her second marriage, to a respected and wealthy man from the city of Metz in France, put an end to her financial independence. She gave all of her money to her new husband — and he lost her assets as well as his own. At times, the couple had no food, and her husband soon died, brokenhearted. Glikl herself, who had been used to a life of independence, wellbeing, and comfort, moved to her beloved daughter Esther's home; Esther supported her and took care of her for the rest of her life. But Glikl never lost faith or hope.

# ADD YOUR VOICE

*"Leaving behind me all of the nothingness of this world, I should have taken myself, with the handful that remained me, to the Land of Our Fathers. There I might have lived as a good Jewess."*

## Explore

Glikl's diaries were written in Yiddish, a language that developed in central and eastern Europe that is a combination of Hebrew and the languages of the countries in which Jews lived, primarily German. In many **Diaspora** communities, where Jews have lived for generations, they spoke a language that was a mixture of the land's language and Hebrew. Yiddish developed in the **Ashkenazi** community in Europe, Ladino in the countries that Jews were exiled to from Spain, Judeo-Yemeni Arabic in Yemen, the Judeo-Arabic dialect in the Middle East and North Africa, and so on.

What language (or languages) did your grandparents and great-grandparents speak? Look into your family heritage. Does someone from your family still know the language? Perhaps they know blessings, prayers, or expressions that were written in the Jewish language that your family spoke.

Does your family have an object or book that has been passed down from generation to generation? Perhaps you have an old album of pictures? Did you ever receive a special gift from your grandparents, that feels in some way like the "gift" Glikl gave her children and grandchildren? Ask the grownups around you about "heritage objects" that are passed down in your family.

## Give Back

Glikl's business acumen was legendary, but she, too, suffered more than once from financial troubles. Jewish tradition states that "all Jews are responsible for one another" (Shevuot 39a), and, indeed, over time Jews have developed mechanisms to care for the those in need. A free loan society is a non-profit organization dedicated to providing interest-free loans to people who are struggling financially. People who are studying, training for work, in need of medical aid or housing, or starting small businesses often are not eligible for loans from a bank. Free loan societies make it possible for such people to move forward without taking on extra debt; they can navigate times of crisis or better their circumstances and then pay back a loan with no interest.

What free loan societies exist in your area? You can raise money for one such society through a rummage sale, bake sale, or other project; your money can then go to helping people in need to advance.

## See Something New

The diary that Glikl wrote was meant to transmit heritage and tradition. Glikl hoped that her children, grandchildren, and those who came after would learn from her experience and follow in her footsteps.

The place that has the longest running Jewish tradition that we know of is the Jewish village of Pekiin in the Galilee, where Jews have been living since the Second Temple Period and until today. Today only one woman is left, the descendant of the last Jewish family to live in Pekiin, Margalit Zinati.

You can visit Pekiin, built atop one of the most beautiful summits in the Galilee. See the Zinati house, and learn about the fascinating Jewish life that took place there. You can sit under the trees near one of the springs, next to the cave where the **Talmud** tells us that Rabbi Shimon bar Yohai hid for twelve years, or in the ancient synagogue, which is some two thousand years old.

And if you happen to visit Germany, in Berlin, right at the entrance to the Jewish Museum, you can see a copy of Glikl's diary, in the meticulous handwriting of her descendants, who copied it by hand.

# Get Out of Your Comfort Zone

What do you know about your family's history? Plenty of resources exist today for research, and oftentimes using such resources you can search back for many generations, connecting with people online to add more and more relatives to your family tree. Get started by asking your family members for all of the information they have (names, birth dates, and locations). You can use a website like MyHeritage, Ancestry, JewishGen, or Geni to learn more (some of the sites require a paid membership for all or some of their services; make sure to check what the different options offer). Create a family tree and try to uncover as much as you can about your family's past.

May 29, 1911–January 15, 1970
2 Sivan 5671–8 Shvat 5730

# 18

# LEA GOLDBERG

## *The Immigrant Who Became a Great Poet*

Lea Goldberg spent her childhood in the city of Kovno (today called Kaunas) in chilly, faraway Lithuania; it was always rainy — even in the summer — and everyone spoke Russian and Lithuanian. But Lea attended a Hebrew school, and at the age of ten decided that she would write only in Hebrew. To write "not [in] Hebrew," she wrote in her diary, would be "not to write completely."

> For all the love I feel for the protagonists of Russian literature, I am not them. The special air that Judaism has created around itself is a magical sphere I cannot, and absolutely do not, wish to leave... My full and complete self, just as it is, I can only find in Hebrew works.

From a young age, she wrote poetry. At age five, she wrote her first poem in Russian; at age twelve, she published her first Hebrew poem in a Lithuanian newspaper. Alongside writing, Lea trained to become a teacher and educator. She studied education and Semitic languages in Germany, and, at age twenty-four, when she moved to Israel, she already had a PhD.

Lea was a gifted teacher. She first taught in high school and later at university. Her students worshipped her, and she cultivated those who were talented, young people who years later became important poets themselves.

During the years of national struggles and wars, when male poets were writing heroic poetry, Lea Goldberg's compositions were personal, sensitive, and full of pain. The men did not understand her, and attempted to explain to her that her poetry should be used for the national effort. "Love has greater value than killing," Lea responded, and kept doing things her way.

It can be said that there were two Lea Goldbergs. The first was sad and somber; at age fourteen, in Lithuania, she already knew that she would never be happy:

> And if, suddenly, all of my dreams were to come true — would I be happy? Of course not. I would find other troubles... I would invent them, and it would be, of course, painful, too. For me, it is already nature not to be satisfied. No matter how good it is — I will always find bad in the good.

The second Lea was an amusing children's author, who gave us *Room for Rent, Where Is Pluto*, and *The Scatterbrain from Upper Maine* (translated from the Hebrew *HaMefuzar MiKfar Azar*):

> He wakes up much to his surprise,
> Frowns a frown and rubs his eyes.
> And wonders: "Did I close my eyes,
> Or did I just lie down in bed?
> Is that the sun or moon in the sky?
> Should I get up or shouldn't I?
> Is it night or is it day?
> Is tick-tock all my clock can say?
> Oh, but now it's clear as day,
> I know what I meant to say.
> Nine o'clock was here last night,
> So today's tomorrow — yes, that's right!

When one writes for children, Lea Goldberg explained, one must have a serious and honest approach to the subject: "the writer must himself see in his creation for children a great artistic duty, exactly like in his writing for adults." In order to write for children, she continued, "you must remember the child you were."

And she remembered, and wrote dozens of poems that are among the most beloved for Israeli children until today. She also edited children's newspapers and books. Her young readers were her only children; she never married and never had her own family.

The decision not to have children was made early on: Lea was an only child. When she was young, her father suffered from mental illness and was hospitalized, and she never saw him again. For her entire life, she feared that she, too, would experience mental illness, and she chose not to have children.

Lea Goldberg did not live to a very old age; she was awarded the *Israel Prize* after her death. The decision to give her the prize was made on the day she died, before the news of her death had been made public.

# ADD YOUR VOICE

## *Explore*

Hebrew — Lea Goldberg's language of choice — has evolved over time. Spoken in biblical times, it remained in use for centuries in Jewish prayer and study, and was brought back to life for modern use by Eliezer Ben-Yehuda. Today Hebrew is essential for studying Jewish sources in their original, but it is also the language upon which the State of Israel functions. You can learn Hebrew — or improve your Hebrew — in a variety of ways, using apps, online programs, or a private tutor.

## Give Back

If you read Hebrew, you can teach Hebrew to those younger than you or read in Hebrew to the elderly in your community. You can also use the language by making a Hebrew newspaper for the people around you to practice theirs; include news, events taking place in the community, a spotlight on someone interesting — and even poetry.

## See Something New

*There are beautiful things in the world. Trees and flowers, people and views,*
*And a person who has eyes open can see at least a hundred wonderful things each day...*

A line from Lea Goldberg's poem, "The Tree," is immortalized on the Burning Bush sculpture, a monument in memory of fallen **IDF** soldiers located at the entrance to the **Knesset**. The Burning Bush, which is always lit — an eternal flame — stands above, and below it, on white stone, are her words, "The morning will rise through their blood."

You can visit the plaza at the Knesset's entrance, see the monument, and from there walk in Jerusalem in the footsteps of Lea Goldberg. In the last twenty years of her life, she lived on Alfasi Street in the Rehavia neighborhood, a neighborhood which today houses the Prime Minister's Residence and the President's Residence. You can even reserve a tour that follows the lives of Jerusalem's female poets from the area.

# Get Out of Your Comfort Zone

Choose songs written by female Israeli poets, and organize a karaoke night in a venue of your choosing. Prepare a playlist and look for the story behind each song; tell your guests about its meaning and narrative. Look up songwriters and poets like Lea Goldberg, Naomi Shemer (see chapter 53), and Rachel Bluwstein (see chapter 9).

January 14, 1858–December 7, 1942
28 Tevet 5618–28 Kislev 5703

# 19

# HANNAH GREENEBAUM SOLOMON

## *Founder of the National Council of Jewish Women*

T he house that Hannah was brought up in, it appears, dictated her path.

Both of her parents were social activists. Her mother, Sarah, founded the Jewish Ladies Sewing Society, a charity that provided clothes for the poor. Her father, Michael, was a human rights activist. These were the days of the Civil War, and one of the memories that followed young Hannah was the night when her father and other human rights activists broke down the door to the jail cell at the local police station to liberate an innocent man.

Michael and Sarah Greenebaum immigrated to the United States from Germany, and were some of the first Jews to settle in Chicago. They had ten children. Because the Jewish education system in the city was not yet developed, Hannah's three older sisters were sent back to Germany for high school. But Hannah insisted on learning at the local school, although she left two years later in order to devote herself to studying music.

From a very young age, Hannah was politically aware. When she was eighteen, she and her sister joined the Chicago Women's Club, which was occupied with education and helping the needy. After a few years of activity, she chose to establish a similar organization, which would focus on the same concerns within the Jewish community.

Hannah's opportunity came with the 1893 celebrations of four hundred years to Columbus's discovery of America. Chicago hosted the World's Columbian Exhibition, the highlight of the celebrations. The event also included an interreligious encounter, the World Parliament of Religions. Hannah Greenebaum Solomon was chosen to organize a congress of Jewish women in advance of the event.

At the time, there were no phones, no radio or television, no computers or internet. In order to gather the leading Jewish women from around the United States, Hannah wrote to rabbis in important cities, and they gave her the names of women who were active in their communities. She then handwrote letters to ninety women — **Orthodox, Conservative**, and **Reform** — and invited them to establish a congress of Jewish women together.

But Hannah did not suffice with the one-time event. Instead, she founded the National Council of Jewish Women — the first organization of Jewish women in the United States. The organization promoted gender equality, education for children, and aid for the vulnerable and poor. The council was made up of ninety women at its inception, but it grew during the thirteen years when she stood at the helm; when she retired, it had thousands of activists from fifty cities in twenty-two states.

One of the National Council of Jewish Women's first activities related to girls' education. For that purpose, it founded Sabbath schools for girls, in which teachers and rabbis broadened the girls' knowledge of prayer, Bible, and Jewish history. Alongside the girls' schools, Hannah made sure to create educational frameworks for their mothers, so that they could impart Jewish values to their children.

No less important was the council's absorption of thousands of Jewish refugees who arrived on the shores of the United States from eastern Europe. Due to the **pogroms** in Russia, a mass immigration began in the early 1880s. Many of those who arrived were very poor, did not speak English, and could not find their place in local economic life. The National Council of Jewish Women offered workshops for women in which they could learn to work and make money to support their families; women from the council specialized in social work to help the needy, taught English, and offered legal aid from top lawyers.

At a time when women had not yet won the right to vote, and a woman could not own property, women's organizations, including the National Council of Jewish Women, were the first to promote laws that would prevent discrimination against women as well as children. At the time, young children who had committed a crime — even if they were only six or seven years old — were judged in regular courts and sentenced to time in prison. Hannah's efforts led to the establishment of a special court for youth in Chicago, which saw the child and not only his actions.

Hannah Greenebaum Solomon, and the organization she founded, united women in the service of the Jewish community; her organization is still active today, fighting to make the world a better place.

# ADD YOUR VOICE

## *Explore*

Hannah Solomon helped found supplementary schools to ensure that girls in her community received a Jewish education. Today, many Jewish children benefit from supplementary education, on Sundays and/or in the afternoons. When did this type of schooling — often referred to as "Hebrew school" — begin? How has it changed over time? Look into Jewish supplementary education in your community: Where does it take place? How many students attend? What subjects do they study?

## Give Back

Hannah Solomon and the National Council of Jewish Women created a sisterhood that reached across communities to do good. The organization is still in operation today, and focuses on social justice, hoping to improve the quality of life of women, children, and families and to protect individual rights. Look on their website to see what their current activities are. Is there a project of theirs that you can get involved with?

## See Something New

The National Council of Jewish Women was born out of a connection between Jewish women of different backgrounds who drew together to serve a cause. The ANU Museum of the Jewish People in Tel Aviv aims to tell the story of the Jewish nation in its own way. You can visit it and take in permanent and temporary exhibitions that reflect Jewish identity and renewal and the multicultural world within Judaism. The museum also offers tours online for groups, if you aren't able to visit Tel Aviv, including one that focuses on women in Jewish history.

## Get Out of Your Comfort Zone

Have you ever seen a patchwork quilt? Many cultures have traditions of such quilts, pieced together by women who, in some cases, would each work on a square of their own and then bring them all together to tell their story. If you are interested in the world of sewing and crafting, you can pay tribute to the spirit of the sewing circle that inspired Hannah and the tapestry of women whom Hannah drew together by creating your own quilt. You can ask women from your community to make squares using a variety of techniques — or make it a family artifact, with family members contributing — and sew them all together. The quilt can be hung on a wall in your home or in a synagogue, telling the story of the people who are important to you and influence your life.

January 20, 1900–July 31, 1968
20 Shvat 5660–6 Av 5728

# 20

# BRACHA HABAS

## *The Land of Israel's First Female Field Reporter*

When the State of Israel was founded in 1948, it contained 197 reporters. Of these, seven were women; all of them worked as editors.

All but Bracha Habas. Bracha was one of the first journalists to report from the field, always stationed where the action was.

Bracha Habas was born in Russia. Her father Israel was a member of the **Hibbat Zion** movement and a founder of the **Mizrachi** movement. Her mother, Nehama, was an educated woman who had been raised speaking Hebrew and knew **Tanakh**, the Bible, inside and out. Bracha grew up speaking Hebrew in her home.

When Bracha was eight, she came to the Land of Israel — then ruled by the Turkish — with her parents. After moving from Petah Tikva to Haifa, the family settled in Neve Shalom, on the outskirts of Tel Aviv.

Bracha was one of the first students at the Levinsky College of Education. Her most revered teacher was the author Yosef Haim Brenner. Brenner quickly recognized Bracha's talent and encouraged her to write.

The college was training her to be an educator; in the years before the land had a compulsory education law, Bracha taught children who otherwise would not be able to learn at all — children from poor families in Jaffa, working youth, young girls who worked in house-keeping. She initiated a program and educated them all in reading and writing; the first stories she published were about them.

When the *Davar* newspaper was founded in 1925, Bracha joined the team, and ended up writing for the paper for decades. Her articles were about everything: social issues (people who needed aid in their everyday lives or their efforts to join the workforce), security (the **Palmach** and **Haganah**, the organizations that preceded the Israel Defense Force), policy (the **Histadrut**, Israel's labor organization, and the **Zionist Congresses**), and on and on.

Bracha Habas's big break as a journalist came in 1936, when the **Arab Revolt** erupted. The Arabs rose up against the British, who had taken over the land from the Turks, but there were also constant terror attacks against the Jewish community in the land, known as the **Yishuv**. And in those turbulent days, when many journalists sat in their homes and described what they were hearing from others, Bracha moved from place to place to collect eyewitness testimony. She reported from the most dangerous locations, from places where Jews were being attacked and the settlements that were being established in response to Arab terror, the **Tower and Stockade** (*Homa UMigdal*) settlements.

Here, for example, is Bracha's description as she traversed "the exposed mountains of **Ephraim**" (northeast of Jerusalem): "From both sides of the way they close in, threatening with the uncertainty that is on them. Up there — boulder or person? And on the other side — stalk or rifle? The eye is vigilant, the heart is vigilant. A shooting machine raises up its maw, soldiers' rifles aim, ready..."

When the Second World War broke out, Bracha traveled by rail to all of the neighboring countries to report on the situation, and when the death camps were liberated at the end of the Holocaust, she interviewed survivors in Italy.

At age twenty-four, Bracha married, but the marriage was not a happy one and she divorced a short time later. Twenty years later, she married David Hacohen, a businessman, writer, and diplomat, and together they lived full lives. David's first wife, Bracha's good friend, had died young; while Bracha never had her own children, she raised her husband's children with him.

Bracha Habas traveled the world and wrote about it all. When the couple went to India, they wrote a book about the trip. And when they lived in Burma (today Myanmar), where her husband was the Israeli ambassador, Bracha shared her experiences with the newspaper's readers, young and old.

Over the course of her life, Bracha wrote dozens of books — biographies of well-known figures, stories of immigrants, stories of heroes, stories of the Holocaust — but all were about real events. She could never understand authors who invented stories.

And she always wrote for children, too. Along with two others, she founded the children's version of *Davar*, called *Davar LeYeladim*; later on, she became a children's books editor at Am Oved publishers, and also wrote books and booklets specially for children.

Bracha Habas treated the children she wrote for with great respect, and shared the problems from the world of the adults — politics and culture — with them. She also wrote moving stories in which children played a central role; once, for example, she reported on a class that had written to the army's chief of general staff to ask him to release their teacher from reserve duty.

Painter and writer Nahum Gutman, one of the cofounders of *Davar LeYeladim*, once said: "The years when I worked in Bracha's company were the best years of my life."

# ADD YOUR VOICE

## Explore

Bracha Habas's most noticeable ability was her eloquence.

Many children, and even adults, are afraid to speak in front of an audience. If you, too, are uncomfortable, perhaps you would like to join a public speaking workshop, either alone or with friends. Here you can learn how to stand in front of an audience, how to construct an argument, how to raise and lower your voice, how to use and read body language, and other tools that can help raise your confidence. Record yourself as you go along in the workshop so you can see your improvement.

You can use your new abilities and give a speech in front of guests at your bat mitzvah celebration, talking about subjects that interest you or that you feel strongly about.

## Give Back

In Bracha Habas's day, journalists had access to information and were able to disseminate it. But today, anyone with a smartphone or access to the internet can research and publish. Journalism plays a major part in bringing the stories of people around the world to the public, and is often crucial in effecting change where it is most needed. What cause can you bring light to? How can you use the tools at your disposal — the internet and social media — to raise awareness and make a change?

## See Something New

If you are a future journalist and love the profession, you can ask to spend a day at a newspaper, to see the journalists, editors, and graphic designers, or to follow a photographer; at night, you can watch the vigorous work that goes into printing the newspaper.

And if you'd like to see history in action, go to the National Library of Israel's website, where you can browse the newspaper collection online. Newspapers in a variety of languages from throughout history can be searched and accessed.

## Get Out of Your Comfort Zone

Edit a newspaper in advance of your bat mitzvah. Choose a theme — your family history, an area of interest, or even just you. If the newspaper focuses on you, you can look up headlines from the day you were born and make a newspaper that includes a headline about your birth. If you're focusing on family, interview relatives and tell their stories. If there's an issue that's important to you that you want to cover, find people you can interview, perhaps even online, and do your research. You can ask friends to contribute columns and add sections like "Business," "Sports," or "Entertainment." Distribute the newspaper as a souvenir at your bat mitzvah party — or, if you'd prefer, challenge your friends to create a newspaper with you at your bat mitzvah celebration.

# 21

# REGINA JONAS

## *The First Female Rabbi*

In 1972, Sally Jane Priesand was **ordained** as a rabbi in Cincinnati, Ohio. The Jewish world was convinced that she was making history as the first female rabbi in the world.

But no one remembered that thirty-seven years earlier, in Berlin, another woman had been ordained: Regina Jonas.

Regina Jonas was born in a poor neighborhood in Berlin, to Wolf, who was a merchant, and Sara, a housewife. Her parents, like all of the neighborhood's residents, were Jews of Polish extraction, **Orthodox** in their worldview and lifestyle.

When Regina was eleven, her father died, and her small family — her mother, her older brother Abraham, and Regina — moved to a different neighborhood and a different synagogue. The rabbi of the new synagogue, Max Weyl, was an Orthodox rabbi, but his views were quite liberal. When he understood that young Regina dreamed of becoming a rabbi, and believed that that was what God wanted of her, he encouraged her to follow her heart. Even years after she had completed her studies at the girls' school he ran alongside the synagogue, Rabbi Weyl continued to teach Regina Jewish religious studies, **Talmud**, and Jewish history.

Rabbi Weyl was one of the only people to hold a bat mitzvah celebration in his synagogue, though the girls were not called to read from the **Torah**; Regina celebrated her bat mitzvah there.

When she finished high school, Regina attended a teachers' seminary and became a Jewish studies teacher at a high school, but she did not feel that she was fulfilling her true destiny. She registered at a rabbinical seminary founded by a leading **Reform** rabbi; despite the fact that her lifestyle and worldview were Orthodox, this was the only seminary that would accept a woman for studies. At age twenty-eight, Regina submitted her thesis. The thesis addressed the question of whether, according to **halakha**, a woman could serve as a rabbi, a debate that had not yet begun at that time in Orthodox Jewish society. Rabbi Max Benath, who reviewed her thesis, graded it and, it appears, planned on ordaining her, but he died suddenly. No other teacher was willing to take on the groundbreaking mission.

Five years later, in 1935, with the Nazis already in power, Rabbi Max Dienemann, the head of the Liberal Rabbis' Association in Offenbach am Main, Germany, agreed to ordain Regina as the first female rabbi in the world.

And still, no congregation would employ her. So, dressed in her purple rabbinical robe (to distinguish her from her male colleagues, with their black robes), Regina cared for the religious needs of Jews in hospitals, nursing homes, and even a women's prison.

With the passing of the **Nuremberg Laws** in 1935, which robbed the Jews of their civil rights, Germany's Jews began to leave, including many of the rabbis. Under these circumstances, there was a need for Regina Jonas's services; she became a wandering rabbi, moving from community to community, trying to provide the frightened Jews with reassurance.

She herself considered leaving Germany, and even turned to famous philosopher Martin Buber, who lived in Jerusalem, asking him whether he thought she could find a place in the Land of Israel and serve as a rabbi. But she ultimately decided not to go; she did not want to leave the persecuted communities.

Regina continued her work until she was taken to the Theresienstadt ghetto in November 1942. There she joined the ghetto's spiritual leaders, including Leo Baeck, who had been her teacher at the rabbinical seminary, and renowned neurologist and philosopher

Viktor Frankl. Her job was to help the deported Jews adjust to their new circumstances. It was not easy for them, recently taken from their homes and living with the threat of death hovering over them. Regina and her colleagues worked to give the community that was forming in the ghetto the sense that life could go on. The cultural life in Theresienstadt was full; plays were put on, operas were written, people studied. Dozens of years later, twenty-four articles that Regina Jonas had written and lectures she had given in the ghetto were found.

On October 12, 1944, Regina Jonas and her mother were deported to Auschwitz, where they were murdered.

With the end of the war, no one remembered Regina Jonas, not even Leo Baeck and Viktor Frankl, who had survived the Holocaust. Only after the fall of the Berlin Wall in 1989, when scholars from the world descended on the eastern part of Germany hoping to find historical documents, did Dr. Katharina von Kellenbach find a tattered envelope with her papers, and restore her title as "the first female rabbi in the world."

# ADD YOUR VOICE

*"To be blessed by God means to give wherever one steps in every life situation blessing, kindness, faithfulness..."*

## *Explore*

Regina Jonas delved into a question that had not been explored until her time: What does religious law say about women serving as rabbis? Her approach was groundbreaking; she made sure to use her halakhic knowledge, following the rules of the game, in order to effect a revolution.

Look into Regina Jonas's approach. What was customary at her time? What was so groundbreaking about her thesis? Do a little research of your own: What rulings or ideas within halakha would not allow women to serve as rabbis? What reasons did Regina give in her thesis to explain why she felt it was permitted? It has been almost a century since she wrote her important work. Interview people in your family and community, including leaders and rabbis, to ask their opinions and see what halakhic sources you can explore to learn more about the question and how answers to it have evolved over time.

## Give Back

Regina Jonas felt that a crucial part of her job as rabbi was bringing comfort to those who needed it. She was a spiritual guide to the ill and the frightened. Aside from visiting the sick, she also tried to create a positive and Jewish atmosphere even when conditions in her ghetto made it nearly impossible. In her spirit, perhaps you would like to take on visiting the sick or elderly on a weekly basis, bringing them joy and comfort.

## See Something New

The Jewish Women's Archive aims to document the stories of Jewish women and bring their voices to the fore. The JWA website has a short documentary film about Regina Jonas (search for "In the Footsteps of Regina Jonas"). It documents a number of rabbis and leaders, from across the Jewish religious spectrum, tracing her past and her story, and their feelings of gratitude to her for her pioneering spirit. If you'd like to learn more about the movie, you can also read some of the linked "Program Resources."

In 1997, a hidden synagogue was uncovered in the Theresienstadt ghetto. The Jews had created a secret house of prayer in a storeroom, and the walls contained inscriptions that included words from prayers and drawings. Search for pictures and videos about the synagogue online.

## Get Out of Your Comfort Zone

The Jewish Women's Archive also carries a variety of activities that amplify women's voices. In the spirit of Regina Jonas, who stood proudly as a woman within her community, find an activity that speaks to you. Listen to the JWA podcast, read along with its book club, follow its blog on feminism and women in society, or even register for one of its online history courses.

# 22

# JUDITH

## *Hero and Savior*

Judith the daughter of Merari, the most impressive woman in the town of Bethulia — clever, beautiful, and wealthy — wanted to keep her neighbors from surrendering to the Assyrian enemy. So the book of Judith, likely composed in the second or first century BCE, tells us.

The town was in terrible crisis. Assyria, with its vast army, wished to defeat it, most likely on its way to conquering Jerusalem. To do so, Holofernes, the army's commander, had taken over the springs that gave the town its water, and the townspeople, young and old alike, were crazed with thirst. The crisis was so great that the residents demanded of the town's magistrate, Uzziah, that he surrender on their behalf. Uzziah negotiated with them, asking for five more days, hoping that those five days would bring a miracle.

Judith, however, felt that they could not wait for a miracle; she took action.

Judith was a widow, and had been wearing black since her husband's death, as was the custom. But that night she bathed, changed into festive clothing, put on her most dazzling jewels, and left the city gates, accompanied by a maid. The two descended the mountain and crossed the valley to the enemy camp. The military guards were stunned to see a beautiful woman at the entrance, and a hundred people escorted her to the commander's tent, where "Holofernes rested on his bed under a canopy, which was woven with purple and gold and emeralds and precious stones" (Judith 10:24).

Judith surprised the Assyrian military commander with an espionage plan: The nation of Israel, she explained, cannot be destroyed by the sword unless it sins against its God. The hunger and thirst that the Assyrians had imposed, she promised, would force the people to sin; with no other choice left, they would use the first fruits and tenths of wine and oil that were reserved for the priests in the Temple. Once they had sinned, and God had removed His protection from them, she suggested, she herself would bring the news to Holofernes and lead him through secret pathways into the town of Bethulia. But in order to know what was happening, when the town's divine protection would end, she would have to leave each night, to pray and listen to the word of God.

Holofernes liked the idea so much that he commanded that the best of foods be served to his guest. But Judith was careful to bring only kosher food from her house, and ate that instead.

For three days, Judith stayed in Holofernes' camp, and for three nights she went to the nearby river to pray. But on the fourth day Holofernes could no longer withstand her beauty; he offered to hold a festive meal in her honor, and plotted to entice her. Judith, in her finest clothing, ate and drank what she had brought from her home, but the besotted commander drank "more wine than he had drunk at any time in one day since he was born" (Judith 12:20). And when he was entirely drunk, Judith approached his bed, seized his sword, and, with two strokes, took off his head. She put his head in the bag in which she kept her food and left, like every night, walking toward the river. From the river, she and her companion turned to the gates of Bethulia, where they were received with joy and rejoicing and Holofernes' head was hung on the city walls.

The Assyrian army, upon discovering their commander's head hanging for all to see, ran for their lives, and the land was quiet for forty years.

# ADD YOUR VOICE

*"And she went before all the people in the dance, leading all the women; and all the men of Israel followed in their armor with garlands, and with songs in their mouths."*

(Judith 15:17)

## Explore

Judith's story is one of a woman who planned and executed a campaign against a bitter enemy. Today, people learn defensive tactics in self-defense courses, which serve to empower women and help prevent physical and sexual assault. Join a martial arts program to learn how to defend yourself and to create a safe environment. Workshops for self-defense may include taekwondo, karate, krav maga, and more.

## Give Back

El HaLev is a Jerusalem-based organization that trains women in self-defense. Its goal is to prevent violence of all types by teaching women and girls of all ages about safety and self-protection, using a method that combines physical and mental skills. Aside from classes in its center in Jerusalem, El HaLev holds personal safety and self-protection programs in schools, boarding homes, special education programs, hostels, shelters, and more.

You can support El HaLev by holding a fundraising drive, collecting money that can finance a program in a school or home, helping prevent violence against women. You may even be able to organize a course in which El HaLev's instructors come to you and your friends.

## See Something New

A monument to female warriors stands at **Kibbutz** Nitzanim, which was established in the year 1943 near the shores of the Mediterranean. One of its founding members, Mira Ben-Ari, was a member of the **Lehi** underground movement briefly and then served in the **Haganah**. When the **War of Independence** broke out, she chose to stay and fight rather than evacuate with the women and children; she was killed in battle.

Visit the Nitzanim beach and the nature reserve to its east. The sand dunes and the sycamores are unique to this part of Israel. Where the kibbutz once stood, there is now a field school, with a bronze statue of three female soldiers who fell in battle, including Mira Ben-Ari. The monument is dedicated to Israel's fighting women, and contains quotes from other famous women who took part in Israel's wars: Sarah Aaronsohn (see chapter 1), Hannah Senesh (see chapter 51), Mira Ben-Ari, Esther Arditi (see chapter 5), Sarah Chizik, and Bracha Fuld.

## Get Out of Your Comfort Zone

Judith is identified with the revolt of the **Hasmoneans** and the holiday of **Hanukah**. The first day of the month of Tevet, which falls on the Hanukah festival, was known in some Jewish cultures as *id el banat* ("the girls' holiday" in Arabic), and recalls the miracle that was performed by a woman. Women from Tunisia, Libya, Algeria, Constantinople, and Thessaloniki (or Salonika) have a custom of not doing any work (sewing, embroidering, and the like) on the first of Tevet. Young women visit each other and hold joyful parties. In some communities, a joint bat mitzvah was held on this day for all of the girls who had reached the age of twelve that year. In other places, a type of bonding activity was held for women of all ages, who celebrated with songs and dancing. There are also motifs of **Yom Kippur**, the Day of Atonement, that have become part of the holiday: in some communities, girls make peace with one another and pray together.

If your bat mitzvah falls on or near Hanukah, you can revive the custom of *id el banat* and celebrate a joint bat mitzvah with your close friends or family. With your friends, you can create your own *id el banat* on the first day of Tevet: cook together, bake honey cakes, and give each other gifts.

# 23

# HELENA KAGAN

## *Jerusalem's First*
## *Female Pediatrician*

H elena Kagan was twenty-four when she completed medical school and a specialty in pediatrics, and the university in Switzerland offered her a job in research. She turned down the rare offer without hesitation, despite the fact that it had never before been offered to a woman, much less so to a Jewish woman. Before his death, her father had made her promise that she would visit the Land of Israel. And what began as a promise to her father ended up becoming her life's mission.

The year was 1914. The Turkish reigned in the Land of Israel, and they had never heard of a female doctor; they categorically refused to give her a permit to work in her field. Helena found herself working as a nurse in the hospital and she quickly trained new nurses in the profession. With no running water and only one bathtub for sixty patients, the young doctor taught the rules of cleanliness and hygiene to Jewish and Arab students. She may have continued to teach nurses for the rest of her life if a medical delegation from Turkey had not arrived in the land and granted her the first license to practice medicine given to a woman in the history of the **Ottoman Empire.**

Immediately after the First World War, when there was great hunger in Jerusalem and children and babies in the city had no milk to drink, Helena Kagan purchased a cow. She would milk the cow every day, boil the milk, and keep it in bottles for hungry children. At the same time, she began to establish clinics within communities to maintain the health of babies and their mothers.

It was at this time that Jerusalem's famed eye doctor, Dr. Ticho, was exiled to Damascus. He left his hospital to Dr. Kagan, who established a Jewish children's hospital there, and later added a day-care center for the small children whom she found wandering the streets of Jerusalem while their parents worked.

In 1924, the Land of Israel's chief rabbi, Rabbi Kook, called Helena Kagan. He had found a baby wrapped in rags on his doorstep with a note: "I am a wretched mother who is forced to abandon the fruit of her womb. I give him to you and place my trust in you." The rabbi turned to Helena, whom he thought of as the person most devoted to babies — and he was not wrong. The baby became the basis for another of Helena Kagan's initiatives, a home for abandoned Jewish babies. In the beginning, the home was so underfunded that the babies slept in padded boxes that had originally carried oranges. In parallel, she worked at the Infants Home for Arab Children, serving as medical director until Jews were barred from the Old City in 1948.

Dr. Kagan founded the pediatric ward at the Bikur Holim hospital in 1936 and ran it for forty years. She worked hard to ease children's pain as much as possible: she allowed parents to remain next to their children, and was the first to create a classroom in the pediatric ward for children suffering from chronic diseases.

Years later, during the **Six-Day War**, Helena met many of the babies she had taken care of twenty and thirty years earlier in the emergency room at the Bikur Holim hospital. They were Jews from West Jerusalem and Arabs from the Old City, now fighting one another. All were her children, and she treated them all with devotion and love.

Helena Kagan passed away with no children of her own, but surrounded by the thousands who had lived thanks to her.

# ADD YOUR VOICE

## *Explore*

---

Helena Kagan saw medical needs around her and created institutions and programs that would save lives and care for those who needed aid. What type of programs today ensure that life-saving measures are available to all? What are the rules about the presence of tools like defibrillators, EpiPens, and first aid kits in public spaces? How else can we take responsibility for those around us and help save lives?

## *Give Back*

---

If you've ever been to a children's ward in a hospital, you may have noticed a room set aside for kids with items like computers, books, toys, games, or musical instruments. These types of spaces make a stay at a hospital feel less threatening and help take kids' minds off of what can be a frightening or painful experience.

Commemorate Helena Kagan's commitment to children's health and wellbeing by collecting items that can be used in a hospital classroom — books, toys, games, instruments, or even used computers. You can reach out to your community, family, or friends to ask them to bring used items to make kids' stays in the hospital a little bit easier.

# See Something New

One of the events that had a huge impact on the world of medicine in the pre-State Land of Israel was the attack on the convoy that departed from central Jerusalem, headed for the Hadassah hospital on Mount Scopus. At that time, when tensions between Jews and Arabs in the city were high, Arab troops often blocked access to Mount Scopus, attacking Jewish vehicles when they attempted to traverse the narrow road.

On April 13, 1948, a large convoy carrying lecturers, medical staff, and patients left for the mountain on which Hadassah hospital and the Hebrew University were located. When it reached the Sheikh Jarrah neighborhood, the convoy was attacked and many were killed and injured. The convoy stood for six hours; the British would not allow **Haganah** members to come to its aid, and after six hours the buses went up in flames. Seventy-eight Jews, some of the finest minds in the land, paid with their lives, including the hospital's director; a British soldier was also killed. From that day on, the hospital ceased its activities, reopening after the Six-Day War, when the eastern part of the city was once again accessible for Jews.

You can follow the convoy, moving from the Hadassah buildings on HaNeviim Street to Shivtei Yisrael Street. From here, turn north, in the direction of the Shimon HaTzadik neighborhood in East Jerusalem and see the monument in memory of the convoy. From the monument, move toward Hadassah Hospital. From Mount Scopus, you have a spectacular observation point — both toward western Jerusalem and eastward to the desert.

# Get Out of Your Comfort Zone

If you are interested in medicine like Helena Kagan, you can join a program for youth. Look around for medical workshops or summer programs in your area. You can learn about the world of medicine and even have hands-on experiences, learning about taking vital signs and patient histories, suturing, and CPR.

*The establishment of "Tipat Halav" baby wellness centers, which have been responsible for the health of babies for one hundred years in Israel, can been attributed to three women: Helena Kagan, the pediatrician who began to give milk to the babies of Jerusalem and cared for sick babies; her sister-in-law, Rachel Cohen Kagan, who was sent by Henrietta Szold (see chapter 55) and the Hebrew Women's Organization to create a series of clinics for women and babies in Jerusalem; and Bertha Landsman, a nurse who had distributed milk to babies in New York and established clinics around the Land of Israel, also at the request of Henrietta Szold and Hadassah.*

# 24

# EMMA LAZARUS

## *The Statue of Liberty's Poet*

Emma Lazarus grew up in a rich and indulgent home. The Lazaruses were a noble Jewish family that had been exiled with Portugal's Jews and arrived in America in the seventeenth century, two hundred years before Emma was born, well before America attained independence.

Emma's loving father would not permit her to go to school; he thought she was too sensitive and sickly. Instead, he hired private tutors for her and her five sisters. Emma wrote poetry from childhood, and, when she reached the age of fourteen, her proud father published her first poetry collection. From that point on, Emma's world revolved around American literature and poetry: she printed books of poetry with respected publishers, translated poetry from German and French, and was praised by the best writers of her time. Her translations of the work of Heinrich Heine, a German Jewish poet who had converted to Protestantism, were considered the best in the English language at the time. She was an American at heart.

Somewhere near the age of thirty, Emma began to connect to her Jewish identity and culture. This may have happened when her good friend Helena gave her George Eliot's famous book *Daniel Deronda*. The book relates to the Jewish national revival in Palestine, the Land of Israel. But the new interest may also have come from her encounter with the refugees from the **pogroms**, Jews who had escaped the horrors of Russia and migrated by the thousands to the United States. Emma understood that she must help her brethren who had come from afar, to teach them to live in their new land.

The great immigration of Russia's Jews to the United States began in the 1880s. Some two thousand people, mostly Jews, arrived each month at the ports of the United States, primarily New York. Many Jewish immigrants were housed on an isolated island, where poverty and filth abounded. There was no running water, nor enough food or work. Instead of working to make money to support themselves, the immigrants lived off of meager donations.

Emma Lazarus visited the refugees and was shocked by their conditions. She wrote about it in newspapers, and would not stop pushing until schools were opened on the island; she even taught English. She was cofounder of the Hebrew Technical Institute, a vocational high school.

Thanks to her articles, factories began to offer the immigrants work. It was, in fact, Emma who was a one-woman factory, bringing salvation to the Jewish refugees.

Emma's poems from that time express the revolution she underwent. The poems in her book *Songs of a Semite* are all about Jews and Jewish heroism as well as the new generation of Jewish agriculturists and their predecessors, the **Maccabees**.

As a journalist, both in Jewish and general media, Emma published a series of articles. The conclusion drawn from her work is clear: a Jewish state must be established in Palestine. In the weekly magazine *American Hebrew*, under the heading "An Epistle to the Hebrews," Emma laid out her idea of establishing a national home for the Jews of eastern Europe in the Land of Israel. Nonetheless, she believed that American Jews should not join, but rather remain loyal citizens in their country.

Emma Lazarus was a **Zionist** Jew fifteen years before the First **Zionist Congress**. But she was also a proud American citizen and grateful for the freedom that America granted her Jewish immigrant brothers and sisters.

It was at that time that the French government gifted the United States an immense statue which would later be called the Statue of Liberty; at the time, it was known as "Liberty Enlightening the World." Embarrassingly, the United States did not have enough funds to build a structure on which the statue could sit. A fundraising event was organized, and New York's writers and poets read their writing. When Emma understood that the statue would be erected in the ocean, greeting the refugees when they arrived in the United States and symbolizing their freedom, she got on board. Her moving sonnet, "The New Colossus," was included in the book published in honor of the event.

But when the statue was erected in New York's south in 1886, Emma was not present at the ceremony. She was fighting cancer, and died of the disease a year later, at age thirty-eight. No one remembered or read the poem that she'd written specially for the ceremony. She, and her poems, seemed to be forgotten.

Fifteen years later, the poem was rediscovered, and her words were inscribed on the base of the Statue of Liberty. These lines greet the millions of people who visit it still today:

Give me your tired, your poor,
Your huddled masses yearning to breathe free,
The wretched refuse of your teeming shore
Send these, the homeless, tempest-tost to me,
I lift my lamp beside the golden door!

Emma Lazarus's legacy even extends as far as Israel; American Jews giving aid for the founding of a neighborhood in Hadera honored her memory by naming it *Nahalat Emma Lazarus* (the legacy of Emma Lazarus) in 1912 — though it has always been known by the acronym "Nahliel."

# ADD YOUR VOICE

## *Explore*

The book *Daniel Deronda*, which influenced Emma Lazarus so strongly, is an important one. Published in 1876, it contains one plotline that relates to Jews and the Jewish homeland. It was first published as eight volumes and has also been adapted a number of times for film and television.

What do you know about the book? Perhaps you can challenge yourself to read it. Why would Emma Lazarus's friend have recommended it for her? What messages does it contain?

## *Give Back*

In the spirit of Emma Lazarus, who toiled to help the Jewish refugees who arrived on the shores of the United States, can you help immigrants? Perhaps you can tutor a student in English? Or serve as a buddy for someone who has joined your school, youth movement, or afterschool program?

You can also look into organizations that offer aid to immigrants. HIAS, the Hebrew Immigrant Aid Society, was founded in 1881 to offer aid to the Russian and Eastern European Jews who were streaming into New York. Today the organization still offers help to immigrants in America and around the world. The Red Cross also offers aid and hope for migrants and refugees. What organizations work with immigrants in your community? What can you do to help?

## See Something New

The Emma Lazarus Project is an initiative of the American Jewish Historical Society to explore Emma Lazarus's life and legacy. On its website, you can read poems submitted as part of its poetry contest, watch a movie about Emma Lazarus's life, peruse an interactive book about her world, and read "The New Colossus" translated into a variety of languages — including Hebrew and Yiddish.

If you live near New York or are visiting, you can visit the Statue of Liberty and see Emma Lazarus's words. And if not, the National Parks Service makes it possible to tour it virtually online.

## Get Out of Your Comfort Zone

Can you write your own poem in the spirit of "The New Colossus"? Emma Lazarus's poem includes motifs of opportunity and hope. What message do you think should greet new immigrants to your country today?

# 25

# LEAH

## *A Mother of the Israelite Tribes*

T he nation of Israel had four mothers, one of whom is known for her eyes. The **Torah** rarely describes a person's physical appearance, yet Leah's "weak" eyes are mentioned in a verse that also states that her sister, Rachel, was beautiful (Genesis 29:17). Commentators debate the meaning of the word; some view it as a medical condition, others believe it was a result of years of crying, still others see her as a sensitive soul.

Leah first appears in the biblical story that recounts Jacob traveling to his uncle, Laban; he had been sent by his parents in the hopes that he would marry a cousin. According to the custom in Haran, Leah, the eldest, should have been the first to marry, but Jacob fell in love with her younger sister, Rachel. Laban insisted on following the local custom and Jacob was covertly and deceitfully wed to Leah. And so Leah became a rejected woman. Was she in on the trick? Did she secretly love Jacob, even while he courted her sister Rachel? Or was the unfair arrangement forced on her, too?

Leah fought for Jacob's love her entire life. She believed that being mother to many children would raise her esteem in his eyes: "Seeing that Leah was unloved, God opened her womb; but Rachel was barren" (Genesis 29:31), the Torah tells us. Leah gave birth to four boys, and their names attest to her hope for love: Reuben (*Reuven*): "It means 'God has seen my affliction (*ra'ah Hashem be-onyi*),' for now my husband will love me" (Genesis 29:32); Simon (*Shimon*): "This is because God heard that I was unloved (*ki snu'ah anokhi*) and has given me this one also" (Genesis 29:33); Levi: "This time my husband will become attached to me (*yelave ishi elai*)" (Genesis 29:34); and Judah (*Yehuda*): "This time I will praise God (*odeh et Hashem*)" (Genesis 29:35; the commentators note that Leah was the first person in the Bible to thank God).

But with Rachel barren, tensions between Leah and her sister were high. When Reuben, Leah's eldest son, brought mandrakes from the field, Rachel asked for them: "Was it not enough for you to take away my husband, that you would also take my son's mandrakes?" Leah cried out (Genesis 30:15). The plant's healing powers — some believed that it could treat infertility — were apparently important to Rachel; she wanted the mandrakes so badly that she agreed to trade a night with her husband for them. And then Leah, who had always been passive, who had always prayed from afar that she might find favor in her husband's eyes, went out to meet him and informed him that he was to come to her and not to Rachel. This action, surprising for someone who had until then appeared meek and obedient, may have been what established her status as the central mother.

Two sons were born after the story of the mandrakes: Issachar to Leah and Joseph to Rachel. Rachel — no longer barren — went on to have one more son, Benjamin, and died in childbirth before the family settled in the land of Canaan. Leah lived a longer life as Jacob's wife and, when she died, was buried in the family burial plot, the Cave of the Patriarchs (*Maarat HaMakhpela*). Jacob, her beloved husband, asked to be buried there alongside her. Leah, who had started out with the deck stacked against her in many ways, set her goals and would not let go, ultimately becoming the mother of six of the Israelite tribes.

# ADD YOUR VOICE

## *Explore*

What were the mandrake plants that the sisters attributed so much importance to? The mandrake is a medicinal root, thought for years to treat infertility. It blooms in the winter, between December and March, in the Mediterranean region. Do you want to learn more? There are plants from which medicines are made, plants that prevent disease, and plants that folk wisdom says have healing powers. Study different plants and what their benefits are. You may want to focus specifically on plants that are native to the Land of Israel, ones that Leah would have been familiar with.

You can decorate your bat mitzvah event with plants and flowers you have studied and share what you learned with your guests, or add a sign with details about each plant. You can also give each of your guests a medicinal plant as a souvenir, or distribute aromatic lavender bags with your name printed on them.

## *Give Back*

Are there any community gardens in your neighborhood? Such gardens are run by groups of people who want to create something new and beautiful in their own environments, but their benefits are far greater; they can also help combat food insecurity by growing vegetables and fight climate change in their own small way. In Leah's spirit, can you make a weekly commitment to help out in a nearby community garden?

## See Something New

Neot Kedumim, the Biblical Landscape Reserve, recreates the land as it was during Leah's time. It focuses on the plants and trees of the ancient Land of Israel and offers tours that connect the landscape and agriculture to the Bible. Here you can learn more about the mandrakes as well as the other plants, see the Seven Species as they are described in the Bible, and even plant trees or herd sheep as Jacob did if you plan ahead.

## Get Out of Your Comfort Zone

Natural plants and flowers are also a perfect basis for a perfume-making workshop. Pick from a variety of flowers whose aromas you like and make perfume with your friends. Look for recipes for perfumes online and prepare all of the ingredients and materials you'll need in advance. You may want to ask around to see if members of your family or friends have experience, or even invite a professional to run the event.

# 26

# NECHAMA LEIBOWITZ

## *Teacher*

N echama Leibowitz was born in Russia and grew up in Berlin, Germany; however, she and her older brother, Yeshayahu, were given an education that focused on the Hebrew language. Their great great grandfather had ordered his children to teach their children and grandchildren only in Hebrew.

And this was no simple task: in the early twentieth century, there were very few children's book that were translated into Hebrew. Nonetheless, Nechama's parents spared no effort, and she and her brother read Andersen's fairy tales and Jules Verne in Hebrew. They even played tag and hide-and-seek in Hebrew. At school, of course, they spoke German.

Nechama stayed in Germany until she received her doctorate, and then she sailed to the Land of Israel with the man she loved and had married, over the opposition of her parents. Her husband, Lipman Leibowitz, was also her uncle, her father's brother. He was thirty years older than she was, and blind.

Jerusalem had already heard of the talented woman from Berlin, and, when she arrived, she immediately found a place as a **Tanakh** (Bible) teacher in the Mizrachi Women's Teacher Seminary in Jerusalem.

Over the years Nechama Leibowitz taught in more and more institutions. She lectured in Israel's first three universities and was the first woman to teach in **yeshivas** ("she is a *talmidat hakham* [**Torah** scholar]," said Rabbi Zvi Yehuda Kook, a prominent rabbi). As an educator, she was an artist, a performer who knew how to bring her material to life.

But this was nothing compared to her life's work, through which she made it possible for anyone who wanted to to learn.

Today, learning is quite simple; students around the world can study together over the internet. But eighty years ago, Nechama needed to send pages by mail to each of the thousands of students who asked to learn Torah. Each worksheet — *gilayon* in Hebrew — was dedicated to the week's Torah portion, or *parasha*. In the worksheets, Nechama presented questions for study, ones that related to the Torah and its commentaries. And each question indicated level of difficulty: simple, hard, and very hard.

People from all over the country heard about Nechama's worksheets: waitresses in cafés, street cleaners, salespeople in stores, and soldiers at the front — thousands of people would sit on Saturday nights and try to answer the weekly questions she had raised. On Sunday, they would send their answers back for her to see and correct. And Nechama, who had sent the pages with the help of her family (her nephews and nieces, her father, and others helped close envelopes and affix stamps), would receive the responses, make her comments, and correct them, teaching and explaining to each sender.

Nechama had some two thousand active students and she knew each one personally; she was interested in their lives and expressed concern if they stopped learning. Many were invited to her home; many became personal friends.

At age ninety-two, Nechama sent the final corrected sheet to her student Chanan Sever, on a **kibbutz** in the Galilee, and wrote: "I am sorry, I cannot anymore. I have no more energy. This is the last paper I am correcting."

Nechama, who was generally a happy person, regretted her whole life that she had not had children. Her brother Yeshayahu's six children, as well as her neighbors' children and her young students from around the country — they were the children she never had. They filled her life.

Thousands attended her funeral, from the greatest of professors to the simplest of people. Yossi, her nephew, stood to recite the mourner's prayer — **Kaddish** — and suddenly turned to the crowd and said "Whoever feels like her son is invited to join me in saying Kaddish."

At her request, her gravestone has only one description on it. It says: "Teacher."

# ADD YOUR VOICE

*"There is one person, one woman, who is worthy of being charged with the task of writing a new commentary to the Torah in our generation: Dr. Nechama Leibowitz." (Prof. Ephraim Elimelech Urbach)*

## *Explore*

What is the Torah portion for your bat mitzvah, the reading for the **Shabbat** after your twelfth birthday in the Hebrew calendar? Read the Torah portion. You can begin with Nechama's commentary — if you read Hebrew, you can find her worksheets on *www.nechama.org. il*; if you'd prefer English, you can find them on the **Jewish Agency**'s archive online or on Sefaria. You can also use the English version of her books, *New Studies in the Weekly Parasha* (in English or in Hebrew). Consult other commentaries on the Torah portion as well. See if something speaks to you: perhaps something from nature (rain, snow, storms, interesting changes in climate), perhaps animals, perhaps family relationships or a moral question (choosing between good and evil, the fate of the righteous and the wicked, impersonation and deceit, etc.). You can present the commentary in artistic ways that speak to you — a story, play, song, or dance — or give a **dvar Torah** or speech on the subject at your bat mitzvah.

## Give Back

The regularity with which Nechama published her sheets was exemplary, and helped people learn Torah on a weekly basis. Challenge yourself to study the Torah portion for one year and publish something about it on a weekly basis. You can start a blog or podcast where you explore elements of the *parasha* that you find meaningful or thought-provoking.

## See Something New

The stories in the Torah that Nechama wrote about all took place around the same region, in today's Israel, Iran, Iraq, or Turkey. Visit the Biblelands Museum in Jerusalem, where you can travel back in time in the lands and capital cities that the Tanakh talks about: Ur of the Chaldees, Susa in Persia, Assyria, Babylonia — the lands in which our patriarchs and matriarchs lived or where they fought over the generations — and learn how they lived.

You can also visit the Biblical Museum of Natural History near Beit Shemesh. There you can see and even touch a variety of animals that are mentioned in the Tanakh — from small insects like locusts, to reptiles like snakes and lizards, to large mounted animals like the lion and tiger. And if you enjoy seeing biblical animals, you can also go to the Carmel Hai-Bar Nature Reserve and visit a variety of biblical animals in nature, many of which can no longer be seen around Israel — the roe deer, dama, and Palestine mountain gazelle.

## Get Out of Your Comfort Zone

The **halakha** recommends that all Jews set aside time to learn Torah regularly, ensuring that it remains a central part of their lives. You can ask a parent, grandparent, or friend to study a subject from world of Judaism regularly with you. It can be the weekly *parasha*, a topic in Jewish law, a philosophical concept, or a book that interests you. Make a weekly date to study and celebrate accomplishments — finishing the study of a book or topic — with family or friends.

April 22, 1909–December 30, 2012
1 Iyar 5669–17 Tevet 5773

# 27

# RITA LEVI-MONTALCINI

## *A Tenacious Scientist despite the Nazis*

F rom a young age, with the loss of her governess to a disease, Rita Levi-Montalcini wanted to study medicine. Her father was opposed; he was worried that a career would interfere with her personal life. But Rita would not be swayed, and decided then and there never to marry or become a mother, but instead to devote herself to science.

Rita Levi-Montalcini was born in Turin, Italy, one of four children in a secular Jewish family whose origins were Spanish and Italian. Her twin sister Paola became a well-known painter.

Rita finished medical school in Turin in 1936 and wished to specialize in psychiatry and neurology. But Fascist Italy would not allow her to work in medicine because she was Jewish, so she shifted her field of interest — and the world gained a gifted and groundbreaking scientist.

When the Second World War broke out, Italian Jews were barred from working in science as well, and so Rita built herself a hidden laboratory in her home, and invited her former teacher, Prof. Giuseppe Levi, to join her. The best of his students gathered in the house; in effect, Rita Levi-Montalcini had opened a small, top-tier university in her home.

In order to buy a microscope, without which she could not work, Rita was forced to ride her bicycle more than 140 kilometers, or 85 miles, from Turin to Milan. On the way back she was caught by police officers, who were certain she was smuggling food. When they saw the strange device she held (they had no idea what it was), they freed her.

At that time, Rita began to study the development of chicken embryos. She had to ride her bicycle from village to village to buy eggs — a hard-to-attain product during the war. Moreover, she needed not just eggs, but fertilized eggs (she used the pretext that they were more nutritious). After she took an embryo from an egg, she would use the yolk to fry an omelet; not everyone in the house liked the idea.

Aside from her scientific work, Rita Levi-Montalcini offered her services to the *partisans*, who were fighting the fascists and the Nazis, and spent time forging documents and certificates.

With Italy's liberation from Nazi occupation, Rita was invited to work at an important university in the United States, and from then until her death she divided her time between the U.S. and Italy.

The work on chicken embryos that Rita had begun during the war continued throughout her life. She revealed how cells of one type secrete substances (proteins) that affect the growth of other cells, and ultimately lead to the differentiation of cells in the embryo. It was her work on chicken embryos that revealed how the brain develops from individual cells into a complicated organ. For her work, Rita Levi-Montalcini was awarded the most important prize in the world of science — the Nobel Prize.

But Rita did not suffice with that. She was always an important activist in political and social causes. She worked in the women's liberation movement; established a non-profit organization with her sister Paola that promoted education for women in Africa; and fought against the use of landmines in war-torn areas.

In 1999, when she reached the age of ninety, she was appointed an ambassador to the UN's Food and Agricultural Organization. At age ninety-two, the president of Italy appointed her a senator for life in the Italian senate. Because she was the oldest member of the senate, she became the chair of the senate in 2006; she should have served as president of the senate, too, but she asked not to because of her age. She was ninety-seven at the time.

Rita Levi-Montalcini was a great friend of the State of Israel, and often gave speeches around the world about the importance of the state to the Jews; she disputed anyone who tried to besmirch it.

At age one hundred, Rita felt that she was as lucid as she had been at age twenty. She slept only two hours a night because she felt that time was short, and she had much work to do.

She died while still active — at age one hundred and three.

# ADD YOUR VOICE

*"Above all, don't fear difficult moments. The best comes from them."*

## Explore

What was it that Rita Levi-Montalcini discovered? Her studies on the body's nervous system led to her discovery and characterization of what she termed the "nerve growth factor." What is the nerve growth factor? Why is it important? What did its discovery give to the world?

## Give Back

The STEM subjects — science, technology, engineering, and mathematics — are essential ones for society and the foundation for many careers, but women are sadly underrepresented in them. In America, women make up 47 percent of the workforce but only 26 percent of STEM jobs. Many organizations are working to level the field, promoting STEM education and women in STEM fields. These types of organizations use mentorships with women in the fields, clubs in schools, afterschool programs, and more.

How can you get involved? What organizations in your community focus on promoting women in STEM fields? Can you start a club in your school or volunteer with younger girls?

## See Something New

Rita Levi-Montalcini rode great distances on her bicycle to buy her first microscope. You can ride from the Technion — Israel Institute of Technology's medical school, near the Rambam Health Care Campus in Haifa, on a marked bicycle path, to the beach and promenade.

From there, you can ride to the Carmel, to the Technion and the Israel National Museum of Science, Technology, and Space (also called the Madatech). The museum has some twenty permanent exhibits and no small number of temporary exhibits, all occupied with various subjects in the world of science. Visit the exhibitions at the science museum; if you choose to, you can even hold a bat mitzvah celebration on a subject of your choice inside the exhibitions.

## Get Out of Your Comfort Zone

The Davidson Institute of Science Education, part of the Weizmann Institute of Science, offers a variety of scientific activities for kids. The institute's website offers online courses, trivia, experiments, and challenges for kids. Take a look!

# 28

# ZAHARA LEVITOV

## *The Pilot with a Tragic Love Story*

Zahara Levitov's life was short, turbulent, and full of loss.
At age one, Zahara was brought to **Kibbutz** Kiryat Anavim; her parents, Zeita and Yehuda, were two of its founders. At age nine, she and her parents left the kibbutz, and she lived in Tel Aviv and Rehovot over the nine years that followed.

Writing was an important part of her life; she kept a diary from her childhood. In one entry, she expressed her anger at the unequal treatment of girls at her school:

> A boy is far freer in his acts, speech, and behavior and is not judged harshly, but when a girl becomes free in her acts, in her behavior, immediately all of the tongues begin wagging at her expense. I object to this injustice. But the answer will always be the same — it is the way of the world...

After finishing her studies at the New High School (Tikhon Hadash) in Tel Aviv, Zahara joined the **Palmach,** an elite underground combat unit. At first, she stayed with the Palmach company on Kibbutz Tel Yosef but afterwards she moved to Ein Harod.

The first important activity that she took part in as a fighter was when she was sent with her comrades to detonate the Akhziv bridge in the Western Galilee. The British caught sight of the group of fighters approaching and shot at them from afar. A bullet hit the knapsack of explosives on one of the fighters' backs. Thirteen people were killed in the explosion, including Zahara's childhood friend, Amichai Klivner. Zahara herself was wounded in the eye.

Before her injury, Zahara had met Shmulik (Shmuel) Kaufman, also a member of the Palmach, who had already been discharged and was planning on going to England to study. But when he came to visit her while she was recovering, love began to blossom between the two. They started to write letters to each other. Both were good at expressing themselves, both loved to write, and the dozens of love letters that passed between them tell us their story.

> You must be cold, though if you walk, you must walk fast. Nonetheless the legs, perhaps the knees, perhaps the entire body is cold? And here is the bed you left, also certainly thinking: Where is he? Why hasn't he come today? (Letter from January 1947)

The time was one of military tension. Shmulik chose to return to the Palmach's forces, at least temporarily. And then, they planned, they would both be discharged together, they would marry, and they would travel to America to study. Zahara dreamed of learning medicine. On the day of their release, Shmulik volunteered to train a group in the use of live grenades. One of the grenades went off, killing Shmulik and two others.

Zahara continued writing him letters:

> My Shmulik!
> ...I am waiting for you, my Shmulik. I cannot know when you will come. Everyone is trying to convince me that you will not come, but despite all the evidence before me, I wait for you, Shmulik, wait for you every moment of every hour, and nonetheless, the terrible thorns of reality are stuck at times in the live flesh and stab with their bitter sobriety: Shmulik will return no more. You have buried Shmulik. You saw how they covered him in heavy stones. His burial stone is set.
>
> (May 31, 1947)

In order to heal, Zahara left on her own for Columbia University in New York to begin studying medicine. But when she heard of a pilot's course that had opened in California, one designated for people from the Land of Israel who were in the United States, she left for Bakersfield, California, where Elynor Rudnick's school was (see chapter 44).

The clandestine course was three months long; the students trained during the day and studied at night. But the course ended midway, when American intelligence discovered the trainees. All of the pilots were given certificates, "wings," and returned to Israel for the **War of Independence**, which was in full swing.

Zahara met Amnon Berman during the course, and a new relationship formed. They returned to Israel together, where Amnon served as a combat pilot and Zahara was a transport pilot and deputy commander of the squadron.

On **Shabbat**, July 3, 1948, Zahara and Amnon were sitting on the beach in Tel Aviv when they heard the click of a camera. Someone had taken their picture. Zahara was immediately on guard. "Has something happened?" Amnon asked. "I was sitting exactly this way with Shmulik on his last Shabbat, on the beach," she answered, "and someone took our picture."

Amnon was killed four days later, on July 7, on his way to the **Negev**. Zahara was killed a month later, in a plane accident in Jerusalem, when she was not yet twenty-one.

# ADD YOUR VOICE

*"Out of lucid and free choice and with great love, I hereby declare my clear agreement — and more, my unconditional commitment — to marry Shmuel K. immediately when the conditions are such that both of us are discharged from active service in the brigade."*

*(Signed on Friday, the twentieth of March, in the evening.)*

## Explore

What do you know about Israel's air force? When was it founded? Take a look into its history and what its contribution has been to Israel's defense. What are its primary branches? Where do women fit in within the air force?

## Give Back

While service in the **IDF** is a requirement for Israel's citizens, the country is also blessed with many volunteers from abroad who want to become part of Israel and its future. These volunteers, known as "lone soldiers," come to Israel on their own. Special non-profit organizations work to ensure that lone soldiers have what they need — a place to live, warm meals, assistance working with Israeli offices, and more. The Lone Soldier Center was founded in memory of Michael Levin, who died in 2006 defending the State of Israel; it helps lone soldiers with housing and basic needs and also creates a sense of community by holding events and Shabbat meals. You can fund one such program in honor of lone soldiers through the center.

## See Something New

Zahara grew up in Kiryat Anavim and was killed in neighboring Jerusalem.

Walk through Kibbutz Kiryat Anavim and try to connect to the landscape of Zahara's youth. You can also traverse the HaHamisha Forest, planted by kibbutz members from Kiryat Anavim and Maale HaHamisha, and walk in the direction of Har Adar. Near the entrance to Har Adar, there is a memorial site with an observation point from which all the communities in the region — all the way to Jerusalem's outskirts — can be viewed. Atop the lookout point there is a monument in memory of the Harel Brigade, which began as part of the Palmach and saw losses during the War of Independence and the **Six-Day War.**

You can also visit the Israel Air Force Museum in Hatzerim, where you can see the old airplanes that were used by the air force from its inception during the War of Independence until today. Take a guided tour, learn about the fleet of airplanes in the past and present, and connect to the past in your own way.

## Get Out of Your Comfort Zone

The relationship between Zahara and Shmulik took place for the most part through letters, written in fountain pen on paper, sent in envelopes through the mail or messengers. Days and even weeks could pass before a letter arrived. But a revolution has taken place in the world of communication; we've moved from long letters to chats and texts and from fountain pens to the cameras on our phones.

Think about the advantages in that type of communication, in which one could write long letters, such as, for instance, love letters.

Hold a letter-writing workshop with friends. Ask the group to be Zahara and Shmulik for a moment, and write a long letter like in the old days. Is it easy to write a letter? Can you communicate using only words, with no emojis? Or perhaps you can do the opposite: fill a page with symbols that you use to write messages (hearts, smileys, angry faces). Are you able to transmit a complete and clear message that way?

Have each person send themselves or a friend the letter they formulated — by mail (addressed, stamped, and put in a mailbox) and see what happens. Check how long it takes for a letter to arrive using the mail today.

# 29

# DEBORAH LIPSTADT

## *Warrior against Holocaust Denial and Anti-Semitism*

N othing in Deborah Lipstadt's childhood indicated that she would work in Holocaust research.

Neither of her parents was a Holocaust survivor. Her father, Erwin, a salesman, had immigrated to the U.S. in the twenties, and her mother, Miriam, a Judaica collector and lecturer, was born in Canada. They met at synagogue. They were both Modern **Orthodox**, and Deborah and her two siblings were raised that way as well. "Judaism was the beat of the drum to which our family marched" is how Deborah defined the atmosphere in her home. She went to a Jewish school on Long Island and spent her summers at a Hebrew-speaking summer camp. When she reached the age of twenty, she spent a very meaningful year in Israel — while studying at the Hebrew University in Jerusalem, she lived through the **Six-Day War**.

Twenty years later, in 1987 — when Deborah already had a doctorate and was a lecturer in the field of Jewish history — two of Israel's most important historians asked her to study Holocaust denial. She laughed; she thought that Holocaust deniers were a joke, and would never be taken seriously. But she soon understood how wrong she'd been.

Deborah rose to the challenge, and her life was transformed: she became the number one expert on **anti-Semitism** and Holocaust denial. Holocaust denial — the attempt to refute or distort established facts about the Holocaust — is a form of anti-Semitism; it often implies that Jews have exaggerated or invented information in order to advance their own interests.

Deborah's book on Holocaust denial made her famous. Aside from being well-written and garnering prizes, it directed attention to one specific Holocaust denier — British historian David Irving. Irving had written that there had been no genocide in concentration camps, that the gas chambers were built by the Poles, that if a few thousand Jews had died in the camps it was of natural causes, and that Hitler was a friend to Jews in Nazi Germany. In her book, Deborah wrote that Irving had intentionally forged documents to serve his anti-Semitic opinions.

Irving sued Deborah Lipstadt and her publisher for libel. Deborah decided that, in her response, she would never put the truth of the Holocaust on trial, but would instead focus on Irving's books and misinformation. Deborah had always made a conscious effort not to engage with Holocaust deniers, in order not to give them a platform. In her trial, she chose not to testify as a witness or to ask Holocaust survivors to speak, but rather allowed the evidence to speak for itself.

Deborah hired another important historian — Richard Evans — who carefully studied Irving's books and the evidence that he had based his research on. The books and papers that he placed on the stand in court prior to testifying, some say, rose to a height of two and a half meters, or over eight feet.

Ultimately the British court was convinced by Deborah Lipstadt's claims and ordered Irving to pay her legal expenses — 2 million pounds (the trial took place in Britain). Irving declared bankruptcy.

Deborah wrote a book called *Denial* about her experiences in the court case. Ten years later, a movie — also called *Denial* — was made about the case.

And Deborah? She served as a consultant for the United States Holocaust Memorial Museum, was appointed to the United States

Holocaust Memorial Council by President Clinton, was made a Special Envoy for Monitoring and Combating Anti-Semitism by President Biden, and aside from her volume about the trial, has written four more important books on the Holocaust.

# ADD YOUR VOICE

*"If the main thing the next generations know about Jewish history is that we were persecuted and suffered, they will lose sight of the tremendous heritage of Jewish culture, theology, and wisdom."*

## Explore

What is Holocaust denial? Take a look at the mechanisms of Holocaust denial, at the people who perpetuate false information about the Holocaust, and at the people who believe such information. Why is it considered a form of anti-Semitism? Does it fall under freedom of speech? Why or why not? What potential dangers do Deborah Lipstadt and others see in Holocaust denial?

## Give Back

There are many ways in which you can get involved and help fight anti-Semitism and Holocaust denial. The Anti-Defamation League, for example, was founded in 1913 to combat prejudice against Jews and ensure fair and equal treatment for all. It fights anti-Semitism in politics, in the public sphere, in the press, in workplaces, in schools, and more. You can support their work financially, or you can learn about their principles and take on a campaign of your own. How can you fight anti-Semitism? Develop your own program to tackle misinformation and prejudice on social media or in the world around you.

## See Something New

Deborah Lipstadt is a powerful speaker. You can check out her lectures online. Among other things, she has given a TED talk in which she tells the story about her legal battle against David Irving. You can also watch the movie *Denial*, which tells Deborah's story.

## Get Out of Your Comfort Zone

Global ARC is a platform that was developed to fight internet anti-Semitism. In order to do so, it democratizes the battle: it creates a global database to collect incidents of anti-Semitism online. You can hold a hackathon with your friends, working with a grownup to report content that denies the Holocaust or defames Jews. This disturbing but worthy project will help you understand how anti-Semitic language works and how you can take a stand against it.

# 30

# ZIVIA LUBETKIN

## *Resistance Fighter in the Warsaw Ghetto*

Few people during the Holocaust chose to go into the **ghetto** of their own free will. And one of those few was Zivia Lubetkin.

Zivia was born in Beten, one of the border towns that was, by turns, part of Poland, Ukraine, and Russia. Jewish life was thriving in the town, and included religious education and **Zionist** youth movements. Zivia, whose family was liberal and religious, joined the **HeHalutz** youth movement and soon stood out. Before the Second World War began, she was one of the movement's leaders, and was sent as a delegate to the Twenty-First **Zionist Congress** in Geneva, Switzerland.

Nazi Germany invaded Poland on September 1, 1939. The Zionist Congress had ended on August 30, two days earlier. Zivia did not need to return to Poland — she had an immigration permit and could have gone to the Land of Israel. But she went back to Warsaw because she understood that she must support her friends.

More than 400,000 people were packed into the Warsaw Ghetto, an area of 4 square kilometers, or 1.5 square miles. They endured hunger, intense diseases, and even unexpected shootings.

Zivia, who somehow managed to make her way into the ghetto, wanted to ensure the residents' welfare. She and her friends from youth movements fed the hungry (in part using agricultural produce they had grown themselves), established clandestine classrooms, published a newspaper, held parties, and ran study seminars. Many of the Jewish writers, poets, and educators who were gathered in the ghetto took part.

Zivia and her friends tried to help people live lives that were as normal as possible, given the circumstances, but did not take part in the ghetto's leadership — and, for the rest of her life, she regretted that the youth movement members had not tried to wrest control of the ghetto from the **Judenrat**, or Jewish council, which cooperated with the Nazis.

Near the end of 1941, two years after the war had begun, rumors of the Germans sending Jews to extermination camps began to rotate in the ghetto. The youth movement members chose to fight the Germans. They had no weapons and they knew their chances of survival were almost nonexistent; still they preferred to die defending themselves.

Zivia took upon herself the task of seeking help outside of the ghetto, on the Polish side of Warsaw. Polish fighters did not respond easily to the Jews' request, and even within the ghetto's Jews it was hard to recruit volunteer fighters.

In the summer of 1942, with the outbreak of the *Grossaktion* (great action) — the terrible deportation of hundreds of thousands of Jews from the Warsaw Ghetto to the extermination camps — the resistance only had two guns. But the *Grossaktion* itself had a surprising result: all of the Zionist bodies understood that the Jews must fight, that they could not be led like sheep to the slaughter. Together they formed the ŻOB (*Żydowska Organizacja Bojowa*, or Jewish Combat Organization). Mordechai Anielewicz, a member of **HaShomer HaTzair**, led the resistance. Zivia took responsibility for collecting money to purchase weapons. She began to collect taxes from the ghetto's wealthy and took over the Judenrat's funds. Some of her associates robbed the bank in the ghetto.

When another *aktion*, or roundup, took place in January 1943, the first true uprising broke out against the Nazis, and it exceeded expectations. The Germans were so surprised by the attack that the *aktion* stopped in the middle.

The Germans returned three months later. This time, they were met by a force that was armed with far more ammunition. The campaign lasted for days, and the Germans retreated once again. The militants had not imagined they would live past the uprising. They had not even prepared food for themselves for the days afterwards, they were so sure they would be killed in battle.

But the Germans' revenge came quickly: they set the ghetto on fire.

The ghetto blazed for many days. People moved from place to place, from where the fire had not yet reached to where the fire had already gone out. And then Zivia had an idea: those who had survived could be freed through the sewers that connected the Jewish ghetto to the Polish city. She began to search for people who knew the complex, branching sewer system. She found that person, meeting him on the night of May 8 — and because of that she was saved.

It was on May 8 that the Germans besieged the revolt headquarters and 120 people, all gathered inside the headquarters, were killed — including the commander, Mordechai Anielewicz.

Zivia, the last remaining officer from the uprising, led dozens of survivors through the sewers to safety on the Polish side a few days later.

In early June 1946, a year after the war ended and only shortly after she had arrived in the Land of Israel, Zivia told the story of the ghetto to thousands of **kibbutz** members and leaders on Kibbutz Yagur. For seven hours, she described the suffering of the people in the ghetto and the fighting, and people sat, speechless. It was the first time that a Holocaust survivor had spoken in front of an audience, the first time that people in the Land of Israel understood even a little of what had happened.

And fifty-eight years after the Warsaw Ghetto Uprising, on the parade grounds of an Israeli air force base, Roni Zuckerman, Zivia Lubetkin's granddaughter, stood out as one of the graduates of the course, making history as the first female combat pilot in the **IDF**.

# ADD YOUR VOICE

*"It was strange to see the twenty plus young Jewish men and women standing against the vast armed enemy happy and joyous. Why happy and joyous? Because we knew: their time would come."*
(Testimony about the beginning of the Warsaw Ghetto Uprising at the trial of Adolf Eichmann)

## Explore

Jewish tradition takes responsibility for fellow Jews very seriously. *Kol Yisrael arevim zeh bazeh*, the entire Jewish people are considered guarantors for one another, the **Talmud** tells us (Shevuot 39a). What does it mean to be responsible for one another? What commandments reflect Jews' mutual responsibility for one another? How do you see it reflected in your community?

## Give Back

In the spirit of Zivia Lubetkin and her undying commitment to the people around her, you can run a toy or clothing drive for shelters in your community. Find a shelter near you that provides aid to victims of domestic abuse or the homeless and recruit your friends and family to help collect the items that are needed.

## See Something New

From Zivia Lubetkin's arrival in the Land of Israel, she was a member of Kibbutz Lohamei HaGheta'ot in the Western Galilee. You can visit the museum founded by the members of the kibbutz and the Ghetto Fighters' House Museum or tour the Western Galilee.

The Ghetto Fighters' House Museum was established with the founding of the kibbutz. The kibbutz members felt that collecting all objects, documents, and photographs in a joint archive was the fulfillment of the will of those who had not been able to escape the ghetto alive. The museum offers tours and even plays for children.

The Western Galilee is a beautiful area in which the kibbutz is located. You can ride a bicycle or hike to the Kabri springs and along the **Ottoman** aqueduct that took water to the city of Akko.

## Get Out of Your Comfort Zone

The Butterfly Project uses ceramic butterflies as symbols of hope and resilience, vowing to never forget the more than a million children who died in the Holocaust by painting ceramic butterflies and displaying them. The program fosters discussions of diversity, inclusion, and justice through the lens of the Holocaust. Groups are invited to paint the butterflies, which become a form of monument, and to learn more about social injustice and hatred and how to combat them. Contact the Butterfly Project to plan an event for your friends, family, or community.

December 25, 1883–March 29, 1972
26 Kislev 5644–14 Nisan 5732

# 31

# HANNAH MAISEL-SHOHAT

## *Agricultural Sustainability Teacher*

Hannah Maisel-Shohat's dream was to train girls and young women in specialized agricultural work. The dream took shape and came to life in Sejera, **Kinneret**, and Nahalal — and even in the urban landscape of Tel Aviv.

Hannah was born to a family of eleven children. Her father was a wealthy merchant in Grodno, which was part of Russia at the time. Like all of her siblings, Hannah was taught at home by private teachers, and in Hebrew. Her father wanted to give his family a basic education, but that was not enough for his talented children. Hannah's sister Sarah went on a hunger strike to get her father to allow her to study at the gymnasium (secondary school). And, because of her, when Hannah reached the same age, nothing stood in the way of her education.

Hannah chose a very unusual subject to study: agriculture. Agriculture, Hannah believed, would contribute greatly to the new society being established in the Land of Israel. She was an active member of **Poale Zion**, a Jewish workers' movement; at age twenty she was appointed head of the organization in her town.

Hannah continued her studies in France, at Besançon University, and in 1909 completed her doctorate in agronomy with distinction. Only then, at age twenty-six, did she immigrate to the Land of Israel. She came with the man she had married three years earlier — Eliezer Shohat.

Eliezer's brother, Israel Shohat, and his wife, Mania Shohat (see chapter 54) were two of the founders of **HaShomer**, a Jewish defense organization. They had moved to Palestine a few years earlier, and were living in Sejera in northern Israel. Mania had founded an agricultural settlement in Sejera; after a short-lived attempt to settle in *moshavot*, Hannah and Eliezer joined the family there. At first, Hannah tried to take part in the agricultural work on the farm — ploughing, sowing, harvesting — but she soon came to the conclusion that women were better suited for a different type of agricultural work, with more skill and less of a concerted physical effort. So she established vegetable and flower gardens and grew glorious plants.

With her firm belief that women must be part of agricultural work in their own way, she began to plan a special farm to train women.

Her first student was Rachel Bluwstein (see chapter 9), who had come to the farm in Sejera. The two moved to the Kinneret Courtyard in April 1911, where three other young women joined them. Hannah named the place the Young Women's Farm. Men who wished to learn farming could study at Mikveh Yisrael, at Kinneret, at Ben Shemen, and at Hulda — but for women, this was a first. And these were not regular agricultural studies; the women specialized in the fields that Hannah felt were better suited to women: coops, barns, and vegetable gardens. At the Young Women's Farm, housekeeping, kitchen work, and cooking were also taught. The women worked in the various agricultural fields during the day and studied the theoretical subjects at night. Under Hannah's guidance, they lived lives of sustainability — years before sustainability was popular.

The farm at Kinneret functioned for seven years, training seventy women and girls. Near the end of the First World War, the Turks seized the farm's buildings and turned them into a hospital; Hannah was banished from the land because of her Russian citizenship.

When Hannah returned after the war, she lived in Tel Aviv, operated an inexpensive and healthy kitchen for workers who had nowhere else to live, and ran cooking courses for women. There, among the pots, she began to plan her next educational venture: a new agricultural farm for young women that would include a school as well. And because she was one of the founders of the first *moshav* (cooperative farming settlement) in the land — Nahalal — it was established in Nahalal. Studies took one year and the requirements for entry were non-negotiable: students needed to be serious and show determination in agricultural work, have good Hebrew, demonstrate an ability to work hard, and be of robust health; girls had to undergo a medical examination before they were accepted.

Young women from around the world waited years for their turn to join the school, which remained small and accessible only to the best, most serious students. But when Hitler rose to power in Germany, the farm's mission shifted. Many students came with the **Youth Aliyah**, the organization that rescued thousands of children from the Nazi regime by bringing them to Palestine. One of the students who was accepted was Hannah Senesh, a poet and paratrooper (see more about her, including the letter she sent to the headmistress, in chapter 51).

With the end of the Second World War, given the great waves of immigration to the Land of Israel and the need for more educational institutions, the agricultural school in Nahalal opened its doors to boys as well.

After her retirement, Hannah Maisel-Shohat returned to her husband Eliezer, who had left Nahalal in 1930. For thirty years, they had been in a long-distance relationship, and kept in touch through correspondence; it was only in the last decade of their lives that they lived together again in Tel Aviv.

# ADD YOUR VOICE

*"One must know how to use a hoe and shears before one knows how to use a microscope."*

## *Explore*

———

"Climate change" refers to long-term shifts in the earth's temperatures and weather. At times, these changes are driven by human intervention, such as the burning of fossil fuel. What do you know about climate change? How does it affect agriculture?

## *Give Back*

———

Environmental awareness begins at a young age. You can take on a project to better the environment. Perhaps you'd like to start a "green" initiative at your school or establish a beach or road clean-up. You can even join "Young Reporters for the Environment"; this group consists of hundreds of thousands of people aged eleven to twenty-five who volunteer in forty-two countries to research environmental issues and report on them.

## *See Something New*

———

If you are a lover of nature, the environment, plants, animals, and birds, you can see all of them up close at the Hula Lake. Twice a year, in the autumn and spring, hundreds of millions of birds fly over the lake on their way to Africa in the south, or on their way back north to Europe. Aside from the birds, fish and other larger animals — even water buffalo — are also found at the lake. Make sure to bring a camera so you can take pictures of the surprises that await you there — you never know what animal or bird you may meet.

You can also visit the **WIZO** Nahalal Youth Village, which is still active today. If you schedule it in advance, you can see Hannah Maisel-Shohat's life work, take in the green spaces, and enjoy an experiential tour in the Center for Agriculture and Sustainability.

## Get Out of Your Comfort Zone

The Hula Lake today is small compared to the great Hula Lake that existed in the past; sadly, it was drained in the 1950s in order to prepare land for agriculture — an act that was later understood to have been a mistake. In the struggle for preserving the lake, over seventy years ago, the Society for the Protection of Nature in Israel was founded.

If you're an environmentalist and care about nature and the climate, focus on the draining of the Hula Lake (act it out, make a video, or use another form of media). Try to understand why it was so harmful to the environment. Perhaps look into what other water sources were drained, and the harm that caused the environment. You can even hold your bat mitzvah celebration with a theme: go green. How can you make your party an environmentally conscious one?

# 32

# SELMA MAYER (SCHWESTER SELMA)

## *Founder of Israel's First Nursing School*

S elma Mayer was five when her mother died in childbirth and, as an adult, she chose to be a nurse in order to save lives. She was one of the first two Jewish nurses licensed in Germany, and worked at a big hospital in Hamburg. When Dr. Moshe Wallach sought a nurse who could help him run the hospital that he had founded — Shaare Zedek — she decided to depart for the faraway city of Jerusalem.

Dr. Wallach nearly turned away the tiny, gentle-looking woman: "I need a big, strong nurse," he said. But he soon learned how wrong he'd been!

Selma arrived in Jerusalem in the middle of the First World War. No nurse had lasted long at Shaare Zedek. The work was abundant, and Dr. Wallach was tough to work with; an **ultra-Orthodox** man, he was diligent, strict, and exceedingly frugal. He worked almost all hours of the day and night, and expected the same of those who worked alongside him. It was thus very hard for him to find professionals who could work with him.

But Selma was not afraid of hard work. Just like him, she worked morning to evening, and then, almost every night, she joined him for house calls, births, and emergency surgeries. At times they walked five or six kilometers (three or four miles) to reach the home of a patient.

Selma was known to all as "Schwester Selma," German for "sister" or "nurse." She brought all of the innovations that were in use in Germany to Jerusalem: she demanded that workers bathe the patients daily, something that was unheard of in the land at the time, and that all staff members, even kitchen workers, wear white gowns, and in general imposed cleanliness and order.

Schwester Selma was so beloved and so loyal to Jerusalem's residents that even the authorities trusted her implicitly. When the First World War ended, she hosted General Allenby, commander-in-chief of the United Kingdom's Egyptian Expeditionary Force, at the hospital and there he signed a document finalizing the surrender of the Turkish; Schwester Selma served tea and cookies.

The hospital had a number of doctors but only one nurse; she was the Operation Room nurse and the midwife, she taught other women to deliver babies and warm preemies, and she was responsible for ridding the ceilings of spiderwebs and for the hospital's **kashrut** — until one day she decided she had had enough and asked for help.

First she hired one nurse and then a second one; by the early 1930s, Selma demanded that a nursing school be built. Dr. Wallach was against it. He did not understand why a person had to be taught to become a nurse; what was so difficult, he thought, about rolling bandages and giving shots? But Schwester Selma persisted, making nursing studies an enterprise that encouraged young Jewish women to move to the Land of Israel from Europe. These were the days of the Nazis' rise to power in Germany, and each student who registered received a permit to enter the land. She thus saved the lives of dozens of Jewish girls. Of course, she took upon herself the running of the school and teaching the practical work.

After the Second World War, an Austrian woman came to the gates of Shaare Zedek seeking Schwester Selma. The woman had traveled all the way from Austria to give the head nurse of the Jerusalem hospital an expensive diamond ring. Her sister, she recounted, had given her the ring before she was taken to her death in a German extermination camp. She had asked that the ring be given to a man or woman who had never married or had children but rather devoted his or her life to others. When a newspaper in Vienna reported on Selma Mayer, the woman understood that she had found the perfect heir.

For seventy years, Schwester Selma lived in a modest, small room in the hospital, along with three girls she had adopted — Simha, Bolissa, and Sarina — all of whom had been left at the hospital. Dr. Wallach adopted them with her. He was the strict father and she the warm and loving mother.

Her second daughter, Bolissa, was killed in a car bombing early in the **War of Independence**. Bolissa, who, like her adopted mother, learned nursing, cared for babies at a **WIZO** center; she was on Ben-Yehuda Street on her way to work when the explosion detonated. Selma never recovered from the loss.

Schwester Selma did not retire. She remained in her small room at the hospital and continued to manage and train nurses until two days after her one hundredth birthday, when she passed away.

# ADD YOUR VOICE

*"Because I lost my mother very early and therefore had quite a difficult youth, a strong need grew in me to give people that which I had missed so much: mother-love and love of human beings. Therefore I chose the profession of nursing."*

## Explore

The first nurses known in history of the nation of Israel were the midwives Shiphrah and Puah, who saved babies from Pharoah's cruel decrees in Egypt, when he commanded that all Israelite boys born be thrown in the Nile. We are told that "in the merit of righteous women, Israel was redeemed from Egypt." It is certain that Schwester Selma was one of the "righteous women." What do these early nurses have in common with today's nurses? What jobs do nurses have on top of the technical things they're trained to do?

## Give Back

OneFamily is an organization that works with Israeli victims of terror and their families to give them the aid they need in order to overcome trauma. Through home visits, financial support, youth programs, support groups, and workshops, the organization aims to ensure the wellbeing of those who are suffering the aftermath of injury and loss. OneFamily's bar/bat mitzvah twinning project makes it possible for you to fund the celebration of a child in Israel, but other options for getting involved with the organization exist. Take a look at the website and see how you can help out.

## See Something New

Take a tour around Jerusalem's old hospitals. The architectural structures are unique and stunning, and their interiors often tell the story of medicine's pioneers.

Walking along HaNeviim Street, for example, you can visit four or five buildings that once served as hospitals. Number 33, which is now Hadassah Academic College, is where the first Jewish hospital in Jerusalem, Rothschild Hospital, was established in 1842. Number 64 is where Helena Kagan (see chapter 23) ran her own hospital. At the building known as Ticho House, on Rabbi Kook Street, right off of HaNeviim Street, you can visit the museum that was once Dr. Ticho's eye clinic and hospital (now an art museum); and on the corner of HaNeviim and Strauss Street, see the Bikur Holim hospital, still one of the most beautiful buildings in the city.

And if you still have energy, you can visit Hansen House in Jerusalem's Talbiya neighborhood. Built in 1887 as a leper asylum, it is now a vibrant design, media, and technology center. A historical exhibition tells the story of the site's history and evolution. You can also visit the gardens and café, which boasts dishes created from sustainable, organic agriculture, as well as the observatory tower.

## Get Out of Your Comfort Zone

While recovering from eye surgery in 1973, Schwester Selma wrote a brief memoir that recounts her life as a nurse in Jerusalem, *My Life and Experiences at "Shaare Zedek."* The book is a wonderful window into her world, and tells the story of what it was like to live and work at the hospital. You can find the entire book online; read it and learn more about this fascinating time and place in Jerusalem's history.

# 33

# GOLDA MEIR

## *Israel's First Female Prime Minister*

"I t isn't really important to decide when you are very young just exactly what you want to become when you grow up... If you are going to get involved in causes which are good for others, not only for yourselves, then it seems to me that that is sufficient, and maybe what you will be is only a matter of chance." This was Golda's advice to girls your age.

Golda's first childhood memory, which she spoke about often later on, directed her life: she remembered her father barricading the door to her house with boards so that rioters could not break in. In Russia, where she grew up, there were violent **pogroms** against Jews. This fate, the fear of attacks on Jews simply because they were Jews, was what she tried to shield Jewish children from for her entire life.

During her childhood in Russia, Golda experienced hunger, cold, poverty, and need, but these were quickly replaced by relative well-being. Her family, like many other Jewish families, immigrated from Russia to the United States. It was there that Golda was raised and went to school, and there that her interest in politics was born; **Zionism** became the center of her life.

When she was eleven, Golda initiated her first public activity, collecting donations to buy schoolbooks for needy classmates. This was the first time she spoke in front of an audience and she learned an important lesson: writing down what she wanted to say was less effective than speaking from her heart. People loved her words — and her. Forty years later, she was still speaking from the heart; representing the newborn State of Israel, she persuaded American Jews to donate funds so that the young country could fight for its life.

Golda loved the United States, freedom, and democracy, but her real goal as a young adult was to get to the Land of Israel and the **kibbutz**.

She and her new husband Morris boarded the *SS Pocahontas* en route to the shores of Jaffa. She was twenty-three when she arrived in the Land of Israel; the couple wished to be accepted to Kibbutz Merhavia in the Jezreel Valley. The kibbutz members were wary of the "American," assuming she would be spoiled and lazy, and did not accept her easily. Golda was hardworking and productive, but Morris did not acclimate well. He did not love kibbutz life, and ultimately they moved to the city.

Many years before the establishment of the state, Golda had already served in senior public roles. First in the Histadrut, the labor union, which served the workers, and later at the **Jewish Agency**, the "government" of the Jews of the Land of Israel before it was a state.

The four most bitter years of her life, Golda said, were the years when she gave up public life to raise her son. And therefore, despite the damage she knew it would cause to her relationship with her beloved husband Morris and to her children — Menachem and Sarah — she returned and took on public roles and missions in distant lands.

Her life was filled with adventures: on the eve of the **War of Independence**, she met twice with King Abdullah of Trans-Jordan and tried to convince him not to join the war. She arrived at his palace in Amman, the capital of Jordan, dressed as a Bedouin woman and wearing a black scarf. The meeting was not a fruitful one, and the Trans-Jordan Arab Legion soldiers waged grave battles against the **IDF**.

Once the war had erupted, it was clear that the young state needed weapons. With the establishment of the State of Israel, after she had signed the Declaration of Independence and before she had even had time to change the ceremonial clothes that she wore, Golda was sent to the United States to raise funds without which the young state would have had no chance of surviving the war. She met with America's Jews, Zionist and non-Zionist, and within a number of weeks she had collected 50 million dollars, a huge amount for the time, which served as the foundation for Israel's first arms deal (with Czechoslovakia).

From the United States, Golda traveled to the USSR to found the Israeli embassy there and reestablish contact with Russian Jewry. The Jews of the USSR were not allowed to openly identify with the State of Israel, but on the first **Rosh Hashanah** (Jewish new year) after the founding of the state, tens of thousands of Jews gathered next to the large synagogue in Moscow. They were all waiting for Golda and her staff, and they were all moved to tears — and so was she. "Thank you for remaining Jews," she told them.

Over the State of Israel's first three years its population tripled. Golda, who had been called back to Israel to join the government as the minister of labor after a year in the USSR, was charged with finding work for hundreds of thousands of new immigrants. She came up with a new plan: work relief. People were given jobs paving roads and planting forests not because paving the road or planting the forest was necessary, but so that they would have work. The roads that were paved during those years were informally known as "Golda's Roads."

Golda exchanged her position for the job of foreign minister, and greatly expanded the circle of countries that supported Israel in Asia and Africa. Then, ill and nearing seventy, Golda decided to retire from public life. She hoped to spend time with her five grandchildren. But things turned out otherwise: Prime Minster Levi Eshkol died suddenly, and all of the government's ministers agreed that only Golda could fill his shoes. And she, ever the good soldier, returned.

Golda became prime minister two years after the **Six-Day War**, after a decisive victory on the battlefield, when Israel felt unbeatable. In 1973, signs of a new war on the horizon were growing. The military promised that all would be fine, and Golda chose to trust the officers.

But the **Yom Kippur War** broke out despite the guarantees, and it was the toughest one in the history of the state. The Egyptian and Syrian armies penetrated Israel's lines, entering Sinai and the Golan Heights, and for many days the situation looked hopeless. One ray of light in the darkness was the airlift of ammunition supplied by America, in no small part due to Golda's great ties with Richard Nixon.

With the end of the war, the nation underwent a harsh self-examination about the complacency that had made it possible for the war to erupt. Israel's citizens demanded that the prime minister who was in office at the time of the war broke out step down, and she did. Five years later, desolate and ill, Golda Meir died.

# ADD YOUR VOICE

*"Not being beautiful forced me to develop my inner resources. The pretty girl has a handicap to overcome."*

## *Explore*

It is clear that fewer women have been involved in politics in the past than have men. Why do you think that is? How has the involvement of women in politics changed over time? Why did it take so long for a woman to be elected as Israel's prime minister? Look at some statistics about women in the world of politics. What do you think the future holds?

## Give Back

Golda Meir passed many welfare laws in Israel. She provided subsidized housing for immigrants and toiled to make sure they were integrated into the workforce. She once stated: "The generation that was privileged to establish the Jewish state must be one that is infused with the great responsibility that hangs over it... We lay the cornerstone for building a society in which there will be no abandoned orphan and no old person crying over his old age." It was clear to her that Israeli citizens must look out for one another and take responsibility for each other. What organizations are there around you that take care of people? How can you get involved? Perhaps you can volunteer for an organization like Habitat for Humanity, ensuring that all people are housed and safe.

## See Something New

Golda Meir, the only woman to serve as prime minister in Israel, was never official immortalized. When I served as a Member of **Knesset**, I tried to advance a bill that would commemorate her. The law still has not passed, but the JNF-Keren Kayemeth LeYisrael has established a park in her memory. At the Mashabim intersection in Har HaNegev, not far from Kibbutz Revivim — Golda's daughter Sarah was one of the kibbutz's founders — is Park Golda Meir.

If you are a lover of the desert — this is the place for you. The park, which ranges over more than 130 acres in area, includes a lake, lawns, local plants, and many charming corners.

And if you are in New York, you can visit the sculpture of Golda Meir located near Broadway and 39th Street.

# Get Out of Your Comfort Zone

Embark on a journey, and write a journal about each of the stations in Golda's life: Russia, Milwaukee, Kibbutz Merhavia, Israel's Knesset, and her time as prime minister of Israel. What did she experience in each? How did each station move her closer to the woman she ultimately became?

# 34

# LISE MEITNER

## *Nuclear Physics Pioneer*

Nothing in Lise's childhood could have predicted the decisive role she would play in shaping physics in the twentieth century. She may have loved the sciences — at age eight, she slept with a math book under her pillow because she did not want to part from it — but Lise was not given a chance to go to school for long. In 1892, at age fourteen, she finished her schooling; girls in Austria, where she was born, were never allowed to learn for more than nine years. An educated woman could serve as a teacher, and that was what Lise did in her young adulthood. But then a revolution took place and the universities' doors were suddenly opened to women. Lise was twenty-three when she passed her entrance exams and was accepted to study physics at the university; at age twenty-nine she earned her doctorate.

But because she was a woman, Lise could not find work in her field.

Lise moved to Germany. It was around this time that she converted to Christianity — though she would remain, in the eyes of the Nazis later on, a Jew regardless. Lise was accepted to work at an experimental physics laboratory, but only under the conditions that applied to women at the time: the room she was given had once been a carpentry workshop, and she was not permitted to leave it; if she needed a bathroom, she had to leave the building to go to a nearby restaurant. She was also not eligible for a salary; her parents supported her instead. But this was enough for Lise. She felt pleased and privileged to work in her chosen field, exploring the behaviors of various materials.

After the First World War, things began to improve. Lise was appointed a professor of physics, the first female to hold the title in Germany, and was finally financially independent. She and her partner, chemist Otto Hahn, ran experiments to unearth the behaviors of radioactive materials and became well-known around the world.

But in January 1933 the Nazis rose to power, and all of Lise's efforts were for naught; it made no difference that she was a world-renowned scientist, nor did it matter that she had left the Jewish religion decades earlier — Lise Meitner was fired and her life was in danger.

Scientists from around the world tried to rescue her, inviting her to conferences or positions outside of Germany, but the authorities would not allow her to leave. Ultimately, Lise escaped; she was fifty-nine, skinny and hungry, and had only one suitcase of clothing and 10 marks to her name, but she made it to neighboring Holland, and from there to Sweden. In her absence, her life's work was stolen from her.

From her exile in Sweden, she maintained ties with her partner, Otto Hahn, and he wrote her about the most important finding to emerge from their laboratory: an atom of a very heavy element (uranium) was "bursting" with molecules that had no electric charge, ones that gathered energy as they accelerated (neutrons). When the neutrons' speed was very high, the uranium disappeared, and, in its place, an entirely different element appeared, one that was far lighter, barium. Hahn was confused; he did not understand what had happened. "You have succeeded in splitting the atom in two," Lise told him from afar, "The barium was created from one part of the atom. We must search for another element created from the split!"

Lise was right; an important part of the discovery was still missing. It emerged that the two molecules that were created at the moment of the nucleus's split weighed only a fifth of the original atom. Where had the missing four fifths gone?

The missing part, the part that would change the face of human history, was found by Lise a few months later with the help of her nephew, physicist Otto Frisch. On a piece of paper that she tore from a notebook, Lise and Frisch made sense of the results that Hahn had received, and discovered that the missing parts had become energy — tremendous power!

The Second World War broke out shortly thereafter. German and American scientists alike hoped to use the new energy to create the most powerful bomb ever, one that would make it possible to secure a decisive victory. Otto Hahn was among the developers of the German bomb, but Lise refused to cooperate with the American developers. She would not be part of killing people on any side.

At the height of the terrible war, the Nobel Prize, the most important scientific honor in the world, was awarded to Otto Hahn. Lise Meitner, the refugee, was not even mentioned.

The Americans were the first to develop the bomb, but it happened only after Germany had surrendered. Japan, Germany's ally, would not surrender, and two of its cities — Hiroshima and Nagasaki — were devastated. The results were catastrophic; from then until today, no one has used an atom bomb.

Lise Meitner was recognized in a number of ways later on — she received many awards, was named a member of the Royal Swedish Academy of Sciences, and received honorary doctorates from a number of universities. Years after her death an element — meitnerium — was named for her, as were an institute, awards, schools, and streets.

# ADD YOUR VOICE

*A physicist who never lost her humanity.*

*(Inscribed on her gravestone)*

## *Explore*

While science and facts are by definition neutral, the application of science can often lead to important ethical questions. When faced with questions relating to science and ethics, scientists — and often-times committees formed for this purpose — must debate whether the application of a new scientific discovery preserves human dignity, rights, or the environment. Scientific ethics asks what scientists' responsibilities are toward the world and the people around them. Lise Meitner, faced with an immense ethical challenge, refused to become part of using science to build a weapon. What other examples of ethical dilemmas arise within the world of science? How do they relate to the question of *tikkun olam*, the Jewish concept of repairing the world?

## *Give Back*

The atom bomb, or nuclear bomb, was developed based on Lise Meitner's discoveries — but Lise herself refused to be a part of developing a weapon. Around the world, people band together to lobby for nuclear disarmament, hoping to reduce the threat of weapons of mass destruction. If this is a cause that is important to you, you can join one of many organizations for youth; for a start, check out Youth-4Disarmament, a UN program that involves today's youth in activism to help create an important change.

## See Something New

If nuclear science interests you, and you see your future as a scientist, you can satisfy some of your curiosity at the Carasso Science Park near Beersheba, which has an exhibition about nuclear power. It is the only one in Israel in which you can experience the splitting of an atom.

If you're ever in Berlin, you can visit the Lise Meitner Memorial, a statue commemorating her contribution to scientific research.

## Get Out of Your Comfort Zone

*The Matilda Effect,* a short video found on YouTube, tells the story of Lise Meitner's contribution to science. It also explains the term "Matilda Effect," which refers to a bias in science in which women and their contributions are overlooked; oftentimes, in the past, women's work was attributed instead to their male colleagues. Learn more about the Matilda Effect and how it has affected women in science throughout the ages. Are there other women in science whose contributions have not been acknowledged? What can you do to bring their work and names to light?

# 35

# DOÑA GRACIA
# MENDES NASI

## *The "Queen" of the Jews*

It was only when she reached her bat mitzvah that Beatriz de Luna of Portugal discovered that her real name was Hannah Nasi, and that she was from a family of **crypto-Jews** who had been expelled from Spain. Jews living in Spain and Portugal, beginning in the fourteenth century, had been persecuted and threatened with death; some chose to convert but to maintain Jewish religious practice in secret. Hannah Nasi's family had been covertly practicing their Judaism, and they passed that information on to her when they felt she was old enough.

The family of Hannah Nasi — known as Doña Gracia — was one of the wealthiest in Portugal, as was the family of her husband Francisco, whom she married at age eighteen. Francisco Mendes — or, by his Jewish name, Tzemah Benvenisti — was close to the king, and his business ranged around the world. Along with his brother and partner, Diogo Mendes-Nasi, he took care of the welfare of the exiles from Spain and Portugal. The bank they owned supported the expellees and made it possible for them to build new lives in the lands they had been forced to run to. A few short years after they married, Francisco died, leaving his fortune to his wife and small daughter.

Due to the changes in her life, Doña Gracia moved to the big city of Antwerp, where her brother-in-law, the partner in the family business, lived. Her young daughter Ana (later renamed Reyna), her two cousins, Samuel and Joseph, and her sister Brianda, who was engaged to Diogo, all came with her.

Diogo also died fairly young. He did not trust his wife Brianda, who he felt was flighty and wasteful, and bequeathed his fortune to Doña Gracia instead. This made Doña Gracia the wealthiest woman of her time. She owned a bank and a spice business that imported from India in the east, through the Turkish Empire, to all of the lands in Europe. Her young and talented cousin João Micas (Joseph Nasi) served as her advisor. Years later, Don João married Doña Gracia's daughter.

Aside from her financial dealings, Doña Gracia also toiled to maintain her husband's life's work defending her brothers and sisters from the persecutions of the Christian Church. She primarily fought against the Catholic Church's **Inquisition**, which persecuted the crypto-Jews, investigating them under terrible torture that at times led to death.

Doña Gracia made use of a kind of international intelligence agency that her husband had begun and that she now headed to care for the crypto-Jews wherever they were. The work included redeeming captives, using the family's ships to help Jews escape, and making it possible for the refugees to preserve their belongings and acclimate in a new land.

The Church's persecution chased Doña Gracia and her extended family out of Antwerp; ultimately they settled in Venice, Italy, an important commercial city at the time.

It was here that the Inquisition caught up with Doña Gracia. Brianda, who had for years been bitter about being financially dependent, reported that her older sister had bought kosher meat in the Venice ghetto — that is, that she was living a Jewish life in private. It is hard to know whether she would have survived the Inquisition were it not for intervention of the ruler of a different city in Italy, the duke of Ferrara. Doña Gracia appealed to him for refuge and he, hoping she would invest money in his city, was happy to receive her. He also agreed that she, as well as any crypto-Jew who wished, could live in his city as Jews for all intents and purposes. It was only then than Doña Gracia unmasked herself and became known by her Jewish name — Hannah Nasi.

Doña Gracia lived in Ferrara for a short time, until Sultan Suleiman the Magnificent, the enlightened conqueror of the **Ottoman Empire**, invited the expellees from Spain and its crypto-Jews to live under his patronage in his empire as proud Jews. But while in Ferrara, she managed to revive Jewish life in the city, had the Bible translated to Spanish and Portuguese, published other Jewish books, and renewed Jewish public life.

When Doña Gracia moved to the Turkish capital, it seemed for a while that she had found her place. She built synagogues and houses of study around the empire, as well as soup kitchens and hospitals, and continued to care for the Jews in Europe as well.

But Doña Gracia had one dream that was greater than the others: to build a state for the Jews who were being persecuted in Europe. She leased the city of Tiberias from the sultan, paying one thousand gold coins each year. Tiberias had stood desolate and destroyed, and Doña Gracia asked the sultan to build the city walls anew and restore its homes. He happily agreed. Her emissaries left for Europe to convince crypto-Jews to move to the Land of Israel and join her new enterprise, in a move that — while similar to the mission of the **Zionist** movement — took place 320 years before Herzl's Zionist vision and the first **Zionist Congress**.

Construction began in Tiberias, Italy's Jews began to immigrate there, and the synagogues in the city began to function. But Doña Gracia's death a few years after the wall was built cut the dream short.

# ADD YOUR VOICE

*"There is nothing similar in Jewish history, or perhaps in any history, until our own day and the organization of the 'underground railway' for saving Jews from the hell of Nazi and post-Nazi Europe and securing the entry...to the Land of Israel."*

*(Cecil Roth)*

## Explore

Hannah Nasi was known by a different name — Doña Gracia — for many years, one that made it possible for her to function in a world that did not accept Jews. Do you have a Jewish name? Is it one that you always use or one that is used only on occasion? Where does your name stem from? Is it biblical? How long has it been in your family? If possible, look through your family tree and see whether it's been used in the past. If you do not have a Jewish name, what name would you choose for yourself? Why are names so important?

## Give Back

Doña Gracia's entire life was given over to her community, rescuing Jews, taking care of them, establishing Jewish institutions, and renewing Jewish life everywhere she went. Among her many enterprises to support her fellow Jews, she ran soup kitchens to feed the hungry. There are many ways to make sure the hungry are fed. Can you volunteer serving food in a nearby soup kitchen? Or perhaps prepare food packages to give to the needy? You may even want to set up a "share table" at your school, where kids can leave extra or unwanted food that anyone can take, making it possible for those suffering from food insecurity to grab a bite with no embarrassment. Arrangements can be made to give food that is left at the end of the day to a nearby shelter or nonprofit program.

## See Something New

Doña Gracia's groundbreaking enterprise, the idea of founding a state for the Jews, focused on Tiberias. In order to get a sense of what life was like at the time, visit 3 HaPrahim Street in the city, the museum dedicated to Doña Gracia. You can get an impression of Hannah Nasi's activities from the sixteenth-century furniture and clothing. You can even try on clothing from the time, and see how you would look if you had been raised in Europe five hundred years ago.

You can also visit the Doña Gracia observation point, inaugurated on **Tu BeShvat** in 2010 by the JNF-Keren Kayemeth LeYisrael, celebrating five hundred years from Doña Gracia's birth. The observation point is found west of the city and the **Kinneret**; it was planted with hundreds of carob and olive trees by Tiberias's schoolchildren.

And if you're in Europe, you can trace Doña Gracia's path to Portugal, or to Belgium (Brussels), or to Venice, all places where she lived and practiced Jewish ritual in private. You can also see Ferrara, where she was finally able to be a proud Jews, and even Turkey.

## Get Out of Your Comfort Zone

Doña Gracia's secret network was only one such network in history that saved people from terrible conditions or death by smuggling them to safety. What other such networks do you know about? How are they similar to Doña Gracia's and how do they differ? What conditions do you think are essential for such networks to exist?

# 36

# MIRIAM

## *One of Three Leaders in the Wilderness*

**M**oses was three months old when his mother put him in a tar- and pitch-coated basket and placed it on the Nile. Miriam, his sister, stood watch over him from afar.

Years had passed since the sons of Jacob had arrived in Egypt; their brother, Joseph, was an important ruler and the Israelites were happily accepted by Pharaoh, the king. But Joseph and that Pharaoh had both died, and a new king now ruled in Egypt, one who had not known Joseph; he was afraid of the Israelites and wished to destroy them. He commanded that all of the Israelite boys be killed. Moses's mother hid her baby from the moment he was born, but when he was three months old, she could no longer conceal him.

Pharaoh's daughter found the baby floating in the basket, and immediately understood that he was an Israelite. Miriam, watching her brother, hiding in the reeds, knew that this was a dangerous moment. Would Pharaoh's daughter rebel against her father's order? Would she kill the baby? Miriam approached the princess as she deliberated and offered to bring a wet nurse from the Israelite community to feed the baby. Her courage paid off; she was quickly dispatched and returned with her own mother, Moses's mother. Pharaoh's daughter commanded that the mother take the baby and nurse him until he grew older.

Years passed and the three siblings — Moses, Miriam, and Aaron — became leaders of the nation that was leaving Egypt. Miriam's role as prophetess and leader is first mentioned in the **Torah** when the Israelites cross the Red Sea and leave Egypt. Pharaoh's chariots, in pursuit, are submerged in the sea, Moses sings the Song of the Sea, and Miriam? She organizes the women and accompanies them: "Then Miriam the prophetess, Aaron's sister, picked up a hand-drum, and all the women went out after her in dance with hand-drums" (Exodus 15:20). This is the first time in the Bible that a woman is called a prophetess.

Miriam was not just a prophetess but also a leader — "all the women went out after her" — and a multitalented artist who drummed, danced, and engaged the women "in dance with hand-drums." It was because of the song of praise that the Israelites were given a well, Miriam's well, which accompanied the Israelites in the desert.

Like all people, Miriam the prophetess had moments of weakness; in one such moment, she spoke critically of Moses. The Torah recounts two claims made in a discussion with Aaron: first about Moses's wife ("because he took a Cushite woman"; Numbers 12:1) and, second, about Moses being selected as the central leader ("Has God spoken only through Moses? Has He not spoken through us as well?"; Numbers 12:2).

When God heard the words in the siblings' conversation, He was angry; He was the one who had picked Moses to redeem the nation. So He called the three siblings to the Tent of Meeting, rebuked the two older siblings who had slandered Moses, and, when the cloud lifted from the Tent, Miriam's was afflicted with *tzaraat*, a disease of the skin.

Moses prayed for her recovery, but God was resolute: her disease would extend seven days and then she would recover. Miriam remained outside of the camp for seven days, and the entire nation — six hundred thousand people — patiently waited for her, not moving on in the wilderness without her.

Miriam is mentioned in the Bible as one of the Israelites' three leaders, but the Scriptures tell us little else about her. We know the names of Moses's wife and sons, the names and fates of Aaron's sons, but nothing about Miriam.

This lacuna has been filled by many **Midrashim** (ancient commentaries). The great number of Midrashim written about her over generations is noteworthy, and tells of her special female leadership and her deep connection with the nation over history. Miriam is known for her connection to water — the waters in the Nile, where we first meet her, the waters of the Red Sea, which the Song of the Sea is about, and the waters of her well.

Right after Miriam's death, as told in the book of Numbers, "the community was without water" (Numbers 20:2). From here, the Midrash concludes that there was water until her death, and it flowed, because of her, from her wondrous well, which moved with the nation through the desert and disappeared with her death.

The nation, tired and thirsty, continued wandering, until they reached a place called Be'er (meaning "well"), on the border of Moab, and there the well again reappeared. In their joy, the Israelites sang a song:

Spring up, O well — sing to it —
The well which the chieftains dug,
Which the nobles of the people started.

(Numbers 21:17–18)

Since then, it is told, Miriam's well has never left the nation. When the Israelites arrived in the land of Canaan, the Land of Israel, it wandered from place to place, from sea to sea. Some sages identified it in the Mediterranean Sea, in the area of Haifa, and there were those who located it in the **Kinneret**. The ill who drink from its waters, the traditions state, are immediately healed.

# ADD YOUR VOICE

*"Oh God, pray heal her!"*

*(Moses's prayer for his sister Miriam's recovery)*

## *Explore*

What is women's leadership? Does it differ from men's leadership, in your opinion? In what ways do you think Miriam's leadership complemented her brothers' leadership in the wilderness? Do you think the world is seeing more leadership on the part of women?

Miriam's drum is well known — in modern Hebrew, the words *tof Miriam*, Miriam's drum, refer to a tambourine — and serves as a symbol of her leadership. Why do you think it is such a strong symbol? What does it represent?

## *Give Back*

How would you like to lead your community in dance? Volunteer to teach a weekly class for younger children or perhaps choreograph a performance that you can put on in retirement homes or other places. Music has an important effect on our world; you can bring music and dance to more people.

## *See Something New*

Some believe that Miriam's well is now found in the Kinneret and others locate it in the Mediterranean Sea near Haifa; you can visit both locations on a "Sea to Sea" trip. Begin at the scenic Akhziv shore north of Nahariya, hike through the Khziv River, and climb Mount Meron. From the Summit Path (Shvil HaPisga) through the Amud River, descend to the Kinneret. This hike takes two or three days. Make sure you're prepared — plan where you will sleep and where you will replenish supplies and water, and make sure you can read the map.

## Get Out of Your Comfort Zone

Tradition ties Jewish women to Miriam's well especially on Saturday nights, after **Shabbat** has ended. Some women would draw water on Saturday nights; some would also utter a prayer before drinking their first cup of water after Shabbat: "I drink this water from the well of Miriam the prophetess who heals all woes...and gives us livelihood without sorrow." Look into the Midrashim and sources about Miriam's well and form a ceremony related to water that speaks to you.

Another tradition — one that has only existed for a few generations — brings Miriam to the **Passover Seder**. Next to the cup of wine for Elijah, families place Miriam's Cup holding water, representing her connection to water and the part of women within the **Exodus** story. It can be filled in various ways and at various points in the Seder, according to different customs, and some say a blessing: "This is the Cup of Miriam, the cup of living waters. Let us remember the Exodus from Egypt. These are the living waters, God's gift to Miriam, which gave new life to Israel as we struggled with ourselves in the wilderness." Learn more about the various customs associated with the tradition and incorporate Miriam in your Seder.

# 37

# RACHEL MORPURGO

## *The First Modern Hebrew Poetess*

R achel Morpurgo was eighteen when she wrote her first poem, and fifty-seven when her first poem was published.

Rachel Morpurgo grew up two hundred years ago in Trieste, Italy, in the Luzzatto family, an educated, deeply rooted Jewish family. She was luckier than most girls in her generation: she was given a Jewish education with a private teacher, who also taught her siblings and her well-known cousin, Samuel David Luzzatto (known by the acronym "Shadal," a Bible scholar and poet). She studied Hebrew, **Torah**, **Talmud**, and mathematics. But when she grew older, she was expected to live like the other women around her: to marry and have children.

Rachel accepted the rules of her society, but insisted on one thing — that she marry a man she loved, one who was less learned and less wealthy than she, despite the objections of her parents.

This was her poem on the day of her wedding to Jacob, the man she married:

Thanks to an awesome God
I will be desolate no more:
I shall cast off all fear,
I will be silent no more.

A bright-eyed bridegroom
Will be the glory of my head:
The Master of the Heavens gave
He whom my soul loves.


But the boy with the beautiful eyes she described in her poem did
not appreciate her gift. He did not want a poet, but a housewife and
a mother for his children. Rachel felt that she was being chained to
housework:

I will try but this time
If I may sing,
From the pot
I have distanced in great fury.


For almost thirty years, Rachel would wake every morning to her
pots and mending, to her children and husband and home. But at
night she would stay up writing poems. Each time, she feared that
she had lost her ability to write, and each time anew stunning compositions would emerge, all in Hebrew.

Her husband and children — she had three boys and a girl —
were not interested in her poetry, so she would send it to her cousin, Samuel David Luzzatto, a philosopher and poet in his own right.
It can be assumed that he sent her his poetry as well, and that they
advised one another. And then, when she was fifty-seven, some
forty years after she had begun to write, her cousin submitted one
of her poems to a journal of Hebrew poetry called *Kokhavei Yitzhak*
(Isaac's stars). The poem was received with enthusiasm. The journal's readers were amazed by the woman who wrote Hebrew poetry — so much so that nine readers wrote poems of praise for her.
Rachel finally received the recognition she had so needed, and continued to publish her poetry.

It was only when she had begun to publish and become known,
and when she received the approval of sages and intellectuals, that
her family began to appreciate her talent as well.

One hundred years after her death, Rabbi Vittorio Castiglioni — a lover of Hebrew from her city, Trieste — collected Rachel's poetry as well as letters she'd written into a book: *Ugav Rahel* (Rachel's harp).

# ADD YOUR VOICE

*Rachel Morpurgo dreamed her entire life of moving to the Land of Israel. When the entourage of Moses Montefiore passed through her city on their way to the land, she expressed her dream to join them "and to serve as one of the handmaids to the honorable woman, his wife, in order to ascend with them and settle there, but I could not."*

## *Explore*

Jewish communities in Italy held bat mitzvah ceremonies in Hebrew, it appears, beginning in the nineteenth century. Rachel Morpurgo was, at the time, older, but it is possible that the education that she and her friends received — which included learning Hebrew and Scripture — was the backdrop for this. Generally, Jewish women and girls in Italy were unique in their education, receiving the same education as the men. Try to learn about Jewish education in Italy since the Renaissance and compare it to education in other **Diaspora** communities. How is a Rachel Morpurgo made? What elements of her education were essential? Could she have become the poet she was without that education? Why is language so crucial within education?

## Give Back

Can you form a Hebrew language club? Perhaps you can meet with friends weekly to study Hebrew poetry, or send out a daily message to them to teach one idiom. Maybe you'd like to focus on modern Israeli slang. What means can you use to teach what you've learned — social media, blog posts, visual art?

## See Something New

Musa, the Eretz Israel Museum, is located in Tel Aviv. On a visit there, you can focus on the Ethnography and Folklore Exhibit, which teaches about Jewish life over generations. You can see an exhibit of pictures from Jewish family life and look at Judaica and sacred items — Torah scroll covers, **tallitot** (prayer shawls), **shofarot**, menoras, and even amulets. In the center of the exhibit stands a Torah **ark** from the eighteenth century, with its doors carved like pictures of the Temple, known as the Heikhal. It was brought in pieces from the town of Trino Vercellese in Italy and rebuilt in the museum. This Torah ark is likely quite similar to the ones that Rachel Morpurgo knew.

You can also visit Rome's Jewish Museum online. Many of its collections can be "toured" on its website and you can learn and visit the synagogues within it. Learn how Italian Jews lived for generations and take a close look at their artifacts.

## Get Out of Your Comfort Zone

Rachel Morpurgo may not have liked housework and distanced herself from her pots in anger, but it is clear that she loved and respected the Italian kitchen.

Jews lived in Italy uninterrupted for over two thousand years, adopting the food of the culture within they lived and adjusting it to accord with **kashrut** guidelines (Jewish dietary laws). Moreover, migrations of Jews from other countries over the centuries meant that new flavors were added within the Italian Jewish kitchen. Try to find a Jewish-Italian cooking workshop. You can even invite a few friends and a chef who can share the secrets of this special kitchen, ultimately telling the story of Italy's Jews through their food.

# 38

# FANNY NEUDA

## *Pioneering Composer of Prayers for Women*

I know that my writings are far from perfect, but nevertheless I hope that, as the product of a female heart, they might echo in women's hearts all the more.

When Fanny Schmiedl was born, prayer in synagogues was conducted in Hebrew; women oftentimes also read supplications in Yiddish at home. But when Fanny grew up, the Jewish women around her spoke German like their non-Jewish neighbors — they did not understand Hebrew, and they did not want to use Yiddish, the language women had prayed in for hundreds of years; it was considered inferior. Women stopped going to the synagogue; if they went, they would mumble ancient texts, not words from the heart.

Fanny, whose parents had both been born to rabbinic families, learned to understand the Hebrew prayers when she was a child. She had been taught German and was fluent, and so she chose to write Jewish prayers for women in German to allow women and girls, who did not understand Hebrew or Yiddish, to appeal to the Creator of the world in language that they understood and words that touched their hearts. Aside from prayers, Fanny also published books of stories for children and youth.

Fanny was born a little over two hundred years ago in the city of Lomnice in Moravia, where her father served as the city rabbi. Fanny, like her brother Abraham, received a broad education at home, one that included German language and literature.

At a young age, Fanny married Rabbi Abraham Neuda, who had also been educated in both **Torah** and general knowledge. The young couple moved to what is today the Czech Republic, and there, in the city of Loštice, Abraham worked as a rabbi.

Life was not kind to them: Abraham died at age forty-two, leaving Fanny, aged thirty-five, a widow with three children. Fanny's father died that same year, and she fell into deep mourning. In earlier years, Fanny had begun to compose exquisite prayers, relating to all subjects and times. She did not write them for publication, but rather to help women who wished to pray from the heart. Abraham, her husband, had been her partner, giving advice, discussing, consulting, and providing support. In her year of grieving, in order not to descend into sadness and despondency, Fanny responded to appeals to publish the collection of prayers in memory of her husband.

The book Fanny published touched the hearts of her community and even became an international bestseller (twenty-eight editions have been published). It was translated to Yiddish and English, and women from all over the Jewish world prayed from it. The prayer book contained prayers for weekdays and holidays, but its true innovation was the inclusion of unique, personal prayers for various moments in the lives of girls and women: for happiness and sadness, illness and recovery, the birth of a daughter and the health of a son joining the army. A prayer for the young woman — essentially a prayer for a bat mitzvah — was also included in the book.

For generations, mothers would bequeath Fanny Neuda's prayer book to their daughters; even one hundred years after it was published, during the Holocaust, Jewish women held on to it in the ghettos and camps.

# ADD YOUR VOICE

*"You have called me, too, Your daughter; to me, too, You extend Your love — an eternal love... You see into my soul; my innermost being is before You as an open book. No emotion that moved my heart, no breath, no utterance of my voice, no thought that animates my soul — none is hidden from Your eyes."*

## Explore

What is the history of Jewish prayer? Where do our prayers come from? How was the Jewish prayer book created? Why are there differences between the prayers of different communities? Take a look at where Jewish prayer comes from and what purposes it is meant to serve.

You may also want to look more generally at the meaning of prayer. How does a person connect to a prayer? What does prayer add to a person's life? Is it still relevant today? Why or why not?

## Give Back

Fanny Neuda never planned to publish her prayers; she wrote individual prayers for her friends for them to say. Can you compose prayers for your friends or family? Use resources like Sefaria to find verses that are fitting. You can also consult Fanny Neuda's book (the translation to English, by Dinah Berland, is called *Hours of Devotion*).

## See Something New

If you are in or visiting Europe, you can plan a trip to the Czech Republic, where you can see the village where Fanny Neuda lived after she married, Loštice. The synagogue where she prayed has been reconstructed and today serves as a center for teaching about Judaism, with an emphasis on religious tolerance. A number of years ago, a girl from Chicago celebrated her bat mitzvah here, and her rabbi brought a Torah scroll that had belonged to the very synagogue during Fanny Neuda's days. The scroll, which had been looted by the Nazis during the Holocaust, was sold by the country's communist leaders, and saved by the Chicago community.

Standing in Fanny Neuda's synagogue, you can read from her prayer book in English or Hebrew and become part of the ongoing chain of women's prayer.

## Get Out of Your Comfort Zone

In some Jewish traditions, a personal verse from the **Tanakh** (Bible) is added to the **Amidah** prayer. This verse relates to a person's name; it begins and ends with the same letters as one's name. Some prayer books contain a list of verses through which you can find the one that matches your name, and there are websites that can help you find the right verse for you (look at **Chabad**, Artscroll, or Sefaria).

Find the verse that matches your name. Where does it come from? What does it mean? What story is it telling? Look at the text around it and see how you connect to its meaning.

September 21, 1925–August 15, 2003
3 Tishrei 5686–17 Av 5763

# 39

# YEHUDIT NISAYHO

## *A Mossad Agent in the Capture of Adolf Eichmann*

Yehudit Nisayho was a spy with thousands of faces. She could sit as any woman at a **Hasidic *tisch* (Shabbat** or holiday celebration), drink with diplomats at a bar, or play the part of a seasoned businesswoman. She remembered every detail about any person she saw and was fluent in six languages.

Yehudit Friedman-Nisayho was born in Holland, but moved to Belgium with her family at age three. Her father, Chaim, worked distributing entry visas, known as certificates, to Jews who wished to immigrate to the Land of Israel; at the same time, he also purchased weapons for the underground **Haganah** organization in Palestine. He served as a role model for his two children, Ephraim (Ben-Haim) and Yehudit, each of whom went on to work in clandestine security activities for the Land of Israel.

With the outbreak of the Second World War, the family moved to the Land of Israel; Yehudit registered at Balfour high school in Tel Aviv and joined the **Bnei Akiva** youth movement. Her friends at the time remember her as mature, intelligent, and reserved.

These were all characteristics that suited the job that the young state's intelligence services gave her.

For her first assignment, Yehudit was part of a team meant to secretly bring Morocco's Jews to Israel in the mid-fifties. She played
a very prominent role, portraying a noisy, wealthy, eccentric Dutch
woman who connected with the elite in Morocco. Her role was essential; she was able to learn important information and gain an understanding of the atmosphere in the country at the time. Ultimately, because of her and her colleagues, twenty-five thousand Jews
from Morocco made it to Israel.

But in most of the classified missions she took part in, Yehudit
played grey, dull women. Because of her ability to fit in and leave no
impression, the head of the **Mossad** — Israel's intelligence and special operations service — chose her for the most important of missions: the capture of Nazi war criminal Adolf Eichmann in Buenos
Aires, Argentina.

Adolf Eichmann had been appointed by Adolph Hitler to oversee
the extermination of the Jewish nation. After the war, he managed
to escape to Argentina. Only the best of the Mossad's agents took
part in the complex campaign to capture him, and Yehudit was the
only woman. She was also the only person permitted to enter Eichmann's room with no accompaniment. Among her tasks, she had
to cook for Eichmann, and she would leave each day to shop in a
neighborhood that was populated by Germans; yet no one recognized that she was different. Because she was an observant woman
who ate only **kosher** food, Mossad Director Isser Harel later noted,
"'Dina' [her alias] had great difficulties with the food. She herself
did not taste the food she made, and most of the time she lived off of
hard-boiled eggs and dry bread, and drank Coca-Cola."

Another famous campaign that Yehudit took part in was of a
completely different nature; an Israeli boy had been kidnapped by
his grandfather, and the Mossad was enlisted to return him to his
parents.

The Shumacher family had immigrated to Israel from the USSR
in 1958 with their son, Yossele, age six. Because they were having
trouble acclimating in a new land, Yossele was sent to live with his
grandfather, who was anti-**Zionist** and **ultra-Orthodox**. When his

parents asked for their son back, the grandfather was opposed; he enlisted the entire Hasidic community he belonged to to smuggle young Yossele out of the country.

Yehudit was sent to Antwerp, Belgium, where there was a large Hasidic community. None of her hosts suspected that she spoke Flemish perfectly; it was one of the six language she was fluent in. She patiently listened to her hosts' conversations to try to discover where the boy had been taken. She also posed as a potential buyer for a house in France to catch the woman who had dressed Yossele as a girl and smuggled him out of the country. Yossele was quickly restored to his parents.

When she returned from the mission, she asked her superiors in the Mossad for permission to marry Mordechai, her boyfriend since her time as a student at the Hebrew University. The two came from vastly different backgrounds: Yehudit was an observant Jew; Mordechai was a secular Jew by choice and had been a communist in his past. They lived together happily for thirty-seven years, with secular Mordechai making the **Kiddush** blessing over wine on Shabbat and religious Yehudit making food on **Yom Kippur**, the most significant fast day of the year, for those who were not fasting.

At age fifty, Yehudit Nisayho retired from the intelligence service; she was the most senior woman to serve in the Mossad. Yehudit returned to university and studied law and, later on, became the head of the Hebrew Writers' Association and a political activist.

Her tranquil life was upended when her only son Chaim, a talented mathematician who had just completed his doctorate and traveled to the United States to continue his education, went to Nepal with his girlfriend and did not return. One night, in a hostel in the Himalayas, the thirty-year-old died, and no one knew why.

Mordechai, brokenhearted, passed away three years later, and Yehudit was left alone. She immortalized her son with awards for outstanding mathematicians and a library that she established in Kathmandu, Nepal's capital, which she and his girlfriend visited each year on the day of his death.

# ADD YOUR VOICE

## *Explore*

---

The Mossad, Israel's intelligence agency, was formed right after the state was founded and is responsible for covert operations and counter-terrorism. What do you know about this secretive organization? How does its work compare to similar intelligence agencies where you live?

## *Give Back*

---

Yehudit Nisayho, as an observant Jew, only ate kosher food. Perhaps you would like to create a recipe book in her honor? You can include only kosher recipes, if you like, or choose to go the vegetarian route. A personal recipe book can focus on old family recipes or can strive for inclusion and contain a variety of foods from different cultures. You can distribute your recipe book as a souvenir at your bat mitzvah celebration or sell it and give the proceeds to charity.

## *See Something New*

---

If the world of intelligence interests you, you can visit the Israel Intelligence Heritage and Commemoration Center in Glilot. Preorder tickets to see a presentation about intelligence strategies, learn more about those who lost their lives, and hear personal stories from veterans of the secret service.

# Get Out of Your Comfort Zone

From the days of the Bible until today, when people want to hide information, they use a code. Some codes are simple and some are intensely complex. In fact, hackers are, in reality, code breakers.

You can create a bat mitzvah celebration around the theme of codes. Your invitations can be written in code, with hints to break the code (not too complex; you want everyone to understand). Explain the history of encrypting to your guests, talk about important milestones in the history of encrypting, discuss the different encrypting techniques — and challenge your guests with encoded riddles, each containing a mission.

# 40

# IDA NUDEL

## *Guardian Angel of the Refuseniks*

Living in unbearable conditions — a small, cold room in an isolated village in exile in Siberia, among criminals and murderers, in −60° weather — Ida Nudel had a wonderful idea: she would adopt a dog.

Her countless friends around the Soviet Union enlisted to help her, and that was how Pizer, a brown collie, joined her, guarding her and serving as her friend and family. They immigrated to Israel together ten years later.

Ida was born in Siberia, in the city of Novorossisk. Her parents, Yakov and Chaya, were very young when she was born — around twenty — and devout communists; they had been sent by the party to work there. But the conditions were so severe that they soon took their baby daughter to live with her grandfather far away, on the Crimean Peninsula.

Ida returned to her parents in Moscow, the capital city, when she was three, and it was then that she first met her little sister Elena. Ida could not play with other children in the neighborhood at the time; she knew no Russian, only Yiddish. So, despite the fact that her parents spoke Yiddish with each other, they forced their girls to speak Russian, and insisted that they speak "without a Jewish accent."

Seven years later, when the Soviet Union joined the Second World War, Ida's father, who had been an officer in the Red Army, was drafted and killed. Ida's grandfather and grandmother in Crimea, as well as her uncles and aunts and their children, were all killed by the Nazis. What had once been a large family now consisted only of Ida's mother and her two girls.

Ida was an active, athletic girl who loved rowing boats and scaling mountains, and she saw her future in engineering. As a university student she was beloved by all and constantly surrounded by friends — at least initially. But a year before she finished her studies, nine Jewish doctors were arrested from around Russia. They were accused of having been sent by the Joint Distribution Committee, a Jewish humanitarian organization, to poison Soviet leaders. This was of course a falsehood, but some of Ida's closest friends were suddenly voicing opinions like "it's a shame that Hitler didn't finish the job."

Ida found herself gradually growing more skeptical about life in the Soviet Union. Her final decision to leave Russia and move to Israel was made when her young nephew, Yakov, experienced **anti-Semitism** for his first time when he was not yet five years old.

Ida Nudel was not alone. Hundreds of thousands of Jews from the Soviet Union had been struggling to leave to Israel, especially after the state's victory in the **Six-Day War** of 1967. Only few were given permits to leave. Others were refused, and the term "refusenik," referring to those who were not allowed to leave, was born. They would gather near Moscow's synagogue, hold protests, and study Hebrew in private, three activities that were forbidden under Soviet law.

In 1970, sixteen **Zionist** activists made a plan to commandeer a small airplane and fly to Israel. They were caught on the runway before boarding the plane and sentenced to many years in prison with forced labor. That was the first the world heard of the Jews' struggle to leave the Soviet Union.

This act gave Ida her first push to become an activist in the movement herself. She organized protests, strikes, and hunger strikes. Her phone took calls from everyone who had been wronged — those who could not get visas, those who had been fired, those whom the **KGB** (the secret police) was harassing.

Ida and her sister applied to emigrate. Her sister and her sister's family were approved and left for Israel, but Ida was told that she could not be given a visa "for security reasons."

Ida was fired from her job as an accountant and was interrogated again and again by the secret police. There were times when she was under arrest for many long days, kept in a damp cell with no water or food.

This of course made Ida fight even harder. Ida became the "mother" of the political prisoners. She kept a detailed list of all of the refusenik prisoners with their birthdates, and would send each one a card on his or her birthday. She also maintained a list of their medical problems, and she reported on them to the prisons' head doctors. She sent packages of provisions, including medications, to the people in jail. She did not hesitate to contact the heads of the Communist Party and ministers to tell them that her friends were being denied their basic rights. She made contacts outside of the Soviet Union, primarily through tourists who were interested in the refuseniks, and formed groups in various places that could fight for prisoners of conscience around the world. The voices of the innocent who were suffering were thus heard in Israel, England, and the United States, and donations were collected for the prisoners. Ida became known to all as the "guardian angel" of the Jewish prisoners.

After six years of tireless activity, on June 20, 1978, Ida was put on trial, imprisoned, and exiled. Her crime? She had hung a sign in her apartment window that said "KGB, give me my visa to Israel."

Ida was sentenced to four years of exile in freezing Siberia, among murderers and other hard criminals. But even there, in icy Siberia, she fought for her rights. When her friend and fellow refusenik, Yevgeny Zirlin, visited, Ida suggested that he film a movie about her life in the village in Siberia. Ida wrote the script, Zirlin taped it, and the movie was smuggled to London and then distributed around the world. Tens of thousands of people wrote letters of support to Ida because of the movie, and heads of state began to take an interest in her fate.

Many refuseniks who served prison sentences were given visas to leave the Soviet Union with their release — but not Ida. On the contrary, after four terrible years of exile, sick and broken, she returned to her home in Moscow to find that she had been banished by the authorities. She was no longer permitted to live in Moscow. For eight months, she went from city to city around the huge country, and was expelled from each. Finally, she found a place to live in a small city in Moldova, where she worked as a street cleaner.

Ida stopped hoping that her life would change. But in 1987, sixteen years after she had first applied to leave the Soviet Union, she was suddenly summoned to the police station and given her long-awaited visa. She was told that she must leave within a few days. Armand Hammer, an American Jewish millionaire who had fought for years for Ida's release, flew her (and her beloved dog) to Israel on his private plane on October 15, 1987, the night after the **Simhat Torah** holiday. She was taken directly to Ben-Gurion airport, where thousands of people awaited her.

Ida had finally come home.

# ADD YOUR VOICE

*"It is the moment of my life. I am at home. I am on the soil of my people. Now I am an absolutely free person among my own people."*

## Explore

What do you know about the struggle to free Soviet Jewry? Learn more about the important movement, much of which took place in the United States. Look into the celebrities and politicians who aligned themselves with the cause. Why do you think it was so important to them? The movement consisted of a political lobby and letter-writing campaigns but also involved people who secretly visited the Russian Jewish community in order to help them from the inside. Ask your parents or grandparents if they remember the struggle to release the refuseniks. Were they involved? If so, how?

## Give Back

The right to freedom of movement — both within a country and between countries — is listed in the United Nations Universal Declaration of Human Rights and in many countries' constitutions. It was
exactly this freedom that Ida Nudel and other refuseniks were denied. Are there other places in the world that restrict their citizen's
freedom of movement? What can you do to help? Can you create a
petition? Protest?

## See Something New

The Museum of Tolerance in Los Angeles was created to combat racism and prejudice — much like the prejudice Ida Nudel faced. Its
goal is to educate people of all ages, especially students, about their
role in creating change, using interactive exhibits and programs. If
you live nearby, you can visit the museum; if not, you can check out
its website and perhaps take part in one of the online programs.

## Get Out of Your Comfort Zone

Interview people who remember the movement to free Soviet Jewry
and create a short movie on the subject. Look especially for people
who were involved in the struggle and who took action. The story
of the women and men who enlisted to help the Jews is a first-rate
example of taking responsibility for brothers and sisters who need
aid. Can you help bring the story to light? You may want to focus on
Ida Nudel, who died during the COVID-19 pandemic in 2021 and had
only a small funeral; her story should be told for coming generations.

# 41

# BERTHA PAPPENHEIM

## *A Life Dedicated*
## *to Advancing Women*

S ometimes overcoming a terrible illness gives a person so much
strength that the patient bursts forth full of energy. This was
the case for Bertha Pappenheim.

Bertha was twenty-one, attractive, and bright when she began to
struggle with mental illness, most likely tied to her father's sickness
and eventual death. Her legs and one arm were paralyzed and at
times she lost the ability to speak; when she was able to speak, it was
generally in foreign languages. Often she refused to eat or drink. She
would certainly have died were it not for her doctor's unorthodox
treatment: the talented, imaginative patient would tell the doctor
stories, and he would analyze and decipher them. Together, the two
created a revolution, written about extensively by the famous psy-
choanalyst Sigmund Freud (she is known as "Anna O." in his work).
Today, millions of patients work with psychologists in a similar
manner; to us, it appears natural. But Bertha entered the medical
research books as the first patient to undergo this type of treatment.

Once she had recovered, Bertha was not still for a moment until
her death. Because she had needed others to care for her for so long,
now she found her calling caring for others. Because, as a woman,

she could not be active, she spent her life occupied with women's rights. Because she had learned to heal through stories, she told stories. Because she had nearly lost her mother tongue, German, and remembered only foreign languages, now she translated works from foreign languages to German.

Bertha began her activism in a Jewish women's organization in Frankfurt, Germany. She worked in a soup kitchen and volunteered telling stories to girls in an orphanage. Eventually, she became the director of the orphanage, which she ran with great devotion. The girls became her daughters; she loved them as a mother and made sure they had a Jewish education and a general education, which would enrich their lives and make it possible for them to be independent women one day.

But Bertha knew that her work in the orphanage was not enough. The fact that the orphanage existed, the fact that there were children who needed a home that was not their parents' home, she knew, was related to a broader crisis that must be fully explored. This realization birthed a new profession in the world: social work.

Social workers attempt to find the source of distress and offer solutions — and Bertha was the pioneer.

Most of the girls at the orphanage, and, in fact, most of the needy people in Germany, hailed from eastern Europe. Bertha traveled to eastern Europe in order to understand why so many children were growing up without parents. She discovered a terrible phenomenon: **pogroms** against the Jews had led to the collapse of families; many girls had been left without the protection of their parents, and were being taken advantage of and sold into prostitution around the world. Many of them became single mothers and could not raise the children they had given birth to.

So Bertha opened a home for young women and unwed mothers and their children. The home was meant to protect the women from the dangers that lurked on the streets and to teach them and their children to stand on their own two feet, to work, and to be proud Jews. In effect, she wanted to create a home that prevented the need for orphanages.

The home was run simply and with an equal division of labor. Each young woman who lived there came of her own free will. The staff and the women divided the housework; they prepared food together and cleaned together. The home's kitchen was **kosher**, and even had a separate kitchen for the **Passover** holiday, when leavened bread is forbidden. Cultural education was also important to Bertha; the home displayed artwork and lectures were given on a variety of subjects. Ultimately, she created four homes, including one that was dedicated to pregnant women.

It was no coincidence that Bertha worked primarily educating young women and girls. Bertha had been born at a time when women had no rights. Very few women learned a profession; women were not permitted to gather; women were not allowed to be involved in political activity, to vote, or to be elected to political bodies. Bertha hoped and believed that through education she would be able to improve the conditions for the women of her time.

Bertha was also well known as a writer and translator. She wrote plays, poems, prayers, and fables for children and translated works from English, French, Italian, Hebrew, and Yiddish to German.

Bertha was a proud Jew, and a proud German. She did not believe in **Zionism** or in immigration to the Land of Israel. She believed that the Nazis must be fought from the inside and disagreed with Henrietta Szold (see chapter 55), whose **Youth Aliyah** was bringing teens to the Land of Israel. Bertha could not have envisioned the fate that awaited those who were not smuggled out of Germany in time; she died in her bed, surrounded by friends and admirers, a few short years before Europe's Jews were taken from their homes to concentration camps.

# ADD YOUR VOICE

*Bertha was particularly proud of translating the rare diary of one of her great great grandmothers, Glikl of Hameln (see chapter 17).*
*No one had drawn a picture of Glikl, so Bertha dressed in clothing typical to Jewish women of the time, sat for a portrait artist, and thereby tried to immortalize her ancestor's outer appearance.*

## Explore

The terms *social invisibility* and *marginalization* refer to society's exclusion of groups of people. These can include the elderly, the homeless, people of different gender identities or physical ability, immigrants, and others. People from these vulnerable groups often feel neglected by society as a whole. In the spirit of Bertha Pappenheim's life's work bringing marginalized groups into society, take a look around and ask yourself what groups in your community are marginalized or socially invisible. What does it mean to be part of such a group? How does it feel? What can society do to help?

## Give Back

Bertha Pappenheim's struggle with mental health was a significant part of her life, and influenced her important work in later years. Today, many people — including teens — face mental health challenges such as depression and anxiety. Oftentimes people keep these difficulties quiet and suffer in silence. What can you do to help raise awareness about mental health challenges? Can you hold an event or hold a fundraising drive for a community organization that promotes mental health?

## See Something New

Bertha began her independent life telling stories to children in an orphanage. In the Western Galilee, not far from Kfar Vradim, an artist named Norman Goldenberg has created an entire world of children's stories in nature. On what is called "Norman's Trail" (*Shvil Norman*), there are winding pathways and even a "yellow brick road" from which you can reach Snow White's cave and places from other beloved children's books. To get there, drive a few hundred meters south of Kfar Vradim and stop in the parking lot.

## Get Out of Your Comfort Zone

Bertha Pappenheim's life was brimming with activity; this chapter gives only an outline of some of her many activities and campaigns. Learn more about her work — her writing, her campaign against human trafficking, her work with rabbis to end the crisis of "chained women" (*agunot*) in **halakha**, her consulting for the Bais Yaakov school network (see chapter 49 on Sarah Schenirer), her translation work, and her founding of the League of Jewish Women. Can you express her seemingly endless activities in writing? Perhaps you can compose a series of poems or a soliloquy that you can perform.

16th century BCE
Ca. 2100, died 11 Heshvan

# 42

# RACHEL

## *A Mother Awaiting the Return of the Children of Israel*

The sun was high in the sky — "it is still broad daylight" (Genesis 29:7) — and Rachel, a shepherdess, drew near the well from which her sheep drank. This was an everyday occurrence. But on this day, Jacob, a cousin she had never met, also arrived at the well in Haran. Jacob looked at the beautiful Rachel and fell in love. More and more flocks arrived, and the sheep waited for water. The stone covering the well's opening was immense, and all of Haran's shepherds were needed to lift it. But Jacob's love for Rachel gave him tremendous power, and he managed to lift the stone on his own. Rachel was not unmoved.

Jacob's love grew. He was willing to work for seven years, with his only recompense Rachel's hand in marriage. And then — when Laban, her father, cheated him and married him to Leah, her older sister, in her place — he was willing to work for another seven years, "and they seemed to him but a few days because of his love for her" (Genesis 29:20).

Long years of marriage followed, and Rachel was unable to become pregnant. She was angry and bitter about her barrenness, and jealous of her sister, who had birthed six boys and a girl. "Give me children," she demanded of her husband Jacob, "or I shall die" (Genesis 30:1). But she found that Jacob could not hear her distress. "Can I take the place of God?" he responded.

The next chapter in motherhood and childbearing in Jacob's family was dictated entirely by the women. Leah's story (see chapter 25) described the mandrakes that her son Reuben brought from the field and how much Rachel wanted them. She did not desire their aroma, or their purple flowers, but rather their medical powers; at the time, mandrakes were thought to be a foolproof remedy for barrenness. Rachel agreed to forgo a night with her beloved Jacob in order to obtain the mandrakes and have a chance at pregnancy — and she succeeded.

Jacob and his three other wives already had eleven children when Rachel gave birth to her first son, Joseph.

"May God add (*Yosef*) another son for me" (Genesis 30:24) was her wish for herself when her first son was born, the wish that gave her son his name — and so He did. But when her second son, Benjamin, was born, while on the way from her father's home in Haran to the land of Canaan, disaster struck: "Rachel was in labor and she had hard labor... Thus Rachel died. She was buried on the road to Ephrath — now Bethlehem" (Genesis 35:16–19).

Jacob, mourning, buried Rachel on the main road: "Over her grave Jacob set up a pillar; it is the pillar at Rachel's grave to this day" (Genesis 35:20).

Jacob never forgave himself for leaving his beloved wife on the road to Ephrath, but her burial on the thoroughfare had significance for generations. Rachel's death transformed her from a real, volatile woman to a symbol of the great mother of the nation of Israel, standing at the crossroads to accompany her daughters and sons.

One thousand years after her death, the books of the Prophets describe Rachel watching the Israelites being exiled, and, from that point on, tradition states that she asks for mercy for her children. "A cry is heard in Ramah," the prophet Jeremiah describes, "Wailing, bitter weeping — Rachel weeping for her children. She refuses to be comforted for her children, who are gone" (Jeremiah 31:15). The

**Midrash** (Lamentations Rabbah, petihta 24) describes her bargaining with God: Rachel recounted how she had had compassion for her sister, helping her when her father married Leah to Jacob, and asked God how He could have no compassion for His nation. God immediately responded to her prayer: "Thus said the Lord: Restrain your voice from weeping, your eyes from shedding tears, for there is a reward for your labor...your children shall return to their country" (Jeremiah 31:16–17).

From then until today this is Rachel's job: she prays for the nation of Israel, weeping and refusing to be comforted until her prayer is answered in full. Hundreds of generations of Jewish women and men have yearned for her, appealing to her for aid when they are in crisis. Even today, if you visit Rachel's Tomb, you can see thousands of men and women visiting her grave any day of the year, but most noticeably on the day of her death, 11 Heshvan.

# ADD YOUR VOICE

## *Explore*

Follow Rachel on a journey throughout the generations. Rachel has never been forgotten; stories about her and her tomb have been told over and over through Jewish history. See what women and men (some who are well-known) have written about her: Nahmanides (Ramban) and his students, Rabbi Benjamin of Tudela, Rabbi Obadiah Bartenura, Judith Montefiore, Rachel Morpurgo (see chapter 37), and Rachel Bluwstein (see chapter 9).

## Give Back

Rachel is the paradigm parent: she watches her children and their children to ensure that they are safe and have what they need. What do your parents do for you? Think about the commitment and work involved in parenting and ask yourself what you can do to show your appreciation. How can you repay your parents? Commit to one activity a week that will ease the burden on your parents or express your love for them.

## See Something New

Rachel's Tomb — *Kever Rahel* — has been a milestone for travelers for many years; it is even marked on the Madaba Map, a sixth-century mosaic map located in Jordan. You can visit Rachel's Tomb in Bethlehem; it is always full of visitors, many of whom are praying for Rachel's intervention in their lives. You can also look online for a virtual tour around the entire location.

Nearby is **Kibbutz** Ramat Rachel. A large statue of Rachel stands on the kibbutz with the words "Your children shall return to their country." You can choose one of a few fascinating tours at the kibbutz: learn about the story of the kibbutz's heroism during the **War of Independence**; visit the biblical palace and citadel that were uncovered in archaeological excavations; or walk through the beautiful groves that surround the kibbutz toward the Olive Columns sculpture that rises to great heights.

# *Get Out of Your Comfort Zone*

Rachel's Tomb has always been part of the link of Jews around the world to the Land of Israel.

Dozens of poems and songs have been written over the years about Rachel; some poets and songwriters have even made biblical verses into songs. Try to read or sing some of the poems and songs about Rachel and learn more about their meaning. You may even want to include them in your bat mitzvah celebration.

Early **Zionism** oftentimes used Rachel as a symbol. Pictures of the building at her tomb appeared on stamps, postcards, artwork, children's games, and more. Look for examples of such objects; if you'd like Rachel to tie together your bat mitzvah celebration, you can even use them to decorate your event.

# 43

# REBECCA

## *A Life of Blessings and Love*

Rebecca's story is the first love story in the **Torah.**
Night has fallen on the spring. Soon the girls of the village will come with their jars to draw water. Far away stands a man, surrounded by dozens of camels overflowing with goods. We know who he is: Abraham's servant, sent there on a mission.

Rebecca draws near, with her jar on her shoulder. The stranger turns to her and asks that she draw a little water for him. Rebecca runs, draws the water, gives the man a drink, and offers to give his camels water, too.

"The man, meanwhile, stood gazing at her, silently wondering" (Genesis 24:21). This is the woman he has been searching for for his master's son, Isaac. She is diligent, good, and beautiful. He removes gold jewelry from his sack — a nose ring and bracelets — and puts them on the local girl. The servant's amazement only grows when he discovers that she is the granddaughter of his master Abraham's brother!

Rebecca, too, is moved, and does not hesitate; when asked, she agrees to join the man and leaves to a strange land to meet her husband.

Upon arriving in the new land it emerges that Rebecca was right to take a chance: at the moment when she first sees Isaac, Rebecca falls from her camel with excitement, and Isaac falls in love immediately. He loves Rebecca so much that he is comforted after the death of his mother.

When, after years of barrenness, Rebecca finally becomes pregnant with twins, "the children struggled in her womb" (Genesis 25:22). The kicks she feels in her stomach are so painful that Rebecca demands an explanation of God, and the answer that she receives is surprising: the two boys in her womb are really two nations, which are beginning, even now, to fight over the birthright. Ultimately, God says to Rebecca, the younger one will overcome the elder.

The differences between the twins that are born, one holding the heel of the other, are noticeable: Esau is hairy and red, and will become a hunter and man of the field, the favorite of his father; Jacob's skin is smooth, and he is a homebody, loved and preferred by his mother Rebecca.

Years pass and Isaac grows old. Before his death, he asks to give his beloved son a blessing and property. He calls for Esau and sends him to bring game from the field to make some delicacies. But Rebecca, instead, cooks a young goat and wraps Jacob's hands in the goat's woolly, hairy skins so that they feel like Esau's. Go, she sends him, bring your father these and get his blessing. "Your curse, my son, be upon me" (Genesis 27:13), she promises.

Rebecca's act has far-reaching consequences: furious Esau vows to kill Jacob, and Rebecca, in one mind with Isaac, sends Jacob to her family in Paddan Aram to find a wife (see chapter 42, Rachel).

Jacob spends twenty years in Paddan Aram; it's doubtful that his loving mother ever saw him again.

# ADD YOUR VOICE

*"May you grow into thousands of myriads."*

*(Genesis 24:60)*

## Explore

When Rebecca left her father's house, her brothers blessed her: "O sister! May you grow into thousands of myriads" — a blessing given to brides until today. How did that blessing play out in her life? And how was the blessing that she insisted that Jacob have related to her blessing?

Think about the moment in which Rebecca dressed her beloved son Jacob as his brother. Why do you think Rebecca did this? Was she concerned for her weaker son? Or did she remember what she had been told years earlier, in her pregnancy, "the older shall serve the younger" (Genesis 25:23)?

## Give Back

Family was the center of Rebecca's world. Her blessing from her family in childhood stayed with her for the rest of her life, and the world of her sons and their future generations was crucial to her. How do you make sure that your family stays united? Can you organize events for your nuclear family (game night, outings) or plan get-togethers for your extended family? Keep in mind that even online activities can bring people together.

## See Something New

Rebecca and Isaac lived in Gerar for many years. When archaeologists began to search for the sites mentioned in the **Tanakh**, or Bible, one of the first places in which the land of Gerar was identified was where the HaBsor National Park now sits.

HaBsor National Park, also called Eshkol Park, ranges over a huge territory, where you can hike or ride along special bike paths. Don't miss the "hanging bridge," near the park's entrance, which is suspended over the river channel. But the park's greatest attraction is the springs, surrounded by stunning meadows and shaded by trees.

## Get Out of Your Comfort Zone

Rebecca appears to have been the first person in the Torah to initiate and design a costume. Can you think of other figures, in the world of scripture or literature, who wore costumes? If clothing defines us, what, in your opinion, is the reason that people choose to dress up? Aside from for fun or for acting, for what other reasons might people wear costumes?

In the spirit of Rebecca and the costume she created, you can hold a costume ball. But first you must learn the secrets of dressing up: costumes, makeup, hair, shoes, other accessories (handbag, umbrella), and even decor. Think about what can and cannot be changed — voice, accent, height, body shape. If you'd like, you can go to a professional dresser or makeup artist in preparation. At your celebration, you can speak to your guests about the meaning of costumes in our lives.

April 2, 1923–May 25, 1996
16 Nisan 5683–7 Sivan 5756

# 44

# ELYNOR "JOHNNIE" RUDNICK

## *Trainer of Israel's First Air Force Pilots*

At age seventeen, Elynor Rudnick had already earned the title of Miss Kern County (California) as a champion equestrian. She was one of twelve children born to one of the richest men in the United States — Oscar Rudnick, an important donor to the **Zionist** cause.

By the time she was twenty-two, Elynor had founded a flight school; three years later she put the school on the line when she made it available, clandestinely, to pilots from the Land of Israel's air force who were preparing for the **War of Independence**. Elynor — often called "Johnnie" — was a pilot, a graduate of a course in aviation mechanics with a private flying license. She was doubtless one of the pillars of Israel's air force, then known as the **Haganah**'s Air Service.

It was late 1947, and the UN had just announced its decision on the establishment of the State of Israel (the United Nations **Partition Plan for Palestine**). The War of Independence had erupted and Teddy Kollek (who would eventually become the mayor of Jerusalem) was serving as the representative of the Haganah — which would later become the **IDF** — in the United States. Kollek knew Elynor's father well; he met with Elynor and the two planned the Haganah's first flight course. The United States had a policy of non-intervention, and would not get involved in the war between the Jews and Arabs. It was clear, then, that the course must take place under cover: if the authorities in the United States found out about its existence, Elynor would pay a high price. Trainees were therefore not brought from the Land of Israel; instead, thirteen candidates (eleven men and two women) who were in the United States at the time were invited to join.

In later years, the course's graduates quivered when they remembered their tough instructor, who dressed like a cowgirl and kept them on a short leash. The course was very focused, much like the courses that had taken place during the Second World War. Three instructors accompanied the thirteen trainees. During the days they practiced flying and at night they learned theory. Nonetheless, two of the cadets — Paltiel Makleff and Sara Guberman — managed to marry, with Elynor Rudnick hosting the couple and their guests and serving as their bridesmaid.

Four months into the course, the police arrived and accused Elynor of smuggling airplane parts overseas; she had been helping the Jews' war effort by dismantling planes to smuggle them to the Land of Israel. Elynor managed to give each of the graduates their wings and help them escape. She was tried, made to pay a large fine, and given a one-year suspended sentence.

And the trainees?

They all joined military efforts — performing in bombing raids, bringing supplies to besieged settlements, and evacuating the wounded. Many were killed, including Amnon Berman, Zahara Levitov (see chapter 28), Emanuel Rothstein, and Meir Hofshi; Paltiel Makleff was shot down near Beit Guvrin and taken hostage by the Egyptians.

But there is another ending to the story. It turns out that it's never too late to say thank you: some forty years after the course ended, in 1986, Air Force Commander Amos Lapidot invited Elynor Rudnick, now aged sixty-three, to the Hazor air force base and gave her a medal in recognition of her service.

She died ten years later.

# ADD YOUR VOICE

## *Explore*

The Haganah's first air training course was run by a woman and women were among the trainees. But in the years that followed women were not permitted to attend flight school. Learn more about the 1995 court case in which a soldier named Alice Miller sued the military in Israel's Supreme Court, demanding that the IDF allow women to participate in the courses. Who were the women and organizations that brought the case to the Supreme Court? What did they expect to accomplish? How did the ruling in the case affect Israel and Israeli women in the years that followed?

## *Give Back*

The Friends of the IDF (FIDF) is an organization devoted to the wellbeing of Israel's soldiers. Donations can be given to support lone soldiers, soldiers facing economic hardship, or soldiers who wish to study for a high school diploma. You can create a campaign to support soldiers in the IDF financially or send letters through the website to soldiers who can use a boost. The FIDF website even includes a series of videos in which you can "meet" Israeli soldiers and learn more about their worlds.

## See Something New

Flight comes in many forms; if you are interested in the world of biology and nature, you can learn about flight from birds. Join a birdwatching course where you live, or experience migrations over Israel.

Israel is a paradise for migrating birds. Flocks pass over the country twice each year — on their way from Europe to Africa and then back from Africa to Europe; in all, some 500 million birds fly over the state annually. The best places to see winged friends in Israel are the Hula Lake in the north, Kfar Qasim in the center, and Eilat in the south. Look at the JNF-Keren Kayemeth LeYisrael's page on the Hula Lake for more information on birdwatching and other activities there and at the Society for the Protection of Nature in Israel's page on birds for other great birdwatching locations. Once a year on **Passover**, Israel holds a huge birdwatching event around the country.

Learn more about bird migration. Why do migrations take place in flocks rather than individually? Try to find parallels between bird communities, in which birds take care of one another, and human ones. Israel takes great pains to protect its birds; Israel's Air Force even uses radar and data collected by birdwatchers to minimize the incidence of birds and planes colliding.

## Get Out of Your Comfort Zone

In order to follow in Elynor Rudnick's footsteps, you can register for a model aircraft course or hold a workshop for your friends. Such courses teach students to fly small crafts and explore the physics of flight.

# 45

# RUTH

## *The First Known*
## *Convert to Judaism*

People in eastern Bethlehem were astonished one morning: coming from the desert were two women — one young, one old. The younger one was not someone they recognized, but she was clearly nobility; she walked upright and proud. The old woman was the one who drew their attention. Could it be? Was this Naomi? She had left the city more than ten years earlier with her family, with her husband Elimelech and her sons Mahlon and Chilion, a respectable and wealthy family escaping the crippling famine to neighboring Moab. Now she returned without them, her clothing worn. And who was the young woman walking erect beside her?

They soon learned that this was Ruth, the wife of Mahlon; he — like his father and his older brother — had died in a foreign land.

After his death, Ruth had refused to return to her father's house; she clung to Naomi. "Wherever you go, I will go," she told her mother-in-law, "Wherever you lodge, I will lodge; your people shall be my people, and your God my God" (Ruth 1:16). Ruth left the gods of Moab and cleaved to the God of Israel.

Whether she was the daughter of a king of Moab, as the **Midrash** believes, or whether she came from a different type of well-connected family, in Judah, Ruth and Naomi lived lives of poverty, alienation, and loneliness. Ruth was forced to glean sheaves of grain behind the reapers; the **Torah** commands those who sow grain to leave the stalks of grain that remain after the harvest for the poor; it was these few seeds, whose harvest requires hard work, that Ruth went to pick.

Ruth found herself in the field of Boaz, "a man of substance of the family of Elimelech" (Ruth 2:1). When he saw the foreign girl, he was curious, and invited her to continue to pick in his field throughout the harvest season. He also offered that she eat and drink with his workers. "Why are you so kind as to single me out," Ruth, surprised, asked the man who was showing her kindness, "when I am a foreigner?" (Ruth 2:10).

"I have been told of all that you did for your mother-in-law," Boaz explained to Ruth, "how you left your father and mother and the land of your birth and came to a people you had not known before" (Ruth 2:11). Boaz's answer evokes God's command to Abraham. "Go forth from your native land and from your father's house" (Genesis 12:1). While Boaz's words invert the order, they draw a parallel between Ruth's brave decision and Abraham's.

With the end of the harvest season, Naomi told Ruth of another important ancient tradition among the Hebrews: a family member can serve as a redeemer for one who has died. Boaz, Naomi reminded Ruth, was a member of Elimelech's family. Go wash and perfume yourself, she suggested to her daughter-in-law, and go down to the threshing floor furtively, and lie at the feet of Boaz as he sleeps; "he will tell you what you are to do" (Ruth 3:4).

Boaz quickly understood what Ruth wanted. Once he had recovered from the shock of finding a woman lying at his feet, he again praised her — this time, for not seeking out a young man of her own age but rather coming to him to continue the line of her deceased husband. Boaz was up to the challenge. Before the city elders, he asked to purchase the land that belonged to Elimelech and his sons and to marry Ruth. The elders accepted Ruth into the nation of Israel, and then the nation and the elders gave the new couple a blessing never before heard in the Bible: "May the Lord make the woman who is coming into your house like Rachel and Leah, both of whom built up the House of Israel" (Ruth 4:11–12).

The marriage of Boaz, of the tribe of Judah, and Ruth, the convert from Moab, was so successful and so blessed that King David was born of their union. The story of kindness — Ruth's kindness to Naomi, Ruth's kindness to Boaz, and Boaz's kindness to Ruth and Naomi — has a happy ending.

Ruth became the symbol for many women and girls who choose to join the Jewish nation. Even today, many consider themselves to be walking in her footsteps when they take upon themselves the Jewish faith and its guidelines.

# ADD YOUR VOICE

## *Explore*

"Wherever you go, I will go. Wherever you lodge, I will lodge; your people shall be my people, and your God my God." Ruth's words to Naomi are well-known; they reflect a resolution to make a change and join the Jewish nation. The **Midrash** imagines Ruth's words as responses to Naomi, creating a conversation between the two in which Naomi describes what her decision will mean and Ruth confirms her commitment to the Jewish people ("You will only be able to walk certain distances on **Shabbat**!" "Wherever you go, I will go"). The commentators view this discussion as her conversion process, with the blessing of the nation at the end of the book serving only as a rubber stamp welcoming her into the nation. Read the commentaries about Ruth's statement. How does it influence our understanding of joining the Jewish nation today?

# Give Back

How can you help care for the hungry? Many organizations are dedicating to feeding those in need. Mazon is an initiative to end hunger in America and Israel, and focuses on community engagement and policy change to combat food insecurity. Leket Israel is an organization that rescues surplus food — agricultural produce and cooked meals — to distribute them to the needy. How can you get involved?

# See Something New

Ruth's story takes place for the most part in wheat fields.

Israel is constantly developing new varieties of wheat that is more durable and better suited to the Israeli climate. The majority of the work takes place at the Agricultural Research Organization — Volcani Institute, the largest center for agricultural research in Israel. You can see the visitors' center and learn more about wheat crops.

You can also visit one of the sites that demonstrates the various stages in the process of turning grain into bread. See, for example, the Old Courtyard on **Kibbutz** Ein Shemer or the **Talmudic** Village in Katzrin.

You may want to contact a kibbutz that grows wheat (there are many in the Lakhish and the western **Negev** areas) and go harvest wheat. (These days, no one walks in the fields; they travel in a special tractor called a combine.)

The Kfar Etzion Field School offers tours to the fields of Bethlehem, which look today much like they did when Ruth and Boaz met. If you take the tour, you can also walk in Amat Habiyar, an aqueduct that took water to Jerusalem and the Temple; the water inside it comes up to your waist!

# Get Out of Your Comfort Zone

The book of Ruth revolves around people's kindness to one another. While many of those kindnesses are acts that are initiated by figures in the book of their own free will, there are also **halakhic** commandments — written in Jewish law — that are intended to create a just and kind society. The obligation to leave wheat in the fields for the poor to pick is one such commandment.

Can you research what other Jewish commandments exist to ensure that there is kindness and social justice within society? Are they found in the Torah, the **Mishnah**, or the **Talmud**?

# 46

# SALOME ALEXANDRA

## *Hasmonean Queen*

S alome Alexandra was one of only two queens to rule the nation of Israel. Her reign is remembered in the chronicles of Israel as a time of goodness, wealth, and security. Even the rains in the time of Salome Alexandra, the **Talmud** tells us, were perfect and brought forth crops that looked like golden coins.

Known as *Shlomtzion HaMalka* in Hebrew and by her Greek name Salome Alexandra, the queen was raised in a home of **Torah** scholars: the Talmud notes that her brother was Simeon ben Shattah, the *nasi*, or head, of the **Sanhedrin** (the Jewish supreme court during the Second Temple period).

Still, in order to become a queen, at that time, she needed to be married to a king. And, indeed, both of her husbands were from the **Hasmonean** dynasty, which ruled Judea and the regions around it from 141 to 37 BCE.

Her first husband, Judah Aristobulus I, was king for only one year; when he died, Salome appointed his oldest brother, Alexander Jannaeus, as king over Israel and married him. Twenty-seven years later, as Alexander Jannaeus neared death, he turned the rule over to her, despite the fact that they had two sons who could have ruled.

What kind of a queen was Salome Alexandra?

The opinions are divided between opposing groups: the Pharisees, who believed in prayer and the study of Torah, and the Sadducees, the priests, or *kohanim*, who clung to the Temple.

Salome Alexandra followed her family's Pharisaic tradition, and the Talmud's sages saw in the strong, God-fearing queen the apex of Hasmonean rule. But the most important historian of the time, Josephus Flavius, who was a priest, felt that while Salome Alexandra ruled her nation and was much beloved, her path was dictated by the Pharisees. He accused her of being power-hungry, and felt that she made poor decisions as a result.

Salome had two sons, Hyrcanus II and Aristobulus II. She appointed Hyrcanus, the elder, as high priest. The appointment made his brother Aristobulus II jealous. When Salome grew sick and weak, her younger son revolted against her and conquered her kingdom from her piece by piece.

After her death, a war erupted between her two sons, both of whom wished to rule over the land. The war was a long one and caused the land to decline, until the Romans conquered it. The conquest led to the end of Hasmonean rule.

Both sources — the Talmud and the books of Josephus Flavius — agree that during the reign of Salome Alexandra, the kingdom prospered and that her military was so large that her enemies were afraid of her. However, Josephus felt that the present was more important to her than the future; the fact that a woman insisted on ruling on her own, instead of transferring power to her son, he believed, was what led to the kingdom's downfall.

# ADD YOUR VOICE

*"Do not be afraid of the Pharisees, and neither from those who are not Pharisees; rather, of the hypocrites..."*
*(Advice from Alexander Jannaeus to his wife Salome before his death, as given in the Talmud, Sotah 22b)*

## Explore

Salome was one of only two queens to rule the nation of Israel. What were her strategies and goals? How did she react to the division among her people, with the Sadducees and Pharisees representing different worldviews? How did her actions diverge from those of her husband? (If you're interested, you can even listen to an episode of a podcast called "What's Her Name" devoted to "The Last Queen of Judea.")

## Give Back

The world of mediation attempts to help people or groups resolve differences through communication and negotiation, preventing escalation. Mediators work in such fields as law (real estate, personal injury, marriage and divorce) and politics (between opposition parties or governments). In the spirit of Salome Alexandra and her attempts to bridge the divide within her nation, you can learn mediation skills and apply them in everyday life; look, for example at programs like "Peer Mediators."

## See Something New

The origins of the Hasmonean dynasty, which ruled the Land of Israel for more than a hundred years, were in the small village of Modiin, today identified with the village el-Midiah. Go visit the graves of the **Maccabees**, the family from which the Hasmoneans descended, and see the place where it all began.

For the adventurous, at the Shilat Cliff, you can organize a hike that includes rappelling.

Nearby, in Shilat, there is a site called the Hasmonean Village, in which the day-to-day lives of the residents of the Hasmonean kingdom are recreated. If you order ahead, you can turn back the clock and see the recreated buildings, the ancient synagogue, and the blacksmith at work. You can also try your hand at squeezing olives using ancient techniques, learn to write in ancient Hebrew script, and even mint Hasmonean coins.

## Get Out of Your Comfort Zone

Hold a historical trial between the talmudic rabbis, who believed in Salome's ability as a woman to rule over them, and Josephus Flavius, who believed that a woman could not rule and blamed her for the kingdom's decline. Formulate a statement of defense in Salome's name and check if there is any truth in the accusations made against her.

# 47

# SARAH

## *Matriarch of the Nation*

Sarah was known to be a beautiful woman — and full of emotion. Laughter and crying appear in the **Torah** for the first time in connection to her.

The first laughs in the Torah came when Abraham and Sarah each learned that in their old age (Sarah would be ninety!) they would have a child together; she laughed once more (a laugh of wonder and enjoyment) when the promise came true. At God's command, Sarah's son was even called *Yitzhak* — Isaac — from the Hebrew word for laughter.

The first crying in the world was heard when Abraham wept in sorrow over Sarah's death: "and Abraham proceeded to mourn for Sarah and to bewail her" (Genesis 23:2).

Sarah, a strong woman, ran her household, took action, and made decisions; at times, Abraham had to abandon his choices in favor of hers.

When Hagar, Sarah's maidservant who had had a child with Abraham, shamed her mistress who was barren, Sarah made her suffer so much that Hagar was forced to flee to the desert. And when the relationship between Isaac and Abraham's eldest son, Ishmael — who prophecy stated would be a "savage" (Genesis 16:12) — was not to Sarah's liking, she demanded that Abraham banish both Hagar and

Ishmael. Abraham did not easily part from his firstborn son, but God demanded that he stand by Sarah: "whatever Sarah tells you," He instructed Abraham, "do as she says" (Genesis 21:12).

Sarah's influence grew and grew and was felt even in her death. Abraham's family had wandered from place to place, and did not settle permanently. When Sarah died and needed to be buried, Abraham purchased the first piece of land in Canaan, a burial site where he and his sons were eventually buried as well: *Maarat HaMakhpela*.

# ADD YOUR VOICE

*"God has brought me laughter; everyone who hears will laugh on account of me."*

(Genesis 21:6)

## Explore

Sarah signals the beginning of a dynasty, and her story is a complicated one. Read Sarah's story in the Torah — you can read it in translation or use a website that offers explanations — and try to understand what motivated her. You may want to study with a parent, and go through some of the commentaries to learn more about how Sarah was understood over time. Allow yourself to learn associatively; move from topic to topic and see where it takes you.

## Give Back

Yad Sarah — while not named for the matriarch — is an organization that began as a free-loan service for medical equipment, seeking to minimize the expenses for items that might only be needed temporarily, such as crutches, oxygen, and wheelchairs. It has since grown into a national Israeli organization with an emergency helpline, a mobile dental unit, repairs of medical equipment, day rehabilitation centers, and more. This private initiative is funded by donations and its policy is to turn no one away. Learn more about Yad Sarah and the services it offers; if you'd like, you can organize a fundraiser to purchase more equipment. If you're visiting Israel, you can take a tour of its flagship location and even schedule a workshop in which you and your family build crutches.

## See Something New

Visit the Cave of the Patriarchs (*Maarat HaMakhpela*) in Hebron, the first piece of land Abraham purchased in Canaan, where he buried his beloved wife. Later on, other matriarchs and patriarchs from the Jewish nation were buried there, all except for Rachel (see chapter 42). The cave is holy to both Jews and Muslims, as Isaac and Ishmael were both Abraham's sons. The cave is open for visitors during most of the year, except for the hall that contains Isaac's tomb, which is open only to Muslims.

And if you're in the neighborhood, see the visitors' center at Beit Hadassah (Hadassah house), which tells the story of Hebron from the time of the **Tanakh** (Bible) until today.

## Get Out of Your Comfort Zone

As noted, Sarah brought laughter into the world. In fact, her entire family was tied to laughter. Abraham "laughed...to himself" (Genesis 17:17), Sarah laughed and the messengers heard her, and their son's name was tied to that laughter.

Invited your friends to a laughter workshop. You can even do a yoga laughter workshop, in which you learn to relax your body and mind using breathing activities.

# 48

# FLORA SASSOON

## *Philanthropist, Businesswoman, and Scholar*

B orn to an influential Indian Jewish family in the nineteenth century, Flora Sassoon always knew she had a duty to her community and would most likely stand at its center — yet her life was even richer and more impressive than she could have imagined.

The Jewish community in Bombay (now Mumbai) was primarily composed of families that had come to India from Iraq, and the Sassoon family was known to be a wealthy family that had come from Baghdad to Bombay in the early nineteenth century. Flora was the eldest of twelve children, and was brought up studying general studies in Catholic schools and Jewish studies with tutors at home. By the time she married at age nineteen, she was fluent in seven languages — Hebrew, Aramaic, Hindustani, English, French, German, and Judeo-Arabic. And her knowledge of Jewish sources was unparalleled.

Flora and her husband, Solomon Sassoon, had three children. Solomon ran the family business; Flora was involved in his professional world but also took on the role of hostess, organizing lavish weekly parties. When Solomon passed away in 1894, she took over his professional duties as well.

Flora worked to ensure a better life for the people around her. She received letters every day asking for money and would respond on the same day, by hand. Aside from the funds she gave to various causes, she provided financial support to Waldemar Mordecai Zeev Haffkine, who was developing vaccines to fight plagues and cholera. Her contribution made it possible for him to save lives — she even chose to be vaccinated in order to set an example. She was also active in the anti-purdah movement, which fought against the idea that Muslim women should be veiled and secluded.

In 1901, Flora moved to London, hoping to find medical treatment for her daughter. She was the center of a social circle, hosting large gatherings at least once a week. Her parties were all strictly **kosher**. She supported Jewish institutions in the United Kingdom, including a **yeshiva** and hospital. She was in contact with British royals and the elite.

Flora's religious life was crucial to her. When she traveled she always brought ten men — a *minyan*, or quorum, required for public worship — as well as a ritual slaughterer, so she could be assured she would have kosher meat. When she visited Baghdad in 1910 with two of her children, she met with important members of the Jewish community and even chanted from the **Torah** scroll in the synagogue. She was a strong supporter of **Zionism** and visited Jerusalem with her son in 1925.

But beyond being a generous donor, the center of her social circle, a pious Jew, and an astute businesswoman, Flora was also known to be an outstanding scholar. She collected Jewish manuscripts; still today, the Sassoon collection is an essential source for research in Jewish studies. She corresponded with the Ben Ish Hai, Rabbi Yosef Hayim of Baghdad, a leading authority on Jewish law. She published articles on Torah commentary and **responsa**. She was a known expert on **Sephardic** traditions.

Flora Sassoon was the first woman to be elected chairperson of the London School of Jewish Studies (then known as Beit HaMidrash L'Darshanim of Jews' College). In her speech, she stated:

> I have been told that since the founding of this institution, it has been unheard of that a woman be honored as Chairperson. This is perhaps

because it says "I have found no woman among all these," or because you recite "Who hath not made me a woman" in your daily prayers. If so, I find it puzzling that you have honored me as Chairperson. ... For, to your mind, men are the basis and principle of the human species, and woman are only the surplus, something extra and inessential... This Beit Midrash was founded seventy years ago, and was always chaired by men — they are the essence, and now, once in seventy years, the time has come to give the honor to a woman, one of the gender that is considered as surplus and not essential. I harbor no grudge toward you for the honor you have bestowed upon me, far from it; I rejoice that you have, once in seventy years, also honored a woman. Nevertheless, I will have you note that this fact is not a good sign...

Today, Flora's grave is on the Mount of Olives; her remains were moved there from London in 1947.

# ADD YOUR VOICE

*"She walked like a queen, talked like a sage, and entertained like an Oriental potentate."*

*(Cecil Roth, The Sassoon Dynasty)*

## *Explore*

What do you know about the Jews in India? How long have they lived there? How did they get there? What are their customs and practices and how do they differ from yours? Learn more about the many different groups of Jews in India, when and how they arrived in India, and what they brought with them. You may want to learn especially about the Jews of Cochin and their tradition of women's singing and dancing.

## Give Back

Flora Sassoon went above and beyond to further medical research for the health of those around her. What can you do to promote awareness of healthy lifestyles and research? Perhaps you'd like to bring light to a health issue or medical research in your community by partnering with an organization to raise awareness.

## See Something New

What does an Indian synagogue look like? Look online for synagogues in India and study pictures of their exteriors and interiors. How do they compare to synagogues where you live? What type of design do you recognize? What different models do you think they were influenced by?

## Get Out of Your Comfort Zone

Flora Sassoon's speech at the London School of Jewish Studies was the first woman's voice to be heard at the center of religious study, and she made how she felt about the lack of women's voices clear. Women's voices and stories have often been missing from history. "Story Aperture" is an initiative created by the Jewish Women's Archive that aims to collect untold women's stories. You can take part in the program by downloading the app and interviewing a woman who you feel has a story that should be heard.

## 49

# SARAH SCHENIRER

*Founder of the Bais Yaakov*
*School System*

**" I** sew beautiful clothing for the bodies of girls and women,"
Sarah Schenirer, a young seamstress, thought to herself, "but
what clothing can I sew for their souls?"

And in order to clothe the souls of Jewish girls, Sarah decided to
create a Jewish educational framework that would fit them. Her first
students were small girls, and her first classroom was in her sewing room. Within a few years she had founded hundreds of schools,
trained thousands of teachers, and educated tens of thousands of
girls aged five to twenty.

Born in Krakow, Poland, Sarah Schenirer studied in a public
school. Polish authorities forced parents to send their children to
school, even if it did not accord with their worldview; otherwise,
they would impose harsh fines on them. But because the Jewish
community had created religious school only for boys, the boys were
raised with a serious Jewish education while the girls were becoming less and less tied to their heritage and practice.

Sarah, who had always had a thirst for knowledge, left school
after eight years in order to help support her family. So she spent
her days by a sewing machine — but spent her nights studying: "I

showed great interest in general knowledge as well... I especially admired the classical works of German and Polish writers... I would go to Polish universities from time to time, to listen to lectures and discussions on various subjects."

With the outbreak of the First World War, Sarah and her family fled to the big city of Vienna. There, in an **ultra-Orthodox** synagogue, she met Rabbi Moshe David Flesch, a student of Rabbi Samson Raphael Hirsch, who believed in education for Jewish women. Rabbi Flesch tried to acquaint the women of his generation with the revered women of the Bible. Sarah was particularly excited when the rabbi spoke about Judith (see chapter 22), the Jewish heroine who had used great resourcefulness to save her nation from the conquest of the military commander Holofernes. Sarah understood that she, too, had a duty to her people: to return to her town and teach the Jewish girls to take pride in their heritage. "Vienna," she wrote in her journal, "was the cradle of the world Bais Yaakov movement."

When she returned to Krakow and tried to convince young women to learn about Jewish tradition and to immerse themselves in Yiddish rather than Polish and Polish culture, she was laughed at. So she chose to focus on the "young seedlings," to begin her educational work with girls of preschool age who had not yet received a general education. And they enlisted with shining faces and sparkling eyes.

Her first group of students numbered twenty-five, equivalent to the Hebrew letters *kaf* (20) and *heh* (5) in **gematria** (which calculates a numerical value for a word based on its letters); this called to mind the command Moses was given at Sinai: "Thus (*koh*, formed by the letters *kaf* and *heh*) shall you say to the house of Jacob (*bait Yaakov*) and declare to the children of Israel" (Exodus 19:3) The name of her institution was taken from the verse: *Bais Yaakov*, the Yiddish pronunciation of the term "house of Jacob."

Her program was blessed by the **rebbe** of Belz, the **Hasidic** sect that Sarah's family belonged to. Once he had given his blessing, Sarah, whose entire formal education had spanned eight years, sat down to write a curriculum; she also trained teachers, managed the accounts, and even traveled from place to place to tell parents about the new institution that she had founded and the possibility of giving their daughters a Jewish education. Her passion and warmth were infectious.

Within a few short years, there were branches of Bais Yaakov all over Poland, and from there the institution spread to other lands — Lithuania, Austria, Germany, and more. The students worshipped Sarah; thousands of students called her "Our Mother Sarah." They would dress in festive **Shabbat** clothes to greet her and bring her flowers. She forbade them from hanging her picture in their rooms or in the school's hallways. "I do not want them to remember my visage," she requested, "but rather my vision."

When stones were thrown at her in one city she visited — not everyone agreed that girls should be educated — she collected the stones and promised: "These stones will be the foundation of the Bais Yaakov school in this city."

Sarah Schenirer died at age fifty-two after suffering from illness. More than fifty thousand students in approximately two hundred and fifty Bais Yaakov schools mourned her death. Her enterprise was at its height. The year was 1935. Four years later, the Jewish world in Europe began to be extinguished, including the hundreds of Bais Yaakov schools. Only a few of her students survived the Holocaust.

But after the Holocaust, after the pieces had been picked up, Bais Yaakov schools were once again established, combining secular and religious studies, around the Jewish **ultra-Orthodox** world. Today there are Bais Yaakov schools in thirteen countries, including the United States and Israel.

# ADD YOUR VOICE

## Explore

How does one woman make a change, especially one that has repercussions around the world? Can you think of other women who faced down challenges to effect change for their communities? What skills did they need? What do you think were the reasons that they were able to accomplish what they set out to?

Because of the Holocaust, much information about Sarah Schenirer and Bais Yaakov has been lost. Learn more about what Jewish communities looked like in Europe before the Holocaust. What institutions did each community have? Do you have a family history in Europe from which you can learn more?

## Give Back

One of Sarah Schenirer's lesser-known activities was writing plays, primarily on topics from the **Torah**. You can combine Sarah Schenirer's love of children and education with her scriptwriting abilities and produce a play on a topic related to Jewish heritage or Torah and put it on for children in kindergartens or schools.

## See Something New

The Bais Yaakov Project is an online archive that collects and digitizes material that relates to Bais Yaakov. It contains photos from Bais Yaakov schools from the past century as well as documents, letters, and journals. You can even learn and hear music that was sung in the schools. Wander around the project's website and learn more about the school system.

You may also want to visit the Heichal Shlomo Museum in Jerusalem, located in the building where the **Chief Rabbinate** of Israel once sat. Today the building contains a synagogue that was transferred from Italy and houses a teachers' college, but also preserves Jewish art — sacred objects, paintings, and sculptures. It represents the world of Sarah Schenirer as well, the world of Jews in eastern Europe immediately prior to the Holocaust. You can visit and take a tour through Jewish heritage.

And if it's possible, you might want to visit Krakow, considered the most beautiful city in Poland. On the outskirts of the city stands a memorial to Sarah Schenirer and her schools, created in the first decade of the twenty-first century.

## Get Out of Your Comfort Zone

"Limmud" is an organization dedicated to promoting Jewish learning around the world. Over eighty communities organize events and festivals with lessons and activities that revolve around Jewish texts and ideas.

In the spirit of Sarah Schenirer and her efforts to bring Torah learning to everyone, look online for Limmud's resources and classes and, if a Limmud event is taking place near you, feel free to sign up — they often include activities and lessons for kids as well.

October 2, 1924–March 6, 2003
4 Tishrei 5685–2 Adar II 5763

# 50

# HANNAH SEMER

## *The First Female Editor of an Israeli Daily Paper*

**"I**n any editors' forum, whether Israeli or international, I found myself alone. There are almost no female chief editors of daily papers," Hannah Semer reported decades ago. Even today she is singular; Israel still has no female editors of daily newspapers.

Hannah Semer was born Hannah Haberfeld in the city of Bratislava, the capital of Slovakia, to an **ultra-Orthodox** but modern rabbinic family. Young Hannah was exposed to modern education, to cinema, theater, and music. She was ten years old when a boy in her class used an **anti-Semitic** slur; her father came to her class and slapped him. "I was embarrassed and proud," she said.

Years later, Hannah returned to her birthplace to search for what remained of the Jews after the Holocaust. In fact, wherever she went overseas, she searched for Jewish history. "We must cling to history with compassion and pride," she claimed, "because no one will do it for us." Her impressions from abandoned synagogues and lost communities were written up in her book, *God Doesn't Live Here Anymore*.

Hannah spent most of the Holocaust in hiding, after which she was sent to forced labor in a brick factory. In autumn of 1944, she was deported to the women's concentration camp in Ravensbrück, Germany, and survived.

Hannah moved to the newly formed State of Israel in 1950. After a short stint as a teacher in a Bais Yaakov school (see chapter 49 on the schools' founder), Hannah began to work as a journalist at a newspaper for new immigrants. She was soon appointed to cover the **Knesset**, Israel's legislature, a field in which she continued to write when she moved to the newspaper *Davar*, where she worked for forty years.

Hannah Semer was considered a brilliant reporter and a gifted interviewer. Before she became editor of *Davar*, she was occupied with politics and state and knew all of the important politicians and diplomats of the young State of Israel: David Ben-Gurion, Levi Eshkol, Moshe Sharrett, and others. She was at times their confidante and advisor, not because of her position at the paper but rather because of her wisdom. For decades she was a presenter on the radio, and, when Israeli television was born, on television as well. She was just as witty and sharp when speaking as she was in writing.

In 1970, Hannah Semer became the editor of *Davar*, the first woman to serve as editor of a paper in Israel. She breathed new life into *Davar*, which was fairly outdated. Hannah recruited some of the best authors and writers and appointed a female journalist to the military beat, a field that had only been open to male journalists previously. She also went far in the world of satire: *Davar Aher*, the satirical newspaper that came out on a weekly basis for twelve years, was groundbreaking.

She soon became the chairwoman of the Editors' Committee in Israel and a member of international journalism bodies.

Hannah's attitude to working women generally and to female editors in particular was a complex one. On one hand, she was a single mother, and raised her daughter alone. On the other, she repeatedly noted that she was not a feminist and even preferred not to employ women (who often had a sick child, or whose nanny hadn't arrived). Ultimately, she admired the work ethic of women, including housewives and mothers: "I see, for example, the work of the housewife, the mother of four children, who wakes each morning to shopping, cleans, organizes, cooks, launders, irons, and I ask myself: How can she? How does she do it?" She once stated that men manage to reach the top because of the women who stand behind them and that "if women had wives," they would outgun the men in every field.

Hannah Semer enjoyed teaching young journalists based on her experience, and they thirstily drank her words.

# ADD YOUR VOICE

## *Explore*

The ANU Museum maintains a special website devoted to synagogues around the world, called Synagogues360. In the spirit of Hannah Semer and her mission to see Jewish houses of worship and communities, you can "visit" these locations online and learn more about their history. What do the synagogues have in common? How do they differ? How does their architecture or design reflect their communities? What draws you to a certain synagogue?

## *Give Back*

The Israel Nature & Heritage Foundation of America aims to protect Israel's nature and heritage sites. One of its projects is the conservation of ancient synagogues in Israel. It supervises the sites and displays their remains to connect Jews today to the Jewish communities of long ago. You can donate a portion of the money you receive in bat mitzvah gifts or run your own campaign to raise funds for the preservation of ancient houses of worship.

## See Something New

Follow in the footsteps of Hannah Semer, who documented the synagogues of the destroyed communities in Europe. Look around Tel Aviv for closed synagogues that have been abandoned and are slated for destruction. A few years ago, artist Brit Yakobi documented some one hundred abandoned synagogues in an initiative she called "Free Space," holding cultural events within them and bringing them back to life. Try to follow these synagogues, or some of them, from the Great Synagogue on Allenby Street south to the Neve Zedek neighborhood. Be a young journalist and document the synagogues' histories in writing or in photographs.

## *Get Out of Your Comfort Zone*

Hannah Semer was part of television when it was established in Israel. In order to appear on television, one must know the secrets of the camera. Invite your friends to a television workshop. Learn how to stand or sit in front of a camera and look directly into the eyes of the watcher at home, what body language tells us and how it is managed, how a complex message can be transmitted in short and simple words, and how makeup is used. You can take advantage of the workshop and film your first movie and screen it at your bat mitzvah celebration.

You can also visit a television studio and learn the secrets of the complex machinery that brings us our news, how to read from a teleprompter, how the cameras are controlled by the control panel, and so on.

July 17, 1921–November 7, 1944
11 Tammuz 5681–21 Heshvan 5705

# 51

# HANNAH SENESH

## *Paratrooper and Poet*

My name: Hannah Senesh. Mother's name: Katherine, maiden name, Salzberger, widow of Bela Senesh, writer... Since 1931 I have been a student at a high school for girls. I will graduate at the end of this term. So far I have completed all my studies with honors...

I longed to live in Palestine, and for the way of life there. I decided to learn this profession so that I could take an active part in the creation of the state and the cultivation of the land... Acceptance to the school would give me great joy and happiness. It would be the first step toward the realization of my life's ambition.

With cordial **Zionist** greetings,
Hannah Senesh

The letter, sent in March 1939, relayed Hannah Senesh's request to be accepted to the agricultural school in Nahalal.

And Hannah was indeed accepted to the agricultural school. She left her beloved mother Katherine in Budapest and tied her life to the Land of Israel. When she finished her studies, she joined a new **kibbutz** on the shores near Caesarea: Sdot Yam. The kibbutz members adored her and trusted her implicitly; she loved the kibbutz and the collaborative work, and even the tent she shared with two friends, although she did dream of having her own room on occasion.

When the day's work ended, Hannah would write. Her outstanding writing abilities were an inheritance from her father, the Jewish Hungarian writer and journalist Bela Senesh. He had died when Hannah was six, and she hoped to follow in his footsteps — "to be worthy of him as a writer, too."

Hannah kept a diary and wrote poetry. From the moment she arrived in the Land of Israel, she wrote only in Hebrew. One of her most beloved poems, known to all, is the poem "Walk to Caesarea," which describes her wonderment at the landscape around the kibbutz:

God — may there be no end
to sea, to sand,
water's splash,
lightning's flash,
the prayer of man.

Despite her love of the land and the life on kibbutz, the news coming from Europe gave her no rest — the Second World War had erupted and the Jewish communities there were being annihilated.

And then an offer came for her to join the paratroopers, who were training to go to Europe and help the Jews there.

May 27, 1943

It's possible they'll call me any day now...leaving the land, leaving freedom... I would like to inhale enough fresh air so as to be able to breathe it even in the **Diaspora**'s stifling atmosphere, and to spread it all around me for those who do not know what real freedom is...

Hannah and her comrades parachuted into forests in occupied Yugoslavia, close to the border with Hungary, the land of her birth. There they made contact with the **partisans**, the underground fighters against the Nazis. Some two weeks after they arrived, the Germans conquered Hungary, and the partisans warned the paratroopers to wait for the right opportunity, not to act in haste.

But Hannah could not wait. In her mind's eye, she saw her beloved mother tortured by the Nazis, taken to a concentration camp; she insisted on moving forward, crossing the border to Hungary —

despite the warnings. Accompanied by a group of young Jews, with the heavy transmitter in her hands, Hannah swam across a river to cross the border. Awaiting them on the other side were Hungarian soldiers, Nazi collaborators, who arrested her and her comrades.

Hannah's actions until that point had demanded tremendous courage — volunteering for a difficult mission, parachuting into enemy territory, living in conditions of terrible hunger and thirst among the partisans. But from that point on, Hannah had a completely different test to withstand.

Hannah was tortured for months in an effort to have her divulge the code of the transmitter that had been caught — but she would not. The only time she nearly gave in was when her mother was brought by her captors, who threatened to kill her if Hannah did not tell them what she knew. Hannah was forced to choose between loyalty to her comrades and her mission and loyalty to her mother. She was lucky; her body betrayed her and she lost consciousness.

She had her twenty-third birthday in prison, and soon after was taken to a military tribunal on charges of treason. "You are the traitors, not me," she protested to the judges, who were collaborating with the Nazis.

Hannah was sentenced to death. She was offered the option of asking for a pardon, but refused. Two hours after the sentence was pronounced, only days before Hungary was liberated from the Nazis and their Hungarian collaborators, Hannah stood, head high, before the firing squad. She would not allow them to blindfold her, as was the custom; she wanted to look into their eyes.

One of her well-known poems, which succinctly describes her life, was written while she was in the partisan camp:

Blessed is the match consumed
in kindling flame.
Blessed is the flame that burns
in the secret fastness of the heart.
Blessed is the heart with strength to stop
its beating for honor's sake.

# ADD YOUR VOICE

## Explore

_____

"*Our promised hour will soon come*
*Our marching steps ring out: 'We are here!'*"
                    *(Lyrics from the Partisans' Song)*

The partisans whom Hannah worked with fought against the Nazis during the Second World War. They were mostly young people who lived in the forests and were constantly moving to keep from getting caught. Learn more about these groups. How many partisans were there? How did they communicate with one another? How many were Jewish? What types of activities were they involved in?

## Give Back

_____

I don't write to Mother at all, so your letters will have to take the place of mine. In fact, I even give you permission to forge my signature... It is unnecessary to tell you how much I would like to see you, to talk to you, or at least be able to write in more detail... Your letters arrive with great delay, but sooner or later they do get here, and I am always so happy when I have news from you.

A thousand kisses, and warmest regards to our friends.

                    (Letter from Hannah to her brother Giora, Yugoslavia, 1944)

Hannah had a very close relationship with her brother and remained in contact with him whenever possible; Giora went on to speak about his sister to many groups and built an archive to preserve her legacy.

What can you do to deepen a relationship with a sibling or siblings? Take on a weekly commitment to do something together — perhaps you can volunteer together or work together on creating family albums.

## See Something New

Visit Kibbutz Sdot Yam and the Hannah Senesh House, where you can see an audiovisual presentation that tells her story in six languages. You can also see the monument with her likeness and the words of the poem "Blessed Is the Match" engraved on it. The monument was brought to the kibbutz from the cemetery in Budapest, where it stood from the end of the Second World War until 2007. The other paratroopers who volunteered with her are also immortalized in the house through pictures, books, and personal items.

You can visit Hannah's grave on Mount Herzl; the Herzl Museum even offers tours of the nation's heroines that include a visit to her grave and the stories of other women in Israeli history.

## Get Out of Your Comfort Zone

The story of Hannah Senesh, a true hero, can be told in a medium you may be familiar with: comics. Can you create a comic book that illustrates her life — from Budapest to Nahalal to Sdot Yam to Yugoslavia and finally back to Hungary?

# 52

# ADA SERENI

## *The Woman in the Black Dress*

T he refugees did not know who she was: A Jewish Italian? A Jew from the Land of Israel? A Christian? But everyone knew that when the "woman in the black dress" arrived at a shore or port, it was a clear sign that a ship would leave for the Land of Israel that night.

"The woman in the black dress" was the name that stuck with the Italian commander of **Aliyah Bet**, the code name for the illegal immigration to the Land of Israel. Tens of thousands of Holocaust refugees owed their journey to the Land of Israel to Ada.

Ada was born in Italy to a well-established and wealthy Spanish Jewish family, as was her husband Enzo. Her husband's father was the personal physician to the king of Italy, and his brother became a minister in the Italian government.

Young Ada and Enzo were **Zionists**, and immediately after marrying they moved to the Land of Israel. They were among the founders of **Kibbutz** Givat Brener, where they raised their three children until the Second World War broke out and the destruction that the war had brought upon the Jews became clear. Enzo Sereni, almost forty years old, was one of thirty-seven Jewish paratroopers from the Land of Israel who elected to parachute behind the Nazi enemy's lines, to give information to the British and to try to help the Jews there.

It had been a year since Enzo had left, and the war in Europe was over; still no sign of life had come from Enzo. So Ada left her three children, the youngest of whom, Daniel, was fifteen, and flew to Italy. While she wore a British military uniform and allegedly was volunteering forming clubs for members of the **Jewish Brigade** from the Land of Israel who had fought in Italy, she really had two entirely different goals: a personal one, to find her husband, and a national one, to organize secret immigration to the Land of Israel for Holocaust survivors.

With the end of the war, hundreds of thousands of Jewish refugees were streaming from all over Europe to France and Italy; they wished to reach the Land of Israel, but the British, who ruled the land at the time, tried to prevent it.

The organization of illegal immigration was the purview of an organization called **HaMossad LeAliyah Bet**, which purchased ships, secretly organized refugees — known as *maapilim* — and tried to send them to the land's shores. Some of the ships made it, but others were caught by the British; those aboard were sent to detention camps.

Ada Sereni knew Italian and could speak easily with leaders and dock workers alike. Immediately after she arrived, she was named deputy to Commander Yehuda Arazi. And when Arazi returned to the Land of Israel, she became commander. She obtained donations to purchase ships, took care of preparing ships for the journey, guaranteed that no passenger was left behind and that each went in his or her turn, and accompanied the ships until each safely landed or was, sadly, caught. Ada was not afraid to tell the Italians the truth she was meant to hide: "My name is Ada Sereni, and I work organizing underground immigration of Jewish refugees in Italy," she announced to all, and she was rewarded with widespread cooperation.

Once, when a group of officers arrived at the dock right when the refugees were boarding ships, she dressed as a doctor and forbade the soldiers who were on the beach to get any closer: "There's a terrible plague," she warned them. The next day, when the health ministry's representatives came to examine the plague-infested passengers, all of the "patients" were already on ships, far away, on their way to the Land of Israel.

Ada was arrested by the Italian police and imprisoned twice. The officers who were forced to arrest the noble, older woman were very embarrassed, but she took it all with calm and humor.

After three years in which HaMossad LeAliyah Bet worked on the shores of Italy, the State of Israel was born, and the world's Jews began to immigrate openly. One of Ada's tasks had been completed.

Her husband Enzo's fate had also become clear: she discovered that he had been murdered in the Dachau concentration camp in late 1944.

Ada's inspiring, sad story might have ended here, with her return to the kibbutz and retirement from public activities. But fate wanted it otherwise.

In 1954, ten years after the parachuting mission into Europe, Kibbutz Maagan, on the shores of the **Kinneret**, held a memorial for the seven paratroopers who had not returned from their mission, including Enzo Sereni. A plane that was meant to drop a scroll in greeting to those at the ceremony lost control and crashed into the guests. Among the dead were Ada's son, Daniel, and his wife.

Ada herself wrote two books about her work, and won the **Israel Prize** in honor of her special contribution to the state. She lived past age ninety.

# ADD YOUR VOICE

*Many women took part in the clandestine immigration, whether directly or indirectly. One woman who stood out for her contribution to illegal immigration was Ruth Klüger, who used her skills, including the eight or nine languages she spoke fluently, to obtain ships for cheap and to raise funds from wealthy Jews for their purchase.*

*When Germany conquered Europe, and the illegal immigration ceased, Ruth was sent to bring Jews to Israel from Syria, Lebanon, and Egypt. She lived in Egypt, and from there was able to make contacts between the Zionist Movement and the French Liberation Army, which was fighting the Nazis.*

*These contacts helped her when France was liberated in the summer of 1944 and the illegal immigration once again began. During the war, thousands of Jewish children had been hidden in monasteries. Ruth went from monastery to monastery to collect them. Fifteen hundred of these were the first illegal immigrants she brought to the Land of Israel.*

*Ruth Klüger so identified with HaMossad LeAliyah Bet that she decided to immortalize the mission by adding a new last name to her previous one: Aliyah Bet or, in one word, Aliav.*

## Explore

---

Aliyah Bet, the clandestine immigration of Jews from Europe to the Land of Israel, extended for fourteen years, beginning in 1934 and concluding with the establishment of the State of Israel in 1948. Why was it necessary? Who was in charge? How many people came to the land through Aliyah Bet? How many were caught and turned away? What was the journey like? Learn specifically about the ship *Exodus*. Why was the story of the *Exodus* one that caught the world's attention?

## Give Back

---

Israel Flying Aid is a non-profit organization that provides aid to communities affected by conflict and natural disasters. It brings medical equipment, food, and even professional training to areas that are in danger. In honor of Ada Sereni and her commitment to her nation's refugees, learn more about Israel Flying Aid and see how you can help out.

## See Something New

---

One detention camp where the illegal immigrants were imprisoned when they were caught was in Atlit, south of Haifa, and serves today as a museum. A huge immigrant ship stands in the center of the Atlit Detainee Camp Museum. Here you can experience what it was like to be an illegal immigrant, see the letters written by the immigrants, and visit the clinic and the dining hall. The site even has a list of immigrants who spent time at the detention camp in Atlit over the seven years in which it was active.

Here you can also comprehend the size of the enterprise that Ada Sereni ran. Not all immigrants came to Atlit. Many were able to escape, some were sent back, many were placed in detention camps in Cyprus, and others who paid with their lives, either as individuals or with an entire ship.

You can also visit and tour the Clandestine Immigration and Naval Museum in Haifa. Here you can learn about the clandestine immigration during its prime. At the center of the display in the museum is the ship *Af Al Pi Khen* ("Nevertheless"), whose journey Ada oversaw personally.

And if you ever find yourself in southern Europe, you can visit the port city of La Spezia, a beautiful city on a gulf, and see the port that is named for two of the commanders of Aliyah Bet: Ada Sereni and Yehuda Arazi.

## *Get Out of Your Comfort Zone*

You can recreate the illegal immigration or play a game of "capture the flag" in the spirit of Ada Sereni: divide your friends into immigrants, volunteers from the Palyam (the **Palmach**'s maritime company) coming to greet the immigrants and hide them, and the residents in the Land of Israel with one flag, and the British officers lurking on the shores under another. The winner is the team that manages to steal the other team's flag.

## 53

# NAOMI SHEMER

*Composer of Israel's
Most Treasured Songs*

B arefoot. Always barefoot. That was how she walked on the **kibbutz** as a child — and in the city as an adult. She was draped in long, flowing dresses and wore her long hair down, even in old age. Such was the mother of Hebrew music, Naomi Shemer.

Naomi Shemer's songs are well known. Israelis grow up with her children's songs but also know her more famous songs; you may have heard *Al Kol Eleh* ("For All These Things"), *Od Lo Ahavti Dai* ("I Have Not Yet Loved Enough"), or *Yerushalayim shel Zahav* ("Jerusalem of Gold").

Naomi Shemer wrote hundreds of songs; dozens were translated into other languages. Most of them are easy to sing — her goal was that people would sing them together.

The first people to sing with Naomi were the members of the kibbutz called Kvutzat **Kinneret**; she had accompanied their singing since she was six, when she received her first piano. Every **Kabbalat Shabbat** (prayer on the beginning of **Shabbat** on Friday night), every celebration on the kibbutz, was accompanied by the talented girl and her piano.

But as a child her life was not easy. She was the first girl born "on the hilltop," in the permanent home of the kibbutz, in one of the

283

first three houses built there. Her mother Rivka was a stern, strict woman. She would wake little Naomi each morning with the sun to practice piano. The entire kibbutz would rise for its daily work to the sounds of the piano.

The efforts, it turned out, paid off. Years later, when Naomi finished her schooling at the Beit Yerah high school near the kibbutz (or almost finished; the outbreak of the **War of Independence** cut it short), she went to study at the music academy in Jerusalem. When she returned from her studies, Naomi began to write songs for the preschool children in Kinneret; at the time, there were very few Hebrew songs for children. After that, she began to write for the grownups as well.

She wrote song that were humorous and playful and songs of sadness and loss, songs of drunks and songs of religion, and chansons in French style.

On **Yom HaAtzmaut** (Independence Day) in 1967, Naomi Shemer had a prophetic moment, one that affected the rest of her life. The mayor of Jerusalem, Teddy Kollek, had asked that she write a song especially for Jerusalem. The song was meant for the night after Yom HaAtzmaut, when a song contest played on the radio (before most houses had a television). That year the competition took place in Jerusalem. It was three weeks before the **Six-Day War** would erupt, before the eastern side of divided Jerusalem would come under Israeli sovereignty; in her song, Naomi lamented the cisterns in Jerusalem's Old City that had dried up, the marketplace empty of Jews. Even before the war, the song *Yerushalayim shel Zahav*, Jerusalem of Gold, made waves and was received with enthusiasm, but three weeks later, when the war broke out and the Old City of Jerusalem returned to Jewish hands, it became an anthem. "You write a truly personal song by yourself in the dead of night, and then it becomes a standard," she said in wonderment.

After *Yerushalayim shel Zahav*, Naomi Shemer was no longer just another songwriter, but a public figure. Her songs provoked strong feelings — both empathy and anger. Her well-known song from the **Yom Kippur War**, *Lu Yehi* ("May It Be"), was sung like a prayer.

From her childhood, Naomi had been exposed to Jewish sources: **Talmud, Aggadah**, and a lot of **Tanakh**. Those responsible were her father Meir, who loved to play **Hasidic** tunes or *niguns*, her traditional grandparents, who lived on the kibbutz, and her teachers Shoshana and Aminadav Yisraeli.

These were the building blocks from which Naomi assembled her words and tunes, songs about the land she so loved, songs that evoked her Jewish heritage and its prayers, songs about the nature that surrounded her. Her songs continue to accompany us many years after her death.

# ADD YOUR VOICE

*The song "To Sing Is to Be Like the Jordan" was inspired by a trip Naomi Shemer took with her mother to Afik HaYarden in honor of her bat mitzvah. Her mother tried to interest her: "Listen to nature; do you hear the rustling of the birds?"*

*And the first person Naomi sent her new song to, twenty-nine years later, was of course her mother. "You see?" she wrote. "Nothing is ever lost."*

*To sing*
*Is to be like the Jordan*
*You begin up in the north*
*Chilly, young, bubbling, and cheeky...*

## *Explore*

Naomi Shemer's "Jerusalem of Gold" has a special place for Jews in the State of Israel. Delve into the song and its meaning. The term "Jerusalem of Gold" is a much older phrase, and stems from the Talmud; take a look at its source. Why is the song so important? What does Jerusalem represent for different people? How do you connect to Jerusalem as a place and as an idea?

## Give Back

In 1979, Naomi Shemer published a poem she'd written for Ida Nudel (see chapter 40), a woman who had been arrested and sent to Siberia, unable to leave the USSR. The poem, "Shalom, Ida Nudel," was read to Ida over the phone by her sister a few years later, when she was still fighting to emigrate to Israel. She felt, she later said, safe and protected knowing that people in Israel were writing about her and remembering her. Naomi even read the poem to Jane Fonda, who went on to become a strong voice in the struggle to free Ida, going so far as to meet Ida in the USSR and to greet her when she was finally freed. The poem (you can find translations online) is a personal one; in it, Naomi notes that they were born the same year, that they come from the same family tree, that they feel the same wind — "the wind...that allows us to form a covenant of twin women..."

Can you write a poem for a hero in gratitude or support?

## See Something New

Naomi Shemer was buried in the Kinneret Cemetery, near Kvutzat Kinneret, where she was born, next to her parents Meir and Rivka Sapir. Her grave has become a destination for many visitors who want to remember her songs, songs that continue to live even after her death. You can visit the grave of the poetess on the shores of the Kinneret and see the graves of some other influential and significant people in Israeli history, including Rachel Bluwstein (see chapter 9).

From there you can continue to the home of Naomi Shemer's grandparents in Kvutzat Kinneret, which tells the story of her songs. You can visit the home, see one of her pianos, and even reserve a "singing tour" that includes Naomi's songs.

## Get Out of Your Comfort Zone

Try to learn one song by Naomi Shemer — learn the words in Hebrew and read a translation — and teach it to your friends. You can
pick one of her more popular songs or look for a song that is less
known but speaks to you personally. If you know her songs already,
you can create a playlist of Naomi's songs that you like and invite
guests to a singalong in true Naomi Shemer fashion.

# 54

# MANIA SHOCHAT

## *Founder of HaShomer and Mother of the Kibbutzim*

M ania Wilbushewitch Shochat was born on her family's estate near the city of Grodno in Belarus. The Wilbushewitch family was wealthy, and Mania could have stayed safe on the estate, gotten an education, and, in time, inherited her parents' property. But she chose to forgo economic prosperity in order to protect the weak and fight first for workers' rights and then for the Land of Israel.

At age fifteen, Mania left home to learn carpentry, and soon found herself teaching her fellow workers reading, writing, and history. Mania did not suffice with that; she became a revolutionary, organizing strikes and protests, and was eventually arrested.

Mania spent a year in jail, locked in a dungeon with only mice for friends. The mice were put there by her jailors, who had hoped to scare her, but Mania was happy to have them; she fed them and they helped her get her mind off of her difficulties, the torture and the hunger.

When she was released from jail, she decided to work within the law. She created the largest and most important trade union in Russia in order to increase the welfare of workers, fighting for a higher salary and less work hours each day.

This all ended suddenly when **pogroms** against Russian Jews began in 1903. Mania went back to working underground, this time obtaining weapons for Jews' self-defense. From then on, throughout her life, no matter what else she was doing, she smuggled weapons for causes she believed in: defending Jews in Russia and Jews in the Land of Israel. She was so determined in her struggle that when she was caught by a Russian police officer when smuggling weapons, she shot and killed him.

When the underground was exposed, all of Mania's friends were arrested and sentenced to death. But she was not arrested. She had received a telegram from her brother Nahum in the Land of Israel, telling her that he was very ill and needed her to come care for him. She boarded the first ship leaving for Jaffa — and when she arrived, her brother Nahum greeted her, healthy and smiling. Mania, understanding that it had been a ploy to save her from her friends' fate, was so angry that she made plans to leave on the next ship for Russia. But, lucky for the entire **Zionist** enterprise, the ship had already set sail.

Mania's great dream was to create a "collective," a group without private property, in which living and working were collaborative, as were salaries.

Mania founded her first collective in Sejera, in the Galilee; it consisted of eighteen members who worked the land together and divided their lives and money. There, in the collective, another dream was born — the dream of an organization for Jewish self-defense. Two crucial institutions were born in Sejera: the **kibbutz**, which followed the ideas of the collective, and **HaShomer**. The kibbutzim are small agricultural settlements that try to preserve absolute economic cooperation and equality between members, although today kibbutz culture has shifted somewhat. HaShomer was an underground organization whose members trained with weapons, guarded the Jewish settlements (before that, all guards had been Arabs), and later took part in the general defense of Jews in the land. With time, members of HaShomer founded the **Haganah**, from which the Israeli Defense Forces was born.

Mania Shochat's life integrated two ideas: she lived most of her life on the kibbutz and stood on the front lines defending the Jewish community in the Land of Israel. In fact, she left her two children on the kibbutz she then lived on, Kfar Giladi, and the nurses in the **children's house** cared for Anna and Gidon (Geda) while she and her husband Israel defended the land.

Mania purchased weapons and distributed them on the different settlements, oftentimes taking great risks. During the riots in 1920, Mania walked around the center of the Arab town of Jaffa, the epicenter of the riots, dressed as a Red Cross representative for two days straight, saving Jews. The beginning of the Israeli munitions industry was in a modest ammunition factory that Mania and her friends established in Afula in the 1920s.

With the eruption of the **War of Independence**, Mania was nearly seventy, but her faith continued to lead her. When she heard that the bloc of settlements in Gush Etzion had fallen and its members had been taken prisoner, she crossed the lines to the Arab Legion soldiers and asked to be taken herself in order to help the hostages. But the Jordanian soldiers sent her back to Jewish Jerusalem.

It was in that same spirit that Mania, now in her eighth decade, volunteered to help immigrants who had arrived in Israel. She left her kibbutz and her life there, and spent the last part of her life in the temporary immigrant camp — the *maabara* — next to Pardes Hannah.

# ADD YOUR VOICE

## *Explore*

The world that Mania Shohat lived in in Russia was rife with pogroms and **anti-Semitism**, leading many Jews to leave in search of safer shores. Look into that period for Jews in Russia. What else was going on? How and when did the pogroms take place? What events preceded the rise in anti-Semitism? Where else did the Jews go?

## *Give Back*

Mania's activism began with her devotion to the plight of workers around her. You can get involved in the fight for workers' rights by speaking out against child labor around the world. Find resources about child labor to inform yourself and then make a commitment to help end it; you can join a global movement online to get some practical ideas or hold an event on World Day against Child Labor (June 12).

## *See Something New*

A visit to the Ayalon Institute, the underground munitions factory that was active on what was known as Kibbutz Hill in the suburbs of the *moshava*, or colony, of Rehovot, can tell you more about the world of Mania, who spent most of her life attaining weapons to defend Jews in Russia and the Land of Israel.

Beneath a laundromat and bakery, meant to conceal the factory, you will find the underground production hall, where you can still see the machines that were used to create bullets and guns. Some bullets are also on display. The workers in the factory were members of groups who were waiting to receive land to build kibbutzim — another of Mania Shochat's dreams.

You can also visit the open, green park in the Carmel neighborhood in Haifa, in which Mania is immortalized, at 2 Moriah Street. Continue from there to Kfar Giladi in the Upper Galilee, the kibbutz where most of the veterans of HaShomer lived and Mania's home for most of her life. In order to immortalize her and her friends, the kibbutz founded the Beit HaShomer Museum, which tells the story of the group and includes a sculpture gallery. The building's roof has a stunning view of the Hula Valley and the Galilee.

## Get Out of Your Comfort Zone

The idea behind collective living that Mania and her husband implemented in Sejera was based on socialism; the goal was to include men and women fully in agricultural work and create a self-sufficient community that had no need of outside aid. Plan your own collective community. What rules would you put into place? What would your goals be? This is an exercise you can do on your own or in which you can involve your friends.

# 55

# HENRIETTA SZOLD

## *Zionist Leader
and Founder of Hadassah*

Henrietta Szold was born and raised in Baltimore, the eldest of four sisters. Her father, Benjamin, was an enlightened scholar, an important rabbi in the city's Jewish community. He wrote about Jewish history and was also occupied with writing a commentary on the Scriptures. When she was a young girl, her father appointed his oldest daughter, whose intelligence and talents were apparent, as his assistant in both thinking and writing.

When she finished her studies at the local high school with honors, Henrietta began to work as a teacher, and at the same time continued writing with her father.

Along with her other occupations — she wrote for various newspapers; taught Russian Jewish immigrants at night; and edited, translated, and proofread books — she was first and foremost her father's devoted daughter and senior assistant.

When he died at the age of forty-two, she was inconsolable. Her mother, seeing her grief, suggested that she publish her father's writings. But in order to do that, Henrietta needed a broader education in **Talmud**, and in order to attain that knowledge she did something very radical, which no woman had done before her: she registered for rabbinical seminary. She was not seeking rabbinical **ordination**, but rather the study of Judaism in the most in-depth manner possible. And there, in the seminary, she underwent emotional upheaval. The strict professional, whose entire life had been devoted to studying and books, fell in love with one of her most important teachers. For a few years, it appeared that he returned her love, but things turned out differently; he married a much younger woman.

From this loss, and from the anger that accompanied it, Henrietta — who was already fifty years old and still living in her mother's home — grew to be an important and influential leader.

Henrietta had joined the **Zionist** Movement years earlier, even before the First **Zionist Congress** in 1897. Now, after her crisis, she visited the Land of Israel for the first time. What she saw there in 1909 shocked her: poverty, disease, and neglect. Those who traveled with her let go of their Zionist dreams because of the visit, but not Henrietta. She returned to the United States resolved to change the state of affairs. She gathered her friends in the Hadassah Study Circle, an organization dedicated to Jewish thought, and convinced them to join her in caring for the health of the Jews in the Land of Israel. Thirty women came to her first meeting. A few years later, thanks to her vigorous leadership, the Hadassah organization included thirty thousand women all over the United States.

Immediately after the First World War, Henrietta organized a delegation to the Land of Israel, a kind of mobile hospital, equipped with the best medical advancements, and with it doctors and nurses. Henrietta herself joined the delegation, this time meaning to make the land her home. The Hadassah delegation set up clinics in all of the Land of Israel's big cities.

And Henrietta? She continued to help develop the Hadassah clinics and hospitals — but that was not enough for her. She also worked in a variety of other areas. The Zionist Movement appointed her to the Palestine Executive, where she was responsible for the health and education of the Jews in the Land of Israel.

Everyone in Jerusalem, where she lived, knew how diligent and meticulous she was. They used to say that people in Jerusalem set their watches based on Henrietta Szold. When she got on the bus in the morning, everyone knew that it was precisely 7:45.

An observant woman, Henrietta Szold would work seventeen hours a day, six days a week, and rest totally on **Shabbat**. She demanded the same commitment from those who worked with her and her assistants.

In 1933, Hitler rose to power in Germany and began to persecute the Jews. Recha Freier, a Zionist activist from Germany, was concerned about the fate of the youth under the Nazis, and initiated her own private immigration program: she contacted **kibbutzim** and institutions and made sure that the adolescents, arriving without their families, would be received. The private initiative eventually became a huge enterprise, the **Youth Aliyah**. And Henrietta Szold, now over seventy, was appointed the head of the program in the Land of Israel. Szold had initially been among those who opposed the program. But with time she understood that the teenagers who did not come to the Land of Israel would ultimately be separated from their parents in far crueler ways. When she visited Germany and saw signs calling for bans on Jews and the Hitler Youth marching and calling "Death to Jews," she was convinced. And from the time she took it upon herself until her death, twelve years later — just months before the end of the Second World War — she was never still. Under her direction, some fifteen thousand teens came to the Land of Israel. She would arrive at the port to greet each of the groups, and so she met the arriving youth, remembering almost all of them.

The day of Henrietta Szold's death, the thirtieth of Shvat, became Mother's Day in Israel, and later came to be known as Family Day. She herself never married, and was never a biological mother. But she had thousands of children, and she knew each by name, and knew what bothered them and what their dreams were. They would write to her, asking for advice about friends and love, pain and longing, and she answered each of them and came to visit them. They would visit her, too, when they came to Jerusalem.

At her funeral, one of the boys said the Mourner's **Kaddish**, and thousands of others stood next to him and cried.

# ADD YOUR VOICE

*"Friends had warned her, before her trip, that visiting Palestine would cure her of her Zionism. On her return voyage, she wrote: 'This prophecy has not been verified. I am the same Zionist I was. I am more than ever convinced that our only salvation lies that way.'"*

(Dvora Hacohen, *To Repair a Broken World*)

## *Explore*

One important part of Henrietta Szold's life was the Youth Aliyah. Recha Freier, originator of the idea of the Youth Aliyah, who fought for it to exist, has almost not been recognized for her acts. Henrietta opposed the idea initially — much like Bertha Pappenheim (see chapter 41) — but ran it devotedly later on, and is often mistaken for the initiator and founder of the project.

Look into the disagreements between Recha Freier and Henrietta Szold. Was one of them entirely right and the other wrong? Did the disagreement between the two get in the way of the immigration program? Or did it perhaps help?

## *Give Back*

Today, Hadassah is over one hundred years old and boasts some three hundred thousand members. Its mission includes advocacy, women's health, Israel, Jewish values, fighting racism and **anti-Semitism**, and more. You can become involved the "Youth Aliyah Mitzvah Project," in which you raise money for programs in Hadassah's Youth Aliyah villages to help immigrant and at-risk students. See the website for details and ideas.

## See Something New

Henrietta Szold's first enterprise was due to her concern for the health of the public, expressed in Hadassah. Visit the nursing school at the Hadassah Medical Center in Ein Kerem, Jerusalem. Learn more about public health and how it has changed between World War I and today.

Despite her abundant activity, Israel contains very few spots that commemorate Henrietta Szold: a small garden in Lod, a youth village named for her, and a research institute. You can also visit the kibbutz that is named for her: Kfar Szold in the Upper Galilee, near the source of the Jordan. If you're in the area, take a trip by car or hike in the Galilee, to the sources of the Jordan with its overflowing water or in the northern Golan, and even the Hermon Mountain, not far away.

## Get Out of Your Comfort Zone

Hadassah Medical Center in Jerusalem prioritizes children's wellbeing in a number of ways. Its Clown Program, now twenty years old, offers humor as a form of healing, helping ease the stress and pain of serious illness.

Invite a medical clown to give a workshop to a group of friends or your class. A medical clown can teach your friends how to create balloon animals and play games that keep you all in stitches — and can also help you and your friends understand why laughter is such an important tool.

# 56

# HANNAH RACHEL VERBERMACHER

## *Leader of a Hasidic Community*

From the moment she arrived in the Land of Israel on her own, near the age of fifty, people stopped pestering Hannah Rachel. **Hasidim**, primarily women, surrounded her with adoration, thirstily drank her words of **Torah**, sat at her table on **Shabbat** toward evening for **Seuda Shlishit** (the evening meal), went with her to the Western Wall and Rachel's Tomb to pray, and received her blessings and were healed. From the moment she arrived in the Land of Israel, no one ostracized her for donning *tefillin*, wearing a *tallit* — both commonly used by men in prayer — and devoting her time to studying and worship. Finally, Hannah Rachel was left alone; no one expected her to act "like everyone else," to marry, to have children.

In Ludmir, the city in Ukraine where she was born, things had been entirely different.

After ten years of marriage in which no children were born, Monish Verbermacher and his wife turned to the Seer of Lublin, one of the greatest Hasidic rabbis, so that he might bless them with offspring. Have no fear, he promised them, you will have a child within a year, and this child will have a very special soul. Monish promised the holy seer that he would raise the child to become a rabbi.

One year later, the embarrassed Verbermachers found themselves the parents of a beautiful baby girl. The father, a wealthy
merchant, kept his promise to the Seer of Lublin, and taught his
child to learn. And she always wanted to learn more. She soon sur-
passed her father in understanding and expertise. She would spend
hours holed up in her room learning — at a time when only men
were scholars in the Hasidic community — and when she wasn't
learning, she was praying.

When she reached the age of twelve, the age when girls take on
a commitment to Jewish commandments, Hannah Rachel's world
fell apart: her beloved mother died of an illness. Hannah Rachel began to spend long hours at her grave. During one of her visits, she
bumped into a gravestone, fell, and lost consciousness. She was unconscious for many days, and the doctors despaired of saving her.
And then one day, she sat up in her bed: I stood before the court of
the heavens, she told her astonished father, and was given a superi-
or soul, a new soul.

Hannah Rachel called off her engagement to a boy of her age from
the village. Calling off an engagement was no small matter: Monish
had to pay the boy's family a steep price in compensation, and Hannah Rachel was shunned by the community. She was not permitted
to pray in the synagogue's women's section. Nevertheless, Hannah
Rachel pushed ahead, creating the future that she now saw as her
path: to serve as a rabbi.

Soon everyone in town had learned of her healing powers. The
common folk would flock to her home to receive a blessing; for the
sick and disabled, she would add homemade tonics to her blessing.
She became known as the "Maiden of Ludmir."

Her father passed away when she was nineteen, and Hannah
Rachel built a structure of red brick to be her own **Beit Midrash**, or
house of study, using her inheritance. For the sake of modesty, she
would sit in her own room, where she also lived, and the Hasidim
would sit in the main hall. Her sermons would be given through a
half-open door, and even the ceremonial meal on Shabbat, Seuda
Shlishit, would be eaten separately in her room. The young woman

who had once been rare for her scholarship now became even more uncommon and groundbreaking: she was also a religious leader.

Her admirers and Hasidim were the simple folk, the poor. But the wealthier community members were both angry at Hannah Rachel and scared of her. They had never met a woman who, instead of marrying and having children, learned Torah. They fought her in every possible way, threatening to excommunicate her and throwing stones at the windows of the Beit Midrash. Finally, they asked Rabbi Mordecai of Chernobyl to come, and he convinced Hannah Rachel to marry.

Hannah Rachel did marry, but she soon divorced; we will never know why. She returned to her Beit Midrash, but she felt that the divine spirit had left her, so she departed for the Land of Israel.

The Maiden of Ludmir arrived in Jerusalem in 1860. In Jerusalem, no one fought Hannah Rachel. The divine spirit returned to her, her face glowed with holiness, women of all backgrounds flocked to her court — **Ashkenazi**, **Sephardic**, and Yemenite — and she once again wrote amulets, healed the sick, and effected miracles. Each morning she would hurry to the Western Wall, where she would don *tefillin* and pray. She was, in essence, the **rebbe** or **rabbanit** of a Hasidic community.

Hannah Rachel was buried on the Mount of Olives, and the women of Jerusalem would ascend to her grave on the anniversary of her death to have a **Hilula**, or celebration — but with time she was forgotten.

Roughly one hundred years after her death, interest in her was renewed, and research uncovered her grave and the writing on the tombstone:

The righteous Rabbanit Hannah Rachel daughter of Monish of Ludmir
22 Tammuz 5648
Most blessed of women in the tent of Torah
May her soul be bound up in the bond of eternal life

# ADD YOUR VOICE

*The only historical reference from Hannah Rachel Verbermacher's time comes from the censuses commissioned by Moses Montefiore in the nineteenth century, which reported on all of the Jews living in the Land of Israel, including in Jerusalem. Hannah Rachel appears twice in the censuses, once as "Rabbanit Rachel Hannah" and once as "The Righteous Rabbanit Hannah Rachel of Ludmir."*

## *Explore*

Aside from Rabbanit Hannah Rachel, Huldah the Prophetess, the poet Else Lasker Schüler, Henrietta Szold (see chapter 55), and Geulah Cohen (see chapter 11) are all buried in the cemetery on the Mount of Olives in Jerusalem, which is the oldest of the cemeteries in the Land of Israel. The mount contains three thousand years of history, with its slopes descending to the Gate of Mercy (or Golden Gate), whose gates are closed and sealed.

Learn more about the mount, its history, and who is buried there. Why have Jews wanted to be buried there for centuries? What does Jewish tradition relate about its special location?

## Give Back

---

Rabbanit Hannah Rachel brought together Jews from all different backgrounds as a community. Find yourself a Jewish pen pal from another country (you can ask parents or teachers to help, or use an initiative like the Global Jewish Pen Pal Program). Through your contact with your new friend, learn what a community looks like somewhere else. How does it differ from yours? What can you learn from your pen pal? How can you use this opportunity to create stronger ties between communities?

## See Something New

---

In her years in Jerusalem, Hannah Rachel would visit the Western Wall each morning. The Western Wall is Judaism's holiest site, the only retaining wall of the Second Temple area on the Temple Mount, built in the first century BCE.

Take a trip to the Western Wall Tunnels, the underground passageways dug over generations along the wall. If you have enough time, you can learn to guide a group of your own guests. Learn the story, thousands of years old, of the Jewish connection to the Temple Mount. You can also invite your guests to a journey through the world of archaeology, a journey that exposes, layer after layer, the history of Jerusalem throughout generations, and experience the multimedia Chain of Generations Center, which highlights the ties of generations of Jewish history to one another.

The Mount of Olives, where Hannah Rachel is buried, rises above the Kidron riverbed, where a number of impressive burial sites are located, including those believed to belong to Jehoshaphat, a king of Judah, and Absalom, one of King David's sons. Visit the promenade inside the riverbed that overlooks the walls of the Old City, the Gate of Mercy, and the Mount of Olives.

## Get Out of Your Comfort Zone

If you'd like to make a longer-term commitment in advance of your bat mitzvah, join the Shahak program online. Run by the Western Wall Heritage Foundation, the program takes you on a journey through a number of sessions that connect you to yourself, your family, the Western Wall, and more.

And if you're musically inclined, learn more about Hasidic music, and specifically the *nigun*, a melody that evokes the joy of prayer. Can you learn one and play it for your family or friends? Or perhaps volunteer to play at a seniors' residence or club?

# 57

# LILLIAN WALD

## *A Nurse Dedicated to Impoverished Immigrants*

N othing in her childhood can explain Lillian's choices. She was the daughter of a wealthy family, born in Cincinnati, Ohio, and was raised in Rochester, New York. She went to the best schools. And yet she chose to spend her life helping the underprivileged. Her grandparents had immigrated to the United States from Germany many years before Germany began to persecute the Jews who lived there. Her father was a successful merchant and her uncle was a well-known surgeon.

When she was twelve years old, Lillian's grandfather took her to a demonstration demanding that the University of Rochester admit women. Perhaps it was there that Lillian first felt the urge to influence and create change.

When she was in high school, Lillian's good friend fell ill and Lillian saw the nurses who cared for her. When her sister was in labor, she went to bring a nurse and bombarded her with questions. It was then that she decided to become a nurse herself.

In order to be accepted to the New York Hospital School of Nursing, Lillian lied about her age. Studies in the nursing school gave Lillian a lot of practical experience but little theoretical learning; she wanted to understand the human body, and therefore registered for a medical college.

In parallel, she began to teach Jewish immigrant women basic hygiene. These were the days of **pogroms** in Russia, and hundreds of thousands of Jews were leaving Russia for the United States. They did not speak English nor did they understand the way of life in the new land, and Lillian took it upon herself to teach them.

In the middle of a lesson, while explaining to the immigrant women how to make a bed and holding a clean sheet in her hand, a small girl burst into the room — changing Lillian's life.

Stuttering, the girl tried to explain what she wanted; Lillian understood that her mother was deathly ill. The two left the class and ran to the girl's home, through the derelict, filthy streets. The stench was so bad that Lillian was forced to cover her nose with the corner of the sheet, which she had brought with her in case she might need a bandage for the ailing mother.

They arrived at a dark home, with a stained, creaky wooden floor. Seven family members, as well as renters, were all crowded into the home's two rooms.

The young mother lay covered in blood along with her baby, born just days earlier. This was the introduction that Lillian — graduate of nursing school and a medical student — first had to the abject poverty of immigrants on the Lower East Side of New York, at the time the most crowded neighborhood on earth.

"That was my baptism of fire," Lillian later recounted.

Lillian took care of the mother and baby, and also scrubbed the floor, cooked for everyone, and promised to return.

Lillian left college and the easy life and moved to the center of the neighborhood with another nurse, Mary Brewster. Only if they lived in the neighborhood, they realized, could they be available at all times. They cared for the sick, but that was not enough for them. Lillian wished to teach the people how to stay healthy, so she tried to understand the reasons behind the illnesses: she would check if there was enough food in a house, if the house had a bathroom inside or only outdoors, and whether the people from the house were going out and working.

Many of the immigrants were proud people who would not accept medical services for free, and therefore Lillian and Mary set a price for their aid: 10 cents. When people did not have enough, they would accept services instead. The tailor would give them an item of clothing for their treatment, the carpenter, an item of furniture.

The need for nurses in the neighborhood was far greater than two women could handle, and more nurses joined their forces. Eventually, they bought a building in the center of the neighborhood, on Henry Street, and the nurses departed from there to their work each morning. From the building, now known as the Henry Street Settlement, Lillian ran other programs: she made sure that schools served meals and she fought to get nurses into schools to care for the students' health.

Lillian was an advocate of rights for many different groups. Children were sent to work at age six or seven, and worked for ten or even twelve hours a day. Lillian made sure they were not exploited, and tried to pass federal laws to protect them. Her dream — which materialized later on — was that child labor would be forbidden by law, and that children would be required to go to school. She also insisted that the classes the Settlement House gave be racially integrated, and became a founding member of the NAACP, hosting the organization's first major conference at Henry Street. Finally, she fought for women: she organized suffrage marches in New York and made sure that the Settlement afforded women job opportunities.

Many years have passed since the Henry Street Settlement was created. The world has changed. Lillian Wald is no longer with us. But the building is active even today, and still serves tens of thousands of people in New York, opening doors of opportunity through social services, arts, and health care.

# ADD YOUR VOICE

## *Explore*

Lillian Wald coined the term "public health," and saw the field as much broader than just treating specific ailments; it encompasses preventing disease and promoting health. Her work included ensuring that there were lunches in public schools, creating parks and playgrounds, and helping women find employment. Learn more about the field of public health and what it has grown into today.

## *Give Back*

Lillian Wald tackled poverty from within the immigrant community. Today, many organizations address the same issues by offering financial education to help people leave the cycle of poverty. What organizations around you help reinforce good financial habits or provide workshops or counseling on finances to help fight poverty? Look at your local Jewish Federation's website and see whether they offer workshops in financial literacy that you can support; you may even want to organize a workshop for your class or a group of friends.

## *See Something New*

The Tenement Museum in New York illuminates the immigrant experience in America, telling stories that include those of the millions of Jews who came from eastern and southern Europe during the late nineteenth and early twentieth centuries. If you can't visit in person, you can still learn more about immigration and immigrant families through their online materials. Only a few blocks away is the Museum at Eldridge Street, which tells the story of the nineteenth-century synagogue and the immigrants who built it; its website also contains online activities that can teach you more about the community.

## Get Out of Your Comfort Zone

Lillian built the playground at Henry Street in order to offer a real recreational space; before that, children spent time in the streets, where real playing was impossible. In honor of Lillian Wald, host a game for your friends — soccer, baseball, or something else that you enjoy.

# 58

# STEFA (STEFANIA) WILCZYŃSKA

## *Mother to Jewish Orphans during the Holocaust*

W hat does the life of a mother of 110 look like?
Think about the life of a parent of three, for example: caring, feeding, soothing, helping with homework, running to meetings with teachers, driving to after-school programs.

Now multiply that by more than thirty-six.

Perhaps that is the reason that very few people have heard of Stefa Wilczyńska; someone who cares for 110 children doesn't have the time to tell her story.

So we'll tell her story instead: Stefa was born to a wealthy family in Warsaw, the capital of Poland. When she finished her studies at a girls' high school, she studied science in two universities, in Belgium and Switzerland.

She returned to Poland and opened an orphanage with Janusz Korczak, a well-known educator, a man who was full of warmth and humor.

Janusz Korczak's story is known to many: when the Nazis demanded that the children in the orphanage be handed over, he refused offers of sanctuary for himself; he walked with the children from the orphanage to death at the hands of the Nazis. But few know about Stefa, who ran the orphanage with Korczak and also perished with the children.

Korczak and Stefa, father and mother to the children, ran the orphanage at 92 Korchmalna Street in Warsaw for thirty years, and it always had 110 children, aged 7 to 14 — children in elementary school, children with their own moods, children who were naughty, children who cried, children who had pain, children who behaved perfectly. Father and mother did not have families of their own.

At six in the morning, Stefa would put on music to wake up the children and everyone would get organized for breakfast. Children were not permitted to miss breakfast. Stefa would sit next to the weaker and skinnier children to make sure they ate well. Children were required to finish all of the food on their plates; Stefa did not allow waste. If there was leftover chocolate milk in their cups, she drank it.

After the meal, Stefa would stand at the door and make sure that each of the children left safely for school, that everyone had their food packed, that their shoes were polished and tied properly, and that no one had forgotten a sweater.

And once the children had left, Stefa would tackle the house: cleaning, washing, bills, ordering food and clothes, and many more tasks that were necessary for a mother of 110. The orphanage had professionals who were responsible for cooking, washing, and teaching. Stefa chose each carefully, and they were all full partners in the children's education and the house's maintenance.

Sick children remained at home. Being sick, the children would say, was the real fun. Stefa would cuddle and coddle them, giving them medications and cooking porridge, spending hours with the patient.

After lunch, the children would sit, as in any other house, and prepare homework and then play. There were also after-school activities and plays and preparation for Jewish holidays.

After dinner and showers — Korczak would oversee the boys and Stefa the girls — the children would get into bed and Stefa would watch over them. The door to her room was always open to hear if someone was crying or coughing, to cover someone whose blanket had fallen off.

Children had to leave at age fourteen, to exit to the wide world, so that there would be more room for new children to join the house. This was not easy — not for the children, who were still quite young, and not for the educators, who were forced to see them encounter great difficulties. Stefa would write letters to her children around the world, from South America to the Land of Israel. They would write to her and tell her about their lives.

In 1938, she left the house and the children after twenty-six years to go to the Land of Israel, spending time in Ein Harod. It seemed that an important and crucial part of her life had drawn to a close. But with troubling news coming from Europe, and Nazi Germany preparing for war, Stefa knew that she had to return to her children — even though her friends at Ein Harod had already arranged for papers for her to stay.

She left the relatively safe Land of Israel and returned to Warsaw. She was with the children when they moved to the ghetto and did everything in her power to keep them from sensing the calamity that was taking place around them; she even took them to summer camp.

And then, in the summer of 1942, the order came: the children and their educators must present themselves to be taken to an unknown destination. Stefa and Korczak were not naïve; they knew what the journey would mean, but they chose to turn it into a celebration.

Stefa selected each child's most festive clothing and put identical blue backpacks on their backs. Together they boarded the train to the Treblinka extermination camp in neat lines. Korczak stood at the head, arms around two of the children; Stefa and the other staff members walked with the group.

None survived.

At the end of the war, a monument was dedicated in Treblinka to their journey; it reads "Janusz Korczak and the children." No one remembered Stefa, who could have remained safe in the Land of Israel but chose to return.

# ADD YOUR VOICE

*"I am convinced that in the current conditions my place is with them [the children] and therefore I am on my way."*

*(Stefa, on her way to the ship from Haifa back to Warsaw, 1939)*

## Explore

Janusz Korczak was a well-known educator who wrote books about pedagogy and works of fiction. The orphanage that he and Stefa helmed put many of his theories into action; the children who lived there remember the children's "self-government," in which even Korczak himself was judged on three occasions. Look into his theories and practice. Do you agree or disagree with the way Janusz and Stefa chose to raise the children in the orphanage?

## Give Back

Emunah is an organization that cares for people in Israel, with a focus on children and families. Among other things, it runs homes for children aged eight to eighteen who cannot be at home with their families. You can fundraise for a home or program or, if you're in Israel, celebrate your bat mitzvah with a joint activity within one of the centers.

## See Something New

The Martyrs' Forest, not far from Jerusalem, is dedicated to the memory of those who perished in the Holocaust; six million trees were planted there to immortalize the dead. Within the immense forest, there is one plot devoted to the children who perished, which holds one and a half million trees. The money for planting the trees was donated by teachers and students, among others. If you visit the forest, you can stand by the impressive Scroll of Fire memorial and hike in the Anne Frank (see chapter 15) area on a pathway along which small signs have been erected with excerpts from her diary and her pictures, leading to a memorial that evokes her empty room. The B'nai B'rith Cave, in the center of the forest's large clearing, serves as a place to commune with the memory of the Holocaust's victims.

You can take a hike in the forest, on paths both visible and hidden. You can even go as far as the Ksalon River, the *moshav* of Beit Meir, the HaMasrek Reserve, and descend along the riverbank to the B'nai B'rith Cave (note: this hike is for experienced hikers only). You can also bike along the forest's pathways and along the Ksalon River, with its many springs.

## Get Out of Your Comfort Zone

While Janusz Korczak is well-known, Stefa's work has gone virtually unrecognized. Not only was she a beloved mother and educator to hundreds of children, but she kept the orphanage running by raising funds from the community, wrote articles, and managed the home's budget. Sadly, her name does not even appear on the monument to Janusz Korczak and the children in Treblinka or the one in Warsaw. Can you use a medium that speaks to you — writing, drawing, social media — to bring her story to light?

June 19, 1914–April 30, 1984
25 Sivan 5674–28 Nisan 5744

# 59

# ZELDA

## *The Poet from a Hasidic Dynasty*

Zelda, everyone called her, friends and readers alike. Zelda —
with no last name — was a brilliant poet who did not dare publish her poetry. She lived in a rickety, leaking house with a paved
courtyard in the Me'ah She'arim neighborhood in Jerusalem. No one
in Me'ah She'arim had published a book of poetry.

Zelda was born in Russia and grew up in the home of her grandfather, a rabbi and the grandson of the founder of **Chabad Hasidic**
movement, surrounded by a loving family. In 1925, when she was
eleven years old, her family moved to the Land of Israel and settled
in Jerusalem, and Zelda experienced an unbearably painful year: her
grandfather and father both passed away during that first year and
Zelda, an only child, said the mourner's prayer — **Kaddish** — for
both of them in the synagogue. In her first school she felt tremendous pressure; even the light of Jerusalem, she wrote in a poem, was
threatening:

> Jerusalem ensnared
> My free spirit.
> I drowned in the light,
> I forgot my name.

But Zelda the girl grew into Zelda the young woman, became accustomed to Jerusalem's light, studied in the Mizrachi Seminar with the best teachers, surrounded by loving friends, and flourished.

When she reached the age of eighteen and finished her studies, the world felt like her oyster. She traveled to the beach in Tel Aviv, studied painting in Haifa, worked as a house painter in Jerusalem, registered for the Bezalel Art Academy, and began her studies.

But circumstances changed. Zelda needed to care for her mother and left the academy. She lived with her mother on the outskirts of Me'ah She'arim — and when she married, her husband moved in with both of them.

Zelda, who had studied in the Mizrachi Seminar for teachers, became a teacher, and was admired and loved by all of the young children she taught. She did not publish a single volume of poetry; she was embarrassed and afraid to share the innermost places in her heart with the world. Fortunately, her poetry was stronger than her embarrassment, and once in a while she would publish a poem in the newspaper supplements.

When she was fifty-three, something happened in Zelda's world — and in the worlds of all poetry lovers in Israel: her first book of poetry, *Leisure*, was published.

And the land was abuzz.

Everyone read the book, everyone talked about it, everyone asked where the incredible poet had been until now. And she never again had quiet in her courtyard or her home. People came on pilgrimages, people wanted to be near her, poets and writers and even common folk, from Jerusalem and from Tel Aviv and from Haifa and from the different **kibbutzim**.

It is said that when she grew old, after she had published another five books of poetry, the little paved courtyard of her old house looked like the courtyards of her ancestors, the **rebbes** of Chabad. People surrounded her and awaited every utterance. And when she grew sick and was near death, she was cared for by dozens of younger friends, a small consolation for the children she had never had. When she passed away, the radio played a song whose lyrics she had written.

Each of us has a name
given by God
and given by our parents...
Each of us has a name
given by the sea
and given by
our death.

# ADD YOUR VOICE

## *Explore*

Poetry written in Hebrew may seem common to us now, but the Hebrew language has undergone many shifts over time. Hebrew was the language used in the Bible and remained in use in Jewish prayer, but it was not used in everyday life for almost two millennia. When Zelda wrote her poetry in Hebrew, it had only recently been reborn. Learn more about Eliezer Ben-Yehuda and the rebirth of the language. What languages were spoken by Jews in the Land of Israel speaking during the end of the nineteenth and the early twentieth centuries? Why did Eliezer Ben-Yehuda feel so strongly about Hebrew? What actions did he take to revive the language? How did the people around him feel about it? How did his children feel about it?

## *Give Back*

Zelda's poetry drew together Jews from around the State of Israel — from many different backgrounds. It was her connection to young poet Yona Wallach, in particular, that finally encouraged her to make her poetry public. In her spirit, form stronger connections with Jews the world over by building relationships with Jews in another country. Encourage your school to join a school twinning program like the **Jewish Agency**'s Global School Twinning Network, which connects Jewish schools across the globe to learn more about other communities and form deeper connections with students in other locations.

## See Something New

Try to uncover the secret of Zelda's magic, the magic that drew people from a variety of communities and worldviews to her. To do so, build a route — either real or virtual — around the different stations in her life.

Her mother's house, which was also her home for many years, was at 31 Tzefania Street in Jerusalem. Here she was visited by a seven-year-old student, Amos Oz, who was in love with his teacher and jealous of her husband. Many years later, when he was a famous author, he wrote about her with longing.

Another station is the Moledet HaYeled school, where she met Amos Oz. It stands near her home, at 5 Zecharia Street.

You can also visit the Shpitzer School, called Yehudioff House, at 24 Ezra Street, where Zelda studied as a girl.

In her home at 24 Ovadiah Street, Zelda first met the young poet Yona Wallach, who worshipped Zelda and her poetry and insisted on collecting and publishing them; together, they got her first book, *Leisure*, published.

In her final home, at 11 HaKalir Street in the Shaare Hesed neighborhood, Zelda lived until her death.

Zelda was the granddaughter of the Lubavitcher Rebbe.

You can celebrate your bat mitzvah in the spirit of Chabad. The final rebbe, Zelda's cousin, wrote that the bat mitzvah celebration must be like a wedding day. According to Chabad's teaching, the bat mitzvah is a girl's true birthday. The young woman should give charity — *tzedakah* — three times that day: once before the morning, or Shaharit, prayer; once before the afternoon, or Minhah, prayer; and a donation to an educational institution. Moreover, she should learn **Psalm** 13 and recite it for her guests.

# MORE INSPIRING
# JEWISH WOMEN

T he stories told in this book are just the tip of the iceberg; Jewish women have made their mark on the worlds of community, culture, feminism, leadership, health, and science for centuries.
Below are some other inspirational women whom you may want
to learn more about. Explore their stories to understand how they
used their talents to effect *tikkun olam* and make the world a better
place. Who else would you include on your list of noteworthy Jewish women?

**Mayim Bialik**
*1975–, U.S.*
Actress, game show host, author, and neuroscientist

**Letty Cottin Pogrebin**
*1939–, U.S.*
Founding editor of *Ms.* Magazine, author, and activist

**Beatie (Bracha) Deutsch**
*1989–, U.S./Israel*
Israeli national champion in the marathon
and half-marathon

**Andrea Dworkin**
*1946–2005, U.S.*
Warrior against pornography and violence against women

**Sandy Eisenberg Sasso**
*1947–, U.S.*
First female **Reconstructionist** rabbi

**Ray Frank**
*1861–1948, U.S.*
First American Jewish woman to preach from a pulpit

**Marcia Freedman**
*1938–2021, U.S./Israel*
First openly lesbian member of Israel's **Knesset**

**Freha bat Avraham**
*18th century, Tunisia/Morocco*
Hebrew poet and scholar

**Betty Friedan**
*1921–2006, U.S.*
Author of *The Feminine Mystique* and cofounder
of the National Organization for Women

**Gal Gadot**
*1985–, Israel*
Miss Israel 2004 and Wonder Woman actress

**Carol Gilligan**
*1936–, U.S.*
Psychologist who brought the female perspective
to the study of ethics

**Emma Goldman**
*1869–1940, Russia/U.S./Europe/Canada*
Anarchist and activist for women's rightsand social issues

**Blu Greenberg**
*1936–, U.S./Israel*
Founder of the Jewish **Orthodox** Feminist Alliance

**Nadine Gordimer**
*1923–2014, South Africa*
Nobel Prize winner and anti-apartheid activist

**Helena of Adiabene**
*1st century, Jerusalem*
Queen and convert to Judaism

**Sara Hurwitz**
*1977–, South Africa/U.S.*
First "Maharat" (female religious leader)
in an Orthodox congregation

**Norma Joseph**
*1944–, U.S./Canada*
Lobbyist for women's divorce rights

**Raquel Liberman**
*1900–1934, Ukraine/Poland/Argentina*
Combatant against human trafficking and prostitution

**Yavilah McCoy**
*1972–, U.S.*
Jewish diversity activist

**Maud Nathan**
*1862–1946, U.S.*
Suffragist and founder of the New York
Consumer's League

**Anne Neuberger**
*1976–, U.S.*
Deputy national security advisor for cyber
and emerging technology

**Sally Priesand**
*1946–, U.S.*
First female rabbi in America

**Aly Raisman**
*1994–, U.S.*
Gymnast and Olympian

**Haviva Reik**
*1914–1944, Israel*
Paratrooper into Nazi-occupied Europe

**Adrienne Rich**
*1929–2012, U.S.*
Poet and essayist on motherhood, sexuality,
and **anti-Semitism**

**Hanna Rovina**
*1888–1980, Israel*
The First Lady of Hebrew theater

**Alice Shalvi**
*1926–2023, Germany/UK/Israel*
Founder of the Israel Women's Network

**Susan Sontag**
*1933–2004, U.S.*
Writer on AIDS, illness, human rights, and morality

**Gloria Steinem**
*1934–, U.S.*
Founder of the National Women's
Political Caucus and *Ms.* Magazine

**Barbra Streisand**
*1942–, U.S.*
Singer and actress

**Sydney Taylor**
*1904–1978, U.S.*
Writer of children's books

**Rebecca Walker**
*1969–, U.S.*
Writer on race, gender, and multicultural identity

**Angela Warnick Buchdahl**
*1972–, South Korea/U.S.*
First Asian American woman to be ordained
as a rabbi and cantor

**Naomi Wolf**
*1962–, U.S.*
Author of *The Beauty Myth*

**Rachel Yanait Ben-Zvi**
*1886–1979, Israel*
**Zionist** activist and groundbreaking educator

# THE WIDE WORLD
# OF BAT MITZVAH CEREMONIES:

## *A Journey through Time and around the Globe*

T he history of bat mitzvah celebrations is a fascinating one. While no fixed ceremony has emerged, different cultures and communities have developed their own rituals and prayers to mark the important moment in a girl's life. In this chapter, we take a look at these ceremonies and prayers. If a custom or ritual speaks to you, you can incorporate it within the celebration you are building for yourself.

Roughly 150 years ago, Italian Jewry created a ceremony for girls who had reached the age of *mitzvot*. Rabbi Isaac Pardo formulated the language for the first ceremony when he served as rabbi of Verona. Leading up to the bat mitzvah, the girls in the Italian Jewish community would study with the rabbi. On a Sunday around the **Shavuot** holiday, a ceremony was held for all of the girls who had reached age twelve. The bat mitzvah girls would dress in long, white dresses (but not down to the floor; they did not want to look too much like brides). They entered in a procession, with crowns of flowers on their heads, accompanied by the singing of a choir, and stood before the open **ark**.

The girls recited a form of the *Sheheheyahu* blessing, a blessing of thanks for great joy, and then a second short prayer.

# Blessings Recited by Girls at the Italian Bat Mitzvah Ceremony

בָּרוּךְ אַתָּה אֱלֹהֵינוּ מֶלֶךְ הָעוֹלָם שֶׁגְּמָלַנִי כָּל טוֹב וְשֶׁהֶחֱיָנִי וְקִיְּמָנִי לַזְּמַן הַזֶּה לָבוֹא בָּאֲנָשִׁים וּלְקַבֵּל עַל מִצְוֹתֶיךָ :

Blessed are You, our God, King of the universe, Who has rendered me all manner of good, and has given me life and sustained me until this time, so as to be counted among adults and to accept the yoke of Your commandments.

יְהוָה יְהוָה אֵל רַחוּם וְחַנּוּן אֶרֶךְ אַפַּיִם וְרַב חֶסֶד וֶאֱמֶת. הִנֵּה הַיּוֹם הַחִלּוֹתִי גֶּשֶׁת אֶל הֵיכַל קָדְשְׁךָ בְּיִרְאָתְךָ לְהִסְתַּפֵּחַ בְּנַחֲלָתְךָ :

Lord, Lord, merciful and gracious God, slow to anger and abundant in kindness and truth: Behold, today I have begun to visit Your holy Sanctuary, with awe of You, to become part of Your inheritance.

Another special prayer was written for the occasion; the entire community blessed the girls with it.

# Prayer for the Bat Mitzvah Girl

מִי שֶׁבֵּרַךְ אִמּוֹתֵינוּ שָׂרָה רִבְקָה רָחֵל וְלֵאָה הוּא יְבָרֵךְ אֶת הַנַּעֲרָה _____ בַּת _____ שֶׁהִגִּיעָה לְפִרְקָהּ.

May He Who blessed our mothers Sarah, Rebecca, Rachel, and Leah bless the girl _____ daughter of _____ who has reached her age.

אָבִינוּ שֶׁבַּשָּׁמַיִם אָב הָרַחֲמָן יָגֵן בַּעֲדָהּ וְיִשְׁמֹר אֶת נַפְשָׁהּ. יָסִיר מִמֶּנָּה כָּל מַחֲלָה וּמִכָּל צָרָה וְנֶזֶק יַצִּילָהּ. יִשְׂמְחוּ בָּהּ אָבִיהָ וְאִמָּהּ וְתִמְצָא חֵן וְשֵׂכֶל טוֹב בְּעֵינֵי אֱלֹהִים וְאָדָם וִיקֻיַּם בָּהּ (בָּהֶן) מִקְרָא שֶׁכָּתוּב "אִשָּׁה יִרְאַת יְהוָה הִיא תִּתְהַלָּל תְּנוּ לָהּ מִפְּרִי יָדֶיהָ וִיהַלְלוּהָ בַשְּׁעָרִים מַעֲשֶׂיהָ" (משלי ל"א, א'–ב'). אָמֵן כֵּן יְהִי רָצוֹן.

May Our Father Who is in heaven, merciful Father, protect her and guard her soul. May He remove any illness and save her from all sorrow and harm. May her father and mother rejoice in her and may she find favor and approbation in the eyes of God and man and may the biblical verse "It is for her fear of the Lord that a woman is to be praised; extol her for the fruit of her hand and let her works praise her in the gates" (Proverbs 31:1–2) be fulfilled in her. Amen, may it be Your will.

The choir then sang **Psalm** 100, and the girls recited the **Ten Commandments** by heart, demonstrating their maturity and Jewish faith, and then they read the Song of Deborah (Judges 5:1–31; see chapter 12).

# Selections from the Song of Deborah
## (Judges 1–7, 12)

וַתָּשַׁר דְּבוֹרָה, וּבָרָק בֶּן-אֲבִינֹעַם, בַּיּוֹם הַהוּא לֵאמֹר.

Then Deborah sang, and Barak, son of Avinoam, on that day, saying:

בִּפְרֹעַ פְּרָעוֹת בְּיִשְׂרָאֵל, בְּהִתְנַדֵּב עָם, בָּרְכוּ, יְהֹוָה.

At a time of tumult in Israel, when the people willingly offered themselves — bless the Lord.

שִׁמְעוּ מְלָכִים, הַאֲזִינוּ רֹזְנִים: אָנֹכִי, לַיהֹוָה אָנֹכִי אָשִׁירָה, אֲזַמֵּר לַיהֹוָה אֱלֹהֵי יִשְׂרָאֵל.

Hear, O kings, give ear, O princes: As for me, I will sing to the Lord, I will sing praise to the God of Israel.

יְהֹוָה, בְּצֵאתְךָ מִשֵּׂעִיר בְּצַעְדְּךָ מִשְּׂדֵה אֱדוֹם, אֶרֶץ רָעָשָׁה, גַּם-שָׁמַיִם נָטָפוּ; גַּם-עָבִים, נָטְפוּ מָיִם.

Lord, when You went forth from Se'ir, when You marched out of the field of Edom, the earth trembled; the heaves also rained, the clouds, too, dropped water.

הָרִים נָזְלוּ, מִפְּנֵי יְהֹוָה: זֶה סִינַי מִפְּנֵי, יְהֹוָה אֱלֹהֵי יִשְׂרָאֵל.

The mountains melted before the Lord, [even] that Sinai, before the Lord God of Israel.

בִּימֵי שַׁמְגַּר בֶּן עֲנָת, בִּימֵי יָעֵל, חָדְלוּ, אֳרָחוֹת ; וְהֹלְכֵי נְתִיבוֹת יֵלְכוּ אֳרָחוֹת עֲקַלְקַלּוֹת.

In the days of Shamgar, son of Anat, in the days of Yael, the highways ceased, and travelers followed crooked byways.

חָדְלוּ פְרָזוֹן בְּיִשְׂרָאֵל חָדֵלוּ עַד שַׁקַּמְתִּי דְּבוֹרָה, שַׁקַּמְתִּי אֵם בְּיִשְׂרָאֵל...

Those of valor ceased, they ceased in Israel, until I, Deborah, arose, arising as a mother in Israel...

עוּרִי עוּרִי דְּבוֹרָה, עוּרִי עוּרִי דַּבְּרִי-שִׁיר ; קוּם בָּרָק וּשְׁבֵה שֶׁבְיְךָ, בֶּן אֲבִינֹעַם...

Awake, awake, Deborah; awake, awake, utter a song; arise, Barak, take your captives...

The figure of Deborah, prophetess and judge, strategic military leader, was chosen by the Italian communities as a symbol for the bat mitzvah girls and the hope for meaningful lives and the ability to grow. The creators of the ceremony saw in Deborah, who stood out as a leader in a generation in which other women were not even named in the Bible, a model for young girls to identify with and a statement that anything was possible.

The Italian ceremony became a tradition within the community. My friend Yonatan Basi, visiting his mother at the seniors' home on **Kibbutz** Sde Eliyahu, asked her how she had celebrated her bat mitzvah. His mother, Fierra Levi, and her friends Nurit and Rita, all three of whom had been born in Italy and are today between the ages of eight-six and ninety, became emotional. They remembered their bat mitzvah parties. They had each come from a different city: Fierra had celebrated in Ferrara, Nurit in Trieste, and Rita in Rome, and each of the cities had slightly different customs. But the experience had been so powerful that seventy-five years later they remembered how they had done their hair and what dress they had worn.

About twenty years ago, I was invited to a private bat mitzvah party in the magnificent synagogue in Milan, Italy. The bat mitzvah girl had been given a gift from her parents — the translation of my book, *A Jewish Woman's Prayer Book*, into Italian. Much like 150 years ago, this time, too, the ceremony was held before the community and took place on Sunday so that **Shabbat**-observant guests could come. Two bat mitzvah girls marched into the sanctuary, where the rabbi awaited them. He led the girls and their families to the ark and opened it. There, before the ancient **Torah** scrolls in their colorful and spectacular adornments, he blessed them in the name of the congregation. Their fathers recited the "Prayer for the Bat Mitzvah Girl" and the girls recited the traditional Italian bat mitzvah prayer, quoted the Song of Deborah, and gave a speech. The ceremony ended with the blessings of the congregation and a *seudat mitzvah*, a festive meal.

In Altona, in northern Germany, a bat mitzvah ceremony was held in the synagogue in 1867 and thereafter; evidence of the ceremony being held exists up until the Holocaust. The ceremony was a "public test in religious studies for girls": the bat mitzvah girls demonstrated their knowledge in Jewish law and commandments for the community. Afterwards, the synagogue's youth choir sang the first sixteen verses of Psalm 119, and the community's rabbi blessed the girls.

# Rabbi's Blessing for Bat Mitzvah Girls, Altona, Germany

יְשִׂימְכֶן אֱלֹהִים כְּשָׂרָה רִבְקָה רָחֵל וְלֵאָה... יְהוָה יְבָרֶךְ אֶתְכֶן וְיִשְׁמֹר עֲלֵיכֶן מִכָּל פֶּגַע, יְהוָה יָאֵר אֶת פָּנָיו עֲלֵיכֶן בִּידִידוּת וְתִמְצֶאנָה נָא חֵן בְּעֵינָיו וּבְעֵינֵי הָאֲנָשִׁים. יְהוָה יִפְרֹשׁ אֶת כַּנְפֵי הַנְהָגָתוֹ עֲלֵיכֶן...

May God make you like Sarah, Rebecca, Rachel, and Leah... May God bless you and guard you from all harm, may God shine His face on you in friendship and may you find favor in His eyes and in the eyes of people. May God spread the wings of His guidance over you...

In my search for women's prayer, I found a rare and special book, a light on my path, and it contained a prayer for the twelve-year-old girl, written by Fanny Neuda (chapter 38) for her community in what is now the Czech Republic. The prayers were written in German, around the same time that girls began to celebrate bat mitzvahs in Italy. Did the prayer accompany a ceremony? Was it read in the synagogue? Unfortunately, so much information has been lost over the years; I could not find any evidence about such a ceremony.

## A Young Girl's Prayer, by Fanny Neuda

תְּפִלַּת הַנַּעֲרָה הַצְּעִירָה,
פָאנִי נוֹיְדָא

שֶׁקֶר הַחֵן וְהֶבֶל הַיֹּפִי
אִשָּׁה יִרְאַת יְהֹוָה הִיא
תִתְהַלָּל.
(משלי ל"א, ל)

Grace is deceiving and beauty is transient; a woman who fears God — she shall be praised. (Proverbs 31:30)

אֱלֹהֵינוּ שֶׁבַּשָּׁמַיִם וּבָאָרֶץ,
הָאֵל הַטּוֹב. אַתָּה דוֹאֵג לְכָל
בְּרוּאֶיךָ, אָב נֶאֱמָן. בְּצֵל כְּנָפְךָ
חוֹסִים כָּל יְצוּרֶיךָ.

Our God Who is in heaven and on earth, God Who is good: You attend to all of Your creatures; faithful Father, all of Your creations take refuge under Your wings.

גַּם לִי קָרָאתָ בִּתְּךָ, גַּם אוֹתִי
מְלַוָּה אַהֲבָתְךָ, אַהֲבַת עוֹלָם.
בִּנְאוֹת דֶּשֶׁא מֹרִיקִים חָלְפוּ
עָלַי יְמֵי יַלְדוּתִי. אוֹדְךָ עַל
נְעוּרַי הַמְאֻשָּׁרִים, אוֹדְךָ
עַל מַה שֶׁאֲנִי. נָתַתָּ לִי מִכָּל
טוֹב, אֵם וְאָב יְקָרִים לְצִדִּי,
מַנְחִים אוֹתִי בְּרֹךְ וּבְאַהֲבָה,
בְּעֵצָה וּבְעֶזְרָה, מְטַפְּלִים
וּמְפַרְנְסִים אוֹתִי, מְעַטְּרִים
אֶת חַיַּי בִּשְׂמָחוֹת מְתוּקוֹת
וְרַבוֹת חֵן.

You have called me, too, Your daughter; to me, too, You extend Your love — an eternal love. My childhood has passed in green pastures; I thank you for my happy youth; I thank You for what I am. You have given me all kinds of goodness: a dear mother and father at my side, guiding me with gentleness and love, with advice and help, caring for me and sustaining me, enhancing my life with sweet and heartwarming joys.

בַּעֲנָוָה, אֵלִי, אֲנִי קְרֵבָה
אֵלֶיךָ, פּוֹרֶשֶׂת צְפוּנוֹת לִבִּי
וּמוֹדָה לָךְ.

With humility, my Lord, I approach You, revealing the hidden secrets of my heart, and offering thanks to You.

330

אַתָּה רוֹאֶה לְנַפְשִׁי, כַּסֵּפֶר הַפָּתוּחַ מֻנָּח תּוֹכִי לְפָנֶיךָ. כָּל סַעֲרַת רוּחַ הַמְּנִיעָה אֶת לִבִּי, כָּל נְשִׁימָה, כָּל הֶבֶל פֶּה הַמַּרְעִיד מֵיתָרִים, כָּל מַחֲשָׁבָה הַמַּסְעִירָה אֶת נַפְשִׁי, אֵינָם נִסְתָּרִים מִנֶּגֶד עֵינֶיךָ. לוּ יִהְיוּ כָּל רִגְשׁוֹתַי, מַחֲשְׁבוֹתַי וּמַעֲשַׂי נוֹשְׂאִים חֵן וָחֶסֶד מִלְּפָנֶיךָ, וְתַצִּילֵנִי מִיֵּצֶר הָרָע וְתֵן בְּלִבִּי הַכְנָעָה וַעֲנָוָה.

You see into my soul; my innermost being is before You as an open book. No emotion that moves my heart, no breath, no utterance of my voice, no thought that animates my soul — none is hidden from Your eyes. If only all my emotions, my thoughts, and my actions might find favor and grace before You. Deliver me from the evil inclination and imbue my heart with submission and humility.

אָבִינוּ שֶׁבַּשָּׁמַיִם, הַנְחֵה אֶת לִבִּי לִבְחֹר בַּדֶּרֶךְ הַטּוֹבָה וְלֹא לִסְטוֹת מִדֶּרֶךְ הַיָּשָׁר. בְּמָקוֹם שֶׁבּוֹ אֲנִי, הֶחָסֵרָה נִסָּיוֹן, לֹא אֵדַע לְהַבְחִין בֵּין טוֹב וָרָע, חָנֵּן אוֹתִי בְּחָכְמָתֶךָ, לַמְּדֵנִי לְהַכִּיר בָּאֱמֶת, לְמַעַן אֶשְׁמֹר עַל צְנִיעוּת וּמִדּוֹת טוֹבוֹת, עַל דְּבָרֶיךָ וּמִצְווֹתֶיךָ אַקְפִּיד בֶּאֱמוּנָה וּבְאַהֲבָה, וּבְנִקְיוֹן כַּפַּיִם וּבַאֲדִיקוּת אֶתְהַלֵּךְ לְפָנֶיךָ.

Our Father Who is in heaven: Guide my heart to choose the way that is good and not to deviate from the straight path. Where I — lacking experience — am unable to distinguish between good and evil, grace me with Your wisdom, teach me to recognize the truth, that I may maintain modesty and good traits, that I may punctiliously observe Your words and Your commandments with faith and with love, and walk before You wholeheartedly and with devotion.

אַל נָא תִּתֵּן אֶת לִבִּי לְהֶבֶל
וּלְרִיק, וְלַהֲנָאוֹת עוֹלָם אַל
תִּתֵּן לְעַרְפְּלֵנִי, שֶׁלֹּא אוֹצִיא
לַשָּׁוְא אֶת עִתּוֹתַי הַיְקָרוֹת,
הָעִתִּים שֶׁעָלַי לְקַיֵּם בָּהֶן
אֶת חוֹבוֹתַי. יְהִי רָצוֹן, שֶׁלֹּא
אָסוּר בְּשָׁעָה שֶׁל קַלּוּת
דַּעַת מֵאִמְרֵי פִּיךָ, שֶׁכְּבוֹד
הַבְּתוּלָה וְהַלֵּב הַזַּךְ יִהְיוּ לִי
לַעֲדִי יְקַר עֶרֶךְ.

בָּרְכֵנִי, אֵלִי, בְּבִינָה וּבִתְבוּנָה,
בִּבְרִיאוּת גּוּף וָנֶפֶשׁ, בְּלֵב
שָׂמֵחַ וּשְׂבַע רָצוֹן. תֵּן שֶׁלְּעוֹלָם
לֹא אָסוּר מִמִּצְוַת כִּבּוּד אָב
וָאֵם, שֶׁלֹּא אֶפְגַּע וְלֹא אַכְעִיס
אֶת הוֹרַי הַיְקָרִים, שֶׁיַּעֲלֶה
בְּיָדִי לְשַׂמֵּחַ אוֹתָם בְּמַעֲשַׂי.
שִׂים בִּרְכָתְךָ, אֱלֹהַי, עַל
יַקִּירַי, שֶׁלְּעוֹלָם אַל יִהְיוּ חֳלִי,
צָרָה וַחֲרָדָה מְנָת חֶלְקָם,
שֶׁיִּשְׂאוּ בְּרָכָה בַּעֲמָלָם
וּבְמִשְׁאֲלוֹת לִבָּם, וּבְמִשְׁלַח
יָדָם וּבְעִסּוּקָם יִשְׂאוּ פֵּרוֹת
לָרֹב. בָּרֵךְ אוֹתָם, אֵלִי,
בַּאֲרִיכוּת יָמִים, וְיִשְׂמְחוּ
בְּחַיֵּיהֶם מְלֵאֵי כֹחַ, בְּרִיאִים
בְּגוּפָם וּבְנַפְשָׁם, אָמֵן.

Let my heart not follow vanity and emptiness, and let the pleasures of the world not cloud my vision, that I not waste my previous life — the life given to me to fulfill my obligations. May it be Your will that I not turn, in a moment of frivolity, from the words of Your mouth; that virginal honor and a pure heart be a precious adornment for me.

Bless me, my Lord, with understanding and insight, with a healthy body and soul, with a heart that is joyful and content. May I never deviate from the commandment of honoring one's father and mother, and not offend or anger my dear parents, so that I may succeed in bringing them happiness through my actions. Bestow Your blessing, my God, upon my loved ones; that illness, trouble, and anxiety never be their lot; that they may enjoy success in their endeavors and fulfillment of their hearts' wishes; and may their occupations and work bear abundant fruit. Bless them, my God, with long life, that they may rejoice in their lifetimes with strength and good health of body and soul. Amen.

Similarly, in early-twentieth-century Alexandria, Egypt, girls were given lessons in Judaism and Jewish history and a joint bat mitzvah celebration was held. The girls came to the large synagogue dressed in white, with white gloves. They sang the Ten Commandments and recited the Thirteen Attributes, the Torah passage that describes God's qualities (Exodus 34:6–7). After the ceremony and speeches, a festive meal — a *seudat mitzvah* — was held.

In the late nineteenth century, the chief rabbi of Baghdad and one of the most important **Sephardic** legal scholars, the Ben Ish Hai (Rabbi Yosef Hayim), recommended that a bat mitzvah girl "wear new clothing and bless the *Sheheyanu* blessing, with the intention [that it be directed at] her entry into the yoke of commandments." Over a half a century later, the Sephardic chief rabbi, Rabbi Yitzhak Nissim, followed the Ben Ish Hai's example and attempted to reinstitute the bat mitzvah celebration. Rabbi Nissim built on the earlier idea, suggesting a ceremony that would take place in the synagogue, and encouraged girls to speak or read a prayer (for example, the Song of Deborah or Hannah's Prayer). Rabbi Nissim also recommended that the girl's father say the blessing "Blessed is He who released me from her punishment," a version of the blessing traditionally said at a boy's bar mitzvah, marking the transfer of accountability to the child with his entry into adulthood. The community, he suggested, would answer with the blessing that Rebecca (chapter 43) was given when she left her father's home "May you grow into thousands of myriads" (Genesis 24:60).

In America, the first bat mitzvah was held in 1922, when Judith Kaplan read her Torah portion, or *parasha*, in New York — which was, at the time, unheard of. Judith was the daughter of Rabbi Mordecai Kaplan, the founder of **Reconstructionist** Judaism. She read the blessings over the Torah in their traditional tune and then chanted in Hebrew and English from a Bible. As the twentieth century progressed, Jewish communities around the world began to hold celebrations for girls on the occasion of their bat mitzvah; in some, girls were called to the Torah or read a prayer and in others they gave a **dvar Torah** or speech. Many included a party with family and friends.

At times throughout history, celebrations have been muted but even more moving. Bilha Sheffer remembered life in the Westerbork transit camp in Holland during the Holocaust: "Mother said: 'We will gather by the bed and eat something.' The family gathers and we sit, and then Mother bends over to her satchel and pulls out a jar of strawberry jam, which I so loved... Everyone marvels, and Mother says to me: 'Mazal tov, [today is] your bat mitzvah.'" My own mother, Miriam Mashiach (Milly Yosefson), always told me about her bat mitzvah; though the family had not planned a celebration, she was surprised by her father, who brought her a rare treat: an orange from the land of Israel — no small feat in Communist Romania in the late 1940s.

The pioneers building the Land of Israel dedicated thought to reinstating Jewish ceremonies and modifying them to suit the life of the working person and the spirit of the Land of Israel. Nonetheless, they did not create a bat mitzvah ceremony or any kind of rite of passage for girls. On kibbutzim and in the settlement movement, they did away with the separation between girls (age twelve) and boys (age thirteen) and the individual celebration; instead, each age group celebrated together during seventh grade. With time, a tradition evolved that included thirteen challenging and educational tasks: working, guarding, meeting different populations in the land, and more. At the end of the year, a communal ceremony was held before the kibbutz families.

After the founding of the State of Israel in 1948, it became commonplace to mark a bat mitzvah. However, no uniform tradition emerged, and the ceremonies and prayers that had been part of the celebrations for the hundred years before the founding of the state were not adopted; they were all but forgotten.

Throughout my research and travels I have seen creativity and innovation. I have visited schools that had their own traditions for celebrating bat mitzvah, communities that instituted ceremonies, and families that marked the occasion over the course of a year. I learned about bat mitzvah girls who integrated big events with a contribution to community and learning and girls who initiated a chal-

334

lenging experience like walking the Israel Trail, doing genealogical research, or teaching language to a new immigrant. I saw an obstacle course built by boys and girls celebrating their bar and bat mitzvahs, which ended with walking through a ring of fire. At the foot of Mount Tabor I took part in a journey of mothers and daughters who recreated the battle of Deborah the Prophetess and Barak the son of Avinoam. I was a guest at a bat mitzvah celebration in an event hall where the bat mitzvah girl had created figures of different women and dressed them in clothing from their eras. Some girls read from the Torah, some take on a challenge, some create their own project for their community. Some connect to ancient texts by reading from the Torah or chanting from one of the five scrolls — and their communities throw soft candies at them and sing.

Some girls read a prayer that speaks to them. In recent years, a number of other prayers have been written for a girl to recite before her community or family upon reaching her bat mitzvah.

# Prayer for the Growing Girl, by Ruth Lazare

| | |
|---|---|
| בָּרוּךְ אַתָּה יְהֹוָה שֶׁעֲשִׂתַנִי אִשָּׁה | Blessed are You, Lord, for having made me a woman |
| שֶׁבָּרָאתָ אֶת גוּפִי בְחָכְמָה | For having created my body with wisdom |
| שֶׁכָּל אֵבֶר יוֹדֵעַ אֶת עִתּוֹ | Such that each organ knows its time |
| וְאַתָּה כּוֹלֵל אֶת אֵבָרַי יַחַד | And You gather my organs together |
| וּמַבְשִׁיל בִּי בַּגְרוּת וּפִרְיוֹן | Bringing maturity and fertility to ripeness within me. |
| עַתָּה אֲנִי אִשָּׁה שְׁלֵמָה | Now I am a complete woman |
| הַמַכִּירָה אֶת מְלֹא חָכְמַת הַבְּרִיאָה | Recognizing all the wisdom of Creation. |
| חָנַנְתָּ אוֹתִי בְּמַתְּנָתְךָ הַבְּרוּכָה | You have graciously granted me Your blessed gift; |
| כָּלַלְתְּ אוֹתִי עִם כָּל נְשֵׁי יִשְׂרָאֵל | You have included me among all the women of Israel |
| וְהִנֵּה אֲנִי לְפָנֶיךָ מְלֵאַת שִׂמְחָה וְהוֹדָיָה. | And here I am before You Full of joy and thanks. |

# Bat Mitzvah Blessing to Be Recited by the Bat Mitzvah Girl, by Rabbanit Oshra and Rabbi Zvi Koren

"בָּרוּךְ יְהֹוָה לְעוֹלָם אָמֵן
וְאָמֵן" (תהלים פ״ט, נ״ג)

"Blessed is the Lord forever, Amen and Amen." (Psalms 89:53)

בְּשָׁעָה שֶׁנִּכְנֶסֶת אֲנִי בְּנוֹעַם
עוֹל מִצְווֹת נוֹשֵׂאת אֲנִי עֵינַי
אֵלֶיךָ בִּתְפִילָה:

At this moment, when I enter the grace of the burden of commandments, I life my eyes to You in prayer:

יְהִי רָצוֹן מִלְּפָנֶיךָ יְהֹוָה
אֱלֹהֵינוּ וֵאלֹהֵי אֲבוֹתֵינוּ,
אֱלֹהֵי אַבְרָהָם, יִצְחָק
וְיַעֲקֹב, שָׂרָה, רִבְקָה, רָחֵל
וְלֵאָה,שֶׁתְּזַכֵּנִי בְּרַחֲמֶיךָ
הָרַבִּים לִלְמוֹד וּלְלַמֵּד,
לִשְׁמוֹר וְלַעֲשׂוֹת וּלְקַיֵּם אֶת
כָּל דִּבְרֵי תַּלְמוּד תּוֹרָתֶךָ
בְּאַהֲבָה עִם שְׁאָר בָּנֶיךָ
וּבְנוֹתֶיךָ, כִּי בָהּ חָפָצְתִּי.

May it be Your will, the Lord our God and the God of our ancestors Abraham, Isaac, and Jacob, Sarah, Rebecca, Rachel, and Leah, that You may enable me in Your infinite mercy to learn and teach, to heed, to do and to fulfill in love all the words of instruction in Your law with the rest of Your sons and daughters, for it is my desire.

פְּתַח לִבִּי בְּתוֹרָתֶךָ, וְאַחֲרֵי
מִצְווֹתֶיךָ תִּרְדּוֹף נַפְשִׁי, "יְהִי
לִבִּי תָמִים בְּחֻקֶּיךָ לְמַעַן לֹא
אֵבוֹשׁ" (תהלים קי״ט, פ׳).

Open my heart to Your teaching, and may my soul pursue Your commandments, "May I wholeheartedly follow Your laws so that I do not come to grief" (Psalms 119:80).

חַזְּקֵנִי וְאַמְּצֵנִי לְקַבֵּל עוֹל
מִצְוֹתֶיךָ בְּאַהֲבָה, "הַדְרִיכֵנִי
בִּנְתִיב מִצְוֹתֶיךָ כִּי בוֹ חָפָצְתִּי
נִשְׁבַּעְתִּי וָאֲקַיֵּמָה לִשְׁמֹר
מִשְׁפְּטֵי צִדְקֶךָ" (תהלים
קי"ט, ל"ה, קי"ו) וְיַחֵד לְבָבִי
לְאַהֲבָה וּלְיִרְאָה אֶת שְׁמֶךָ,
כַּכָּתוּב:
"וְאָהַבְתָּ אֵת יְהֹוָה אֱלֹהֶיךָ
בְּכָל-לְבָבְךָ וּבְכָל-נַפְשְׁךָ וּבְכָל-
מְאֹדֶךָ" (דברים ו', ה').

Strengthen me and make me resolute in accepting the yoke of your commandments with love, "Lead me in the path of Your commandments, for that is my concern... I have firmly sworn to keep Your just rules" (Psalms 119:35, 106), and unite my heart to love and fear Your name, as it is written: "You shall love the Lord your God with all your heart and with all your soul and with all your might" (Deuteronomy 6:5).

"וְאָהַבְתָּ אֵת יְהֹוָה אֱלֹהֶיךָ
בְּכָל-לְבָבְךָ וּבְכָל-נַפְשְׁךָ וּבְכָל-
מְאֹדֶךָ" (דברים ו', ה').

"הוֹדוּ לַ יְהֹוָה כִּי טוֹב כִּי
לְעוֹלָם חַסְדּוֹ" (תהלים
קי"ח, א').

"Praise the Lord, for He is good; His steadfast love is eternal" (Psalms 118:1).

And for all of my days I will cry in a great voice and not be ashamed:

וְכָל יָמַי אֶקְרָא בְּקוֹל גָּדוֹל וְלֹא
אֵבוֹשׁ: "שְׁמַע יִשְׂרָאֵל יְהֹוָה אֱלֹהֵינוּ
יְהֹוָה אֶחָד" (דברים ו', ד').

"Hear, O Israel! The Lord our God, the Lord is one" (Deuteronomy 6:4).

You have all of the tools; you can use them to connect to the past or to create something new. Mazal tov — and welcome to the world of Jewish women.

# TIMELINE
# OF ICONIC JEWISH WOMEN

|  | YEARS | HEBREW YEARS | ERA |
|---|---|---|---|
| SARAH | 18th century BCE | Ca. 1950 | Biblical Matriarchs and Patriarchs |
| REBECCA | 17th century BCE | Ca. 2000 | |
| LEAH | 16th century BCE | Ca. 2100 | |
| RACHEL | 16th century BCE | Ca. 2100 | |
| MIRIAM | 14th century BCE | Ca. 2300 | Exodus from Egypt |
| DEBORAH | 11th century BCE | Ca. 2650 | Judges (Land of Israel) |
| RUTH | 10th century BCE | Ca. 2750 | |

| | | | |
|---|---|---|---|
| JUDITH | Between 6th and 2nd century BCE | Between 3200 and 3600 | Second Temple Period |
| ESTHER | 5th century BCE | Ca. 3300 | |
| SALOME ALEXANDRA | 140–67 BCE | 3614–3694 | Hasmonean Period |
| BRURIAH | 2nd century | Ca. 3900 | Roman Rule in the Land of Israel |
| DOÑA GRACIA MENDES NASI | 1510–1569 | 5270–5329 | Early Modern Period |
| OSNAT BARZANI | 1590–1670 | 5350–5430 | |
| GLIKL OF HAMELN | 1646–1724 | 5405–5485 | |
| RACHEL MORPURGO | 1790–1871 | 5550–5631 | Late Modern Period |
| HANNAH RACHEL VERBERMACHER | 1805–1888 | 5566–5648 | |
| GRACE AGUILAR | 1816–1847 | 5576–5608 | |

| | | | |
|---|---|---|---|
| FANNY NEUDA | 1819–1894 | 5579–5654 | |
| EMMA LAZARUS | 1849–1887 | 5609–5648 | |
| HANNAH GREENEBAUM SOLOMON | 1858–1942 | 5618–5703 | |
| BERTHA PAPPENHEIM | 1859–1936 | 5619–5696 | |
| FLORA SASSOON | 1859–1936 | 5620–5696 | Late Modern Period |
| HENRIETTA SZOLD | 1860–1945 | 5621–5705 | |
| LILLIAN WALD | 1867–1940 | 5627–5700 | |
| LISE MEITNER | 1878–1968 | 5639–5729 | |
| MANIA SHOHAT | 1878–1961 | 5639–5721 | |
| SARAH SCHENIRER | 1883–1935 | 5643–5695 | |
| HANNAH MAI-SEL-SHOHAT | 1883–1972 | 5644–5732 | |

| | | | |
|---|---|---|---|
| SELMA MAYER | 1884–1984 | 5644–5744 | |
| STEFA WILCZYŃSKA | 1886–1942 | 5646–5702 | |
| HELENA KAGAN | 1889–1979 | 5649–5738 | |
| SARAH AARONSOHN | 1890–1917 | 5650–5678 | |
| RACHEL BLUWSTEIN | 1890–1931 | 5651–5691 | |
| ADA FISHMAN MAIMON | 1893–1973 | 5654–5734 | Late Modern Period |
| GOLDA MEIR | 1898–1978 | 5658–5739 | |
| BRACHA HABAS | 1900–1968 | 5660–5728 | |
| REGINA JONAS | 1902–1944 | 5662–5705 | |
| NECHAMA LEIBOWITZ | 1905–1997 | 5665–5757 | |
| ADA SERENI | 1905–1998 | 5665–5758 | |
| RITA LEVI-MON-TALCINI | 1909–2012 | 5669–5773 | |

| | | | |
|---|---|---|---|
| LEA GOLDBERG | 1911–1970 | 5671–5730 | |
| ZIVIA LUBETKIN | 1914–1978 | 5674–5738 | |
| ZELDA | 1914–1984 | 5674–5744 | |
| MIRIAM BEN-PORAT | 1918–2012 | 5678–5772 | |
| BELLA ABZUG | 1920–1998 | 5680–5758 | |
| HANNAH SENESH | 1921–1944 | 5681–5705 | |
| ELYNOR RUDNICK | 1923–1996 | 5683–5756 | Late Modern Period |
| HANNAH SEMER | 1924–2003 | 5685–5763 | |
| GEULAH COHEN | 1925–2019 | 5686–5780 | |
| YEHUDIT NISAYHO | 1925–2003 | 5686–5763 | |
| ZAHARA LEVITOV | 1927–1948 | 5688–5708 | |
| SHULAMIT ALONI | 1928–2014 | 5688–5774 | |

| | | | |
|---|---|---|---|
| ANNE FRANK | 1929–1945 | 5689–5705 | |
| NAOMI SHEMER | 1930–2004 | 5690–5764 | |
| IDA NUDEL | 1931–2021 | 5691–5782 | Late Modern Period |
| RUTH BADER GINSBURG | 1933–2020 | 5693–5780 | |
| ESTHER ARDITI | 1937–2003 | 5697–5763 | |
| DEBORAH LIPSTADT | 1947– | 5707– | Contemporary Period |
| RACHEL FREIER | 1965– | 5725– | |

# Glossary

| | |
|---|---|
| **AGGADAH** | Rabbinic writing that relates not to Jewish law but rather to ethics, parables, and traditions |
| **ALIYAH BET** | The code name for Jewish illegal immigration to Palestine between 1920 and 1948 |
| **AMIDAH** | Central Jewish prayer, also called the *Shemoneh Esreh*, traditionally recited three times a day on weekdays |
| **ANTI-SEMITISM** | Discrimination against or hatred of Jews |
| **ARAB REVOLT** | Arab uprising against British control of Palestine, 1936–1939 |
| **ARK** | The place in which Torah scrolls are kept at the front of a synagogue, known as an aron kodesh in Hebrew |
| **ASHKENAZI (ADJ.)/ ASHKENAZIM (V.)** | Jews whose families lived in the area along the Rhine in western Germany and France during the Middle Ages who then migrated to lands like Poland, Lithuania, and Russia |

| | |
|---|---|
| **BAR KOKHBA REVOLT** | Rebellion of the Jews in Judea against the Roman Empire in the years 132–136, named for its leader, Simon bar Kokhba |
| **BASIC LAWS** | Thirteen constitutional laws in the State of Israel; many are based on individual liberties outlined in Israel's Declaration of Independence |
| **BEIT MIDRASH** | House of study, a building or hall dedicated to Torah study |
| **BNEI AKIVA** | Global Religious Zionist youth movement founded in 1929 in the Land of Israel |
| **BOBOV** | Hasidic community originating in Bobowa (Poland) |
| **CHABAD** | Hasidic movement, also called Lubavitch, founded in 1775 by Rabbi Schneur Zalman of Liadi, known for its network of institutions around the world, outreach, and humanitarian aid |
| **CHALLAH** | Braided, yeast-based bread typically served at Shabbat meals |

| | |
|---|---|
| **CHIEF RABBINATE** | Israel's rabbinic authority for Jewish law, recognized as the legal and administrative body responsible for religious Jewish life in the country, including marriage and divorce, burial, kashrut, and religious courts |
| **CHILDREN'S HOUSE** | Shared living quarters of children on kibbutz, in which groups of children around the same ages had lessons, slept, and ate together |
| **CONSERVATIVE JUDAISM** | Also called Masorti Judaism, the movement that aims to preserve traditional Judaism while allowing for modernizing some religious practices, based on the ideology of Zacharias Frankel, who lived in the nineteenth century |
| **CRUSADES** | Religious wars of the eleventh, twelfth, and thirteenth centuries that aimed to reconquer the Holy Land from the Muslims |
| **CRYPTO-JEWS** | Jews who practiced their Judaism only in secret, while pretending to belong to another faith in public |

| | |
|---|---|
| **DAF YOMI** | Daily study of one folio (both sides of a page) of the Talmud, in a cycle that takes seven and a half years |
| *DAVEN* | Pray (Yiddish) |
| **DIASPORA** | Jewish communities outside of the Land of Israel |
| **DVAR TORAH** | Words of Torah, or an idea imparted that relates to Torah |
| **ETZEL** | Also known as the Irgun, Zionist para-military organization that operated between 1931 and 1948 in the Land of Israel, which used violent acts in an attempt to liberate the Jewish homeland |
| **EXODUS** | The migration of the Israelites from slavery in Egypt to freedom |
| *GABBAI* | Beadle or sexton; the person responsible for running services in synagogue |
| **GEMATRIA** | Jewish numerology, which attributes a numerical value to each of the Hebrew letters |

| | |
|---|---|
| GHETTO | Part of a city restricted to a specific minority group, first made for Jews in Europe in the sixteenth century |
| HAGANAH | Zionist paramilitary organization in the Land of Israel from 1920 to 1948 and the predecessor of the Israel Defense Forces |
| HALAKHA/ HALAKHOT (PL.)/ HALAKHIC (ADJ.) | Jewish law, made up of both the Written and Oral Torah |
| HAMOSSAD LEALIYAH BET | The Haganah's arm for clandestine immigration to the Land of Israel and the State of Israel between 1938 and 1952 |
| HANUKAH | The Festival of Lights, an eight-day holiday marking the victory of the Maccabees against the Seleucid Empire and the rededication of the Temple |
| HASID (SING.)/ HASIDIM (PL.)/ HASIDIC (ADJ.) | Sub-group of ultra-Orthodox Judaism that began with a spiritual revival in the eighteenth century, formed around courts of rebbes, or rabbis |
| HASHOMER | Jewish defense organization in the Land of Israel between 1909 and 1920 |

| | |
|---|---|
| **HASHOMER HATZAIR** | Labor Zionist secular Jewish youth movement born in 1913 |
| **HASMONEANS** | Dynasty that ruled Judea and its surroundings from 140 to 37 BCE |
| **HEHALUTZ** | Jewish youth movement that trained young people for agricultural settlement of the Land of Israel |
| *HESED* | Lovingkindness or giving |
| **HIBBAT ZION** | A group of organizations founded in the late nineteenth century in eastern Europe that responded to the pogroms and anti-Jewish atmosphere by promoting Jewish settlement of the Land of Israel |
| **HILULA** | Celebration of a wedding or the anniversary of a death, sometimes with a pilgrimage |
| **HISTADRUT** | Israel's General Federation of Labor, a trade union founded in 1920. |
| **IDF** | The Israel Defense Forces, the state's military, founded in 1948 |

| INQUISITION | Spanish tribunal requiring that all citizens convert to Catholicism, under threat of death; some 150,000 people were prosecuted and between 3,000 and 5,000 were killed between 1478 and 1834 |

| ISRAEL PRIZE | The State of Israel's highest honor, awarded to people who show excellence in their fields (humanities, Jewish studies, natural sciences, culture, etc.) |

| JEWISH AGENCY | Jewish non-profit body, founded in 1929, initially created to help Jews settle in the Land of Israel and develop it; today it also connects Jews to Israel and their Jewish identities and supports vulnerable populations |

| JEWISH BRIGADE | Military formation within the British Army during World War II made up of Jews from the Land of Israel, formed in 1944 |

| JUDEA | Ancient name for portion of today's Israel that belonged to the Israelite nation (called *Yehuda* in Hebrew), spanning from Jerusalem to Beersheba from 934 BCE to 586 BCE; today, it refers to the area called Judea and Samaria (*Yehuda veShomron*), also known as the West Bank |

| | |
|---|---|
| **JUDENRAT** | Jewish council, mandated by the Nazis among the Jewish communities in the areas they occupied |
| **KABBALAT SHAB-BAT** | Prayers recited on Friday evening to welcome Shabbat, made up of Psalms and hymns |
| **KADDISH** | Aramaic prayer of praise recited during prayer services; the Mourners' Kaddish is recited for eleven months after the death of a parent |
| **KASHRUT/ KOSHER (ADJ.)** | Jewish dietary laws originating in the Torah and with rabbinic interpretations and application to today's world; laws include a separation between meat and milk, the prohibition of eating the meat of specific animals, and a specific process for the killing of animals and preparation of their meat |
| **KGB** | The Soviet Union's security and intelligence agency from 1954 until 1991 |
| **KIBBUTZ/ KIBBUTZIM (PL.)** | Communal form of living, originally formed around agricultural work, based on egalitarian principals and a social contract in which all income generated goes into a common pool |

| | |
|---|---|
| **KIDDUSH** | Ritual blessing recited over wine on Shabbat (literally translated as "sanctification") |
| **KINNERET** | Sea of Galilee, the largest freshwater lake in Israel, located in the country's northeast |
| **KNESSET** | Israel's legislature (literally translated as "assembly") |
| **LAG BAOMER** | Holiday celebrated on the thirty-third day of counting the Omer (the forty-nine days counted from Passover to Shavuot). It may celebrate the end of a plague in which Rabbi Akiva's students were killed or commemorate the death of Rabbi Simeon bar Yochai; in some communities, mourning customs end on this day. The day is celebrated with bonfires and pilgrimages to Meron. |
| **LEHI** | Acronym for *Lohamei Herut Yisrael* (Fighters for the Freedom of Israel), terrorist organization that used violence to try to remove the British from the Land of Israel; founded in 1940 and disbanded in 1948 |

**MACCABEES**  Jewish priestly family that rebelled against the Seleucid rulers to take control of Judea during the second century BCE, founders of the Hasmonean dynasty

**MAPAI**  Israel's workers' party, founded in 1930 and dissolved in 1968

**MARRANOS**  Jews who converted to Catholicism in Spain or Portugal during the fourteenth and fifteenth centuries under duress but continued practicing their Judaism in secret

*MEGILLAH*  Literally "scroll," usually referring to the five books in the Bible known as the *megillot*: Song of Songs, Ruth, Lamentations, Ecclesiastes, and Esther

**MESSIAH**  Figure expected to redeem the Jewish nation in the future, generally believed to be from the family of King David

**MIDRASH**  Interpretive commentary on biblical texts, often used in the Talmud, which can relate to ethics and values (*Midrash Aggadah*) or religious law (*Midrash Halakha*)

| | |
|---|---|
| *MIDRASHA* | Seminary of Jewish religious learning for women |
| **MISHNAH/ MISHNAIC (ADJ.)** | First collection of Jewish religious oral traditions compiled around the year 200; it collects hundreds of years of traditions and religious laws |
| *MITZVAH/ MITZVOT* | Jewish religious commandments |
| **MIZRACHI** | Global religious and Zionist movement founded in 1902 |
| *MOSHAV* | Israeli settlement or town, often agricultural in nature and sometimes cooperative |
| *MOSHAVA/ MOSHAVOT* (PL.) | Colony of independent Jewish farmers in the Land of Israel during Ottoman rule |
| **MOSSAD** | Israel's national intelligence agency, responsible for collecting intelligence, counter-terrorism, and undercover operations |
| **NEGEV** | Desert region in southern Israel |

| | |
|---|---|
| **NUREMBERG LAWS** | Racist laws enacted by Nazi Germany in 1935, which revoked Jews' citizenship and banned marriage between Jews and Germans |
| **ORDINATION/ ORDAIN (V.)** | Process through which a person becomes a rabbi (called *semikha* in Hebrew) |
| **ORTHODOX JUDAISM** | The branch of Jewish practice that advocates strict adherence to Torah and talmudic law |
| **OTTOMAN EMPIRE** | Also known as the Turkish empire, domain that controlled areas of the Middle East, Eastern Europe, and North Africa for over six hundred years; the Land of Israel was under its control from 1517 until 1917 |
| **PALMACH** | The Haganah's elite fighting force, established in 1941 to protect the Jewish community in the Land of Israel in the event of attacks that might take place as a result of events in the Second World War |
| *PARNAS* | Lay leader in a synagogue |

| | |
|---|---|
| *PARASHA* | Weekly Torah portion, read on Shabbat and, in shortened form, on Mondays and Thursdays; many communities complete the entire Torah reading over the course of a year while others have a triennial cycle, completing the reading of the Torah over three years |
| PARTISANS | Armed groups of fighters who battled the Nazis during the Second World War |
| PARTITION PLAN FOR PALESTINE | The 1947 United Nations proposal to split the land of Palestine into two states, one for the Arab community and one for the Jews |
| PASSOVER | Springtime holiday that commemorates the Exodus of the Israelites from slavery in Egypt to freedom |
| POALE ZION | Zionist Marxist movement founded in the early twentieth century in Europe and the United States |
| POGROM | Violent riot against Jews, especially during the nineteenth and twentieth centuries in the Russian Empire |

| | |
|---|---|
| **PSALMS/ PSALM (SING.)** | Biblical book of hymns, many of which are used in prayer |
| **RABBANIT/ RABBANIOT (PL.)** | Feminine form of the word "rabbi"; in the past, it was primarily attributed to wives of rabbis but in modern times it can also refer to female rabbinic leaders |
| **RECONST- RUCTIONIST JUDAISM** | Movement founded in 1922 by Mordecai Kaplan that views Judaism as a civilization that evolves over time |
| **REBBE** | Central rabbi around whom a Hasidic community revolves |
| **REFORM JUDAISM** | Movement that began in Germany in the nineteenth century that advocates adapting Jewish practice to the changing world |
| **RESPONSA** | A form of halakhic writing that was used for some 1,700 years, usually in letter form as answers to questions, known in Hebrew as *Shu"t*, short for *She'elot* (questions) *UTeshuvot* (and answers) |

| | |
|---|---|
| **ROSH HASHANAH** | Jewish New Year, a two-day holiday during the month of Tishrei (around September) |
| *ROSH YESHIVA* | Rabbinic leader of a yeshiva |
| **SANHEDRIN** | Assembly or council of sages during the period after the destruction of the Second Temple with religious and legislative authority (the Great Sanhedrin was composed of seventy-one judges; the Lesser Sanhedrins, sitting within cities, had twenty-three apiece) |
| **SATMAR** | Hasidic dynasty founded in 1905 characterized by stringent religious observance and opposition to Zionism |
| **SECOND ALIYAH** | Wave of immigration of Jews to the Land of Israel between 1904 and 1914; roughly 35,000 Jews came, primarily from Russia and Poland, with some from Yemen |
| **SEDER** | Ritual feast observed on Passover (once in Israel, twice outside of Israel), including the retelling of the Exodus story, eating matza, drinking four cups of wine, and eating a festive meal |

**SEPHARDIC (ADJ.)/ SEPHARDIM (PL.)**   Jews whose families stem from the Diaspora communities in Spain and Portugal; at times the word refers to Jews from Arab lands and North Africa as well, though they are more commonly known as Mizrahi

**SEUDA SHLISHIT**   Also known as *Shaleshudes* (in Yiddish), the third meal of the Shabbat, eaten near the end of Shabbat in the afternoon or evening

**SHABBAT**   The Sabbath, the seventh day of the week, which the Torah describes as a day of rest from work

**SHAVUOT**   Holiday celebrating the giving of the Torah to the nation of Israel as well as the grain harvest, seven weeks after Passover; the Book of Ruth is read and dairy foods are customarily eaten

*SHOFAR*   Instrument made of a ram's horn, blown during services on Rosh Hashanah and Yom Kippur

**SIMHAT TORAH**   Holiday celebrating the end and beginning of the annual Torah-reading cycle

| | |
|---|---|
| SIX-DAY WAR | War fought between June 5 and 10, 1967, between Israel and a group of Arab states (primarily Jordan, Syria, and Egypt) |
| SUKKAH | Temporary structure built out of doors with a roof made of plant material; it is customary to eat and even sleep in a Sukkah during the Sukkot holiday |
| SUKKOT | Holiday celebrating the fruit harvest in which it is customary to sit in temporary booths or dwellings (Sukkahs) built out of doors |
| *TALLIT* | Fringed shawl worn during prayer |
| TALMUD/ TALMUDIC (ADJ.) | Rabbinic text relating Jewish law and tradition compiled between the third and sixth centuries, made up of sixty-three tractates and structured around the Mishnah; the Jerusalem Talmud, composed in the Land of Israel, is written in Hebrew while Babylonian Talmud, composed in the Jewish community in Babylonia, is written partially in Aramaic |
| TANAKH | The entire Hebrew Bible; the word is an acronym for the three sections of the Bible — Torah, Neviim (Prophets), and Ketuvim (Writings) |

| | |
|---|---|
| TANNA/ TANNAIM (PL.) | Rabbinic sage whose opinions are recorded in the Mishnah, lived between the years 10 and 220 |
| *TEFILLIN* | Phylacteries; two square boxes attached to leather straps and used in prayer, with one affixed to the head and the other placed on the arm |
| TEN COMMAND- MENTS | Set of foundational principles given to the nation of Israel at Mount Sinai, appearing in Exodus 20:2–17 and Deuteronomy 5:6–21 |
| *TIKKUN OLAM* | Literally "repairing the world," the Jewish concept that people can and should perfect the world in partnership with God |
| *TISCH* | Yiddish for "table," a gathering of Hasidic Jews around their rebbe, who is sitting at a table, with singing and words of Torah, usually on Shabbat or holidays |

| | |
|---|---|
| **TORAH** | The first five biblical books — Genesis, Exodus, Leviticus, Numbers, and Deuteronomy — telling the story of the world's creation, the patriarchs and matriarchs, and the development of the Israelite nation |
| **TOWER AND STOCKADE (*HOMA UMIGDAL*)** | The form of founding settlements in which a tower and enclosure were built overnight; fifty-two such settlements were founded between 1936 and 1939 in the Land of Israel, in response to the British restrictions on building and the Arab Revolt |
| **TU BESHVAT** | The fifteenth day of the month of Shvat, the "New Year" for trees, celebrated as the time that the trees begin to bloom again after the winter; in Israel, trees are often planted |
| *TZENA* | Austerity (economy) policies in the State of Israel between 1949 and 1959, when emergency measures were in place and food was rationed due to food and foreign currency shortages |

| | |
|---|---|
| **ULTRA-ORTHODOX** | Also known as "haredi" Judaism, the group within the Orthodox community that is characterized by a degree of segregation from general society and strict adherence to Jewish law |
| **WAR OF INDEPENDENCE** | Also called the Arab–Israeli War, the war that began on May 15, 1948, with the withdrawal of the British from the Land of Israel; it ended with armistice agreements signed between the State of Israel and its neighbors in 1949 |
| **WIZO** | Women's International Zionist Organization, founded in 1920 to advance the status of women |
| **YESHIVA** | School for religious study |
| **YISHUV** | The Hebrew word for "settlement," referring to the Jewish community living in the Land of Israel near the end of the nineteenth century and until the State of Israel was established |
| **YOM HAATZMAUT** | Israeli Independence Day, held on 5 Iyar |

| | |
|---|---|
| **YOM KIPPUR** | The Day of Atonement, an annual day of fasting and prayer considered the holiest day of the Jewish year |
| **YOM KIPPUR WAR** | War fought from October 6 (Yom Kippur) to October 25, 1973, between Israel and a group of Arab states led by Egypt and Syria |
| **YOUTH ALIYAH** | Rescue of thousands of Jewish children from Nazi Germany and their resettlement in the Land of Israel |
| **ZIONISM/ ZIONIST (ADJ.)** | Movement for the establishment and support of a state for the Jewish nation in the Land of Israel |
| **ZIONIST CONGRESS** | Regular conference dedicated to Zionist activity, first inaugurated by Theodor Herzl in 1897 |

# Sources

\*     Berland, Dinah, ed. *Hours of Devotion: Fanny Neuda's Book of Prayers for Jewish Women*. New York: Schocken Books, 2007. Cambridge, MA: Harvard University Press, 2021.

\*     Falk, Marcia, trans. *The Spectacular Difference: Selected Poems of Zelda*. Cincinnati: Hebrew Union College Press, 2004.

\*     Frank, Otto H. and Mirjam Pressler, eds. *Anne Frank: The Diary of a Young Girl: The Definitive Edition*. Translated by Susan Massotty. New York: Anchor Books, 1996.

\*     Goldberg, Lea. *The Scatterbrain from Upper Maine*. Translated by Amos Mitchell. Illustrations by Avner Katz. Tel Aviv: Sharon, 1972.

\*     Hacohen, Dvora. *To Repair a Broken World: The Life of Henrietta Szold, Founder of Hadassah*. Cambridge, MA: Harvard University Press, 2021.

\*     Kagan, Helena. *The Voice that Called*. Jerusalem, 1978.

\*     Keller, Tsipi, trans. "Entries from the Diaries of Lea Goldberg." https://intranslation.brooklynrail.org/archive/israel/.

\*     Lavie, Aliza, ed. *A Jewish Woman's Prayer Book*. New York: Spiegel & Grau, 2008.

\*     Lavie, Aliza. *Women's Customs: A Journey of Jewish Customs, Rituals, Prayers and Stories*. Tel Aviv: Miskal, 2012. Hebrew.

\*     Lowenthal, Marvin, trans. *The Memoirs of Glückel of Hameln*. New York: Schocken Books, 1977.

\*     Mann, Jacob. *Texts and Studies in Jewish History and Literature*. New York: Ktav Publishing House, 1972.

\*     Mayer, Selma (Schwester Selma). *My Life and Experiences at "Shaare Zedek."* Jerusalem: Shaare Zedek Medical Center, 1973. Available online at: https://www.szmc.org.il/Uploaded-Images/11_2015/MyLifeAtShaareZedek-Eng.pdf.

\*     Nadell, Pamela. *America's Jewish Women: A History from Colonial Times to Today*. New York, NY: W. W. Norton & Company, 2019.

\*     Nadell, Pamela. "Feminism, American Style: Jewish Women and the Making of a Revolution." http://ajs.haifa.ac.il/images/Nadell_Research_Paper_final.pdf.

\*     Roth, Cecil. *The House of Nasi: Doña Gracia.* New York: Greenwood Press, 1969.

\*     Roth, Cecil. *The Sassoon Dynasty.* London: R. Hale, 1941.

\*     Senesh, Hannah. *Hannah Senesh: Her Life and Diary.* Woodstock, VT: Jewish Lights, 2004.

## *About the Author*

Aliza Lavie, PhD, is a former Member of the Israeli Knesset, lecturer, writer, chair of the Israel Film Council, and founder of the Shaycha venture for educational technology.

Dr. Lavie served as chair of the Committee on the Status of Women and Gender Equality and chair of the Committee to Combat Women Trafficking and Prostitution in Israel's Knesset. She is the recipient of the Outstanding Parliamentary Award for her contribution and ground-breaking legislation.

Lavie served as senior lecturer at Bar-Ilan University, chairperson of the Herzl Center, and general director of the Public Council for Youth Exchange.

In her writings, Lavie expands the Jewish-Israeli bookshelf, often restoring and reclaiming what has almost been lost. Her book *A Jewish Women's Prayer Book* was awarded the National Jewish Book Award.

Lavie's public activity focuses on social and gender equality, the intersection between religion and state, reinforcing the connection between Israel and the Diaspora, and strengthening the image of the State of Israel as Jewish and democratic. She seeks to engender connection and unity based on common identity, culture, and history and reduce tribalism, sectoral politics, and rifts in the Israeli sphere.

Aliza is the CEO of Shaycha – a first-of-its-kind virtual journey that connects users to their Jewish heritage.

Made in the USA
Middletown, DE
03 March 2025

72119639R00203